BEN BLACK was born in Scotland and first travelled to Israel when he was three years old, just before the outbreak of the 1973 Yom Kippur War. By the mid 1980s, his passport was virtually cover-to-cover Israeli entry and exit stamps. Then, in 1988–89 he lived on Kibbutz Rosh HaNikra and fell in love with the country. After graduating from university and several more trips to the Middle East, he returned to live in Jerusalem from 1994 to 1995. Following a brief trip to Australia, he immigrated to Israel in 1996 and lived in Tel Aviv for two and a half years.

As a writer and editor, he travelled extensively across Israel. As a traveller, he left his tracks in the Palestinian Territories, the Sinai Desert and Jordan.

He currently resides in Australia with his wife. *Breaking Ranks* is his first book.

BREAKING RANKS
BEN BLACK

TURBULENT TRAVELS IN THE PROMISED LAND

LONELY PLANET PUBLICATIONS
Melbourne • Oakland • London • Paris

Breaking Ranks: Turbulent Travels in the Promised Land

Published by Lonely Planet Publications
    Head Office: 90 Maribyrnong Street, Footscray, Vic 3011, Australia
                      Locked Bag 1, Footscray, Vic 3011, Australia
    Branches: 150 Linden Street, Oakland CA 94607, USA
                      10a Spring Place, London NW5 3BH, UK
                      1 rue Dahomey, 75011, Paris, France

Published 2001
Printed by The Bookmaker International Ltd
Printed in China

Edited by Bryony Cosgrove
Designed by Simon Bracken
Maps by Natasha Velleley

National Library of Australia Cataloguing-in-Publication entry

Black, Benjamin, 1970– .
    Breaking ranks: turbulent travels in the promised land.

    ISBN 1 86450 361 0.

    Black, Benjamin, 1970– - Journeys. 2. Israel –
    Description and travel. I. Title.

915.694

Text © Benjamin Black 2001
Maps © Lonely Planet 2001

For Lucy and Ziggy

CONTENTS

ACKNOWLEDGEMENTS

THIS BOOK started life as a collection of letters and diary entries. The idea to transform them into a manuscript had been brewing in my brain for two years, and I am grateful to Susan Keogh and Lonely Planet Publications for giving me the opportunity to put finger to keyboard.

Bryony Cosgrove, Carolyn Proctor, Viv Ulman, Jez Frankel and John Hinman all read draft copies of the manuscript and offered invaluable comments and criticisms.

Suzy Jaffe, Tanya Boyden Yarkoni, Meg Ulman, Dave Collins, Moshe Lederman, Sharon Rosen, Linda Robinson, Ros Steen, Joe Hallgarten, Dan Cohen, Juliet Levy, Ric Cantor, Mark Freedman, Adam Kay, Colin Krikler, Marc Cowan, Geoff Stringer, Michelle Glynn, Benji Wajcman, Simon Black and Ray Simonson all assisted me with their contributions, large and small.

Utmost apologies to my family and friends for being incommunicado while I was writing this book, and enormous thanks to my parents, brother and sister for their unconditional love and support.

But, mostly, I owe a debt of gratitude to the people of the region, Jews and Arabs alike, whom I befriended on my journey and whose warmth, openness and insights enriched this contemporary portrait of Israel and its environs.

And last – but first – to my wife, best friend, soul mate and travelling companion for the last eight years, Lucy, whose critical eye, patience, love and crystal-clear memory helped transform the first draft into the final product.

This book is dedicated to you, *habibi*.

AUTHOR'S NOTE

NOT ALL decisions in life are clear-cut. Some are lost in those misty shades of grey between the white and black of right and wrong.

This story is one of them. It is based on a true story, although some of the characters' names have been changed to protect their anonymity, and a couple of the place names have been changed to protect their sanctity.

I moved to Israel in the 1990s as the country, already at peace with Egypt since 1979, was on the threshold of a peace treaty with Jordan and what seemed like a heartbeat away from the end of the conflict with the Palestinians. In that sense, my life there was caught inside the bubble of hope as the country began to grapple with the peace process.

ISRAEL CHRONOLOGY

1004 BC King David conquers Jerusalem.

952 BC King Solomon builds the First Temple.

586 BC King Solomon's Temple is destroyed by Nebuchadnezzar; Jews are exiled to Babylon until 537.

63 BC The Romans arrive and conquer the Holy Land.

20 BC The Second Temple is built by King Herod.

AD 70 The Second Temple is destroyed; Jews are cast into exile again.

638 Arabs, led by Umayyad Caliph Omar, invade the Holy Land and impose Muslim rule.

692 The Mosque of Omar, the Dome of the Rock, is completed; the Church of the Holy Sepulchre is destroyed.

1099 Crusaders invade the Holy Land; Jews and Muslims are massacred.

1187 Muslims return to power under Saladin.

1517 The Ottomans conquer the Holy Land; the walls of Jerusalem are erected under Suleiman the Magnificient.

1881– 82 Zionists from Eastern Europe, suffering from pogroms and persecution, begin to immigrate to Palestine in mass numbers.

1896 Theodore Herzl publishes *The Jewish State*, stating that only the establishment of a Jewish state can solve the Jewish problem.

1917 Jerusalem is surrendered to the British. The Balfour Declaration backs the idea of a homeland for the Jews in Palestine.

1936	The Arab revolt against a Jewish homeland sparks violence between Jews and Arabs.
1939–45	Six million Jews perish under the Nazis in World War II, prompting increased pressure to create a Jewish state.
1947	The United Nations passes Resolution 181, which proposes partitioning the land between the Jews and the Arabs; the Jews accept the decision, the Arabs reject it.
1948	The War of Independence is sparked after Israel declares an independent state and the surrounding Arab armies attack her. Jerusalem is divided: Jordan occupies the Old City
1956	The nationalisation of the Suez Canal by Egyptian leader Gamal Abdel Nasser prompts an Israeli response. Within 100 hours, the IDF captures the Gaza Strip and drives the Egyptians from the Sinai Desert. Israel then relinquishes its gains under a UN-brokered cease-fire.
1964	The Palestine Liberation Organisation (PLO) is founded in Cairo.
1967	Israel recaptures the Old City of Jerusalem and the West Bank from Jordan, the Gaza Strip from Egypt and the Golan Heights from Syria in the Six-Day War.
1973	Egypt and Syria launch a two-pronged attack that almost defeats Israel, catching her unawares on Yom Kippur, the holiest day of the Jewish calendar.
1977	Egyptian President Anwar Sadat visits Jerusalem and addresses the Knesset, Israel's parliament.
1979	Prime Minister Menachem Begin and President Sadat sign a peace deal.
1982	As part of the peace agreement with Egypt, Israel withdraws from the Sinai Desert in April; in June, Israel invades Lebanon, with the declared aim of driving the PLO from bases near the border where it has been launching missile attacks on Israeli settlements.
1985	Israel withdraws from most of Lebanon, maintaining a 'security zone' in the south.

1987   The Intifada, a Palestinian uprising against twenty years of military rule, ignites in the Gaza Strip. It spreads immediately to the West Bank.

1988   The PLO recognises Israel's right to exist.

1993   Israel and the PLO sign the declaration of principles, leading to the Oslo Accords; the Intifada ends.

1994   Israel and Jordan sign a peace treaty.

1995   Yigal Amir, a Jewish extremist, assassinates Prime Minister Yitzhak Rabin.

1996   Likud leader Benjamin Netanyahu defeats Labour's Shimon Peres by 0.9% – the slimmest margin in the history of the state.

1999   Labour's Ehud Barak defeats Netanyahu in a landslide victory.

2000   Israel withdraws unilaterally from southern Lebanon; Yasser Arafat and Ehud Barak come close to finalising a deal, but fail to agree over Jerusalem and the Palestinian right of return. A new uprising, the Al-Aqsa Intifada, begins.

2001   Likud's Ariel Sharon defeats Ehud Barak in a landslide victory.

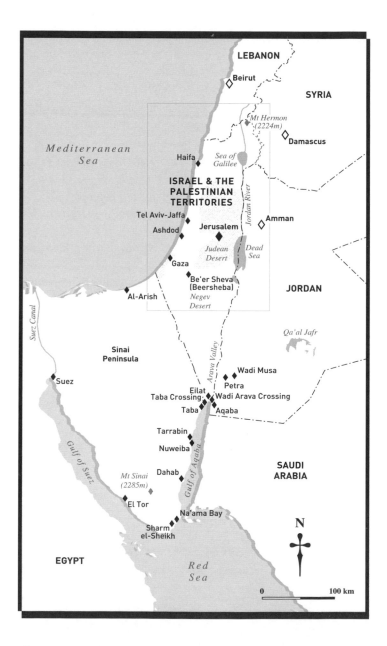

LEBANON

Kiryat Shmona

Rosh HaNikra
Nahariya
Akko (Acre)
Karmi'el
Tzfat (Safed)

Golan Heights

Mediterranean Sea

Haifa
Nazareth
Tiberias

Sea of Galilee

SYRIA

Afula

Um al-Fahm
Hadera
Jenin

Mikmoret
Magal

JORDAN

Netanya
Herzlia

Nablus

Tel Aviv-Jaffa
West Bank

Holon
Ramla
Ramallah
Jericho

Amman

Ashdod
Jerusalem
Allenby Bridge Crossing

Ashkelon
Bethlehem

Kiryat Gat
Judean Desert

Dead Sea

Gaza
Hebron
Kiryat Arba

Gaza Strip

Masada

Be'er Sheva (Beersheba)

Dimona

ISRAEL & THE PALESTINIAN TERRITORIES

N

EGYPT

Negev Desert

Mitzpe Ramon

0   40 km

Jordan River

'In peace sons bury their fathers,
but in war fathers bury their sons.'

HERODOTUS

CHAPTER ONE

SPARKY was uncharacteristically quiet as we awaited our departure from London's Heathrow airport. His handsome face was partially concealed behind his head of dreadlocks and he wore a weird smile that made him look like he'd just had major dental surgery. I sensed that something was amiss.

He was one of the boys. But to me, Sparky – who earned his nickname because he was constantly sparking up a cigarette or a joint – was more than that. He was one of an inner circle of mates who had grown up together and who were close enough to be my brothers.

Sparky had an independent streak that set him apart. We all talked about tattoos. He went out and got one – a Mayan tribal design on the back of his left shoulder. We had one ear pierced, he had both done – and wore at least two earrings in each. We consumed twenty cigarettes a day; he chain-smoked thirty. We dabbled in hash and grass. He sold the shit.

He was just one of those cheeky characters bent on living life on the edge. Wherever we went, he would go one step further.

We were a group of twenty or so 18-year-olds heading for Rosh HaNikra, a 400-member kibbutz in northern Israel that virtually straddles the border with Lebanon. Most of us had spent our teenage years together as members of an international Zionist youth movement, meeting twice a year at national camps where we got to know each other from the inside of a leaking tent somewhere in the British countryside. That's where I had first met Sparky and some of the others several years before.

After our final year at school, a year-long, kibbutz-based program organised by the youth movement was dangled, carrot-like, in front of us. Even though it was dressed up as an educational program, including seminars and tours, we were more interested in the big picture: this would be our opportunity to leave home and lose our innocence in a hedonistic haven of hippies, pseudo-hippies and wannabes, where money plays no intrinsic role, where food, clothes and shelter are provided in return for manual labour, and where the dream of living a carefree life on a secluded farm would become a reality.

Because the Middle East is synonymous with some of the world's most wanted terrorists, security is as tight as it is tough.

Undercover Israeli secret service agents sporting sunglasses and earpieces, gun-toting British policemen in bullet-proof vests and airport security personnel are all on the prowl for suspicious-looking characters.

Airline staff question us meticulously. 'Did you pack your bags? Have they been with you since you packed them? Did anybody give you anything to take? Could anyone have slipped something inside? Where are you going in Israel? What are you doing there? Why? How long for? When will you return? . . .'

One slightly unconvincing response can result in your underwear being dissected in front of a line of bemused passengers. Likewise, if you look as though you've just spent a month in a guerrilla training camp in Iran or Afghanistan, you'll be on a fast track to a bag – and full body – search.

No matter where you are travelling from in the world, you know you've arrived before you've even taken off for, let alone landed in, Israel.

Surprisingly, Sparky attracted no attention whatsoever. He waltzed through without a problem.

I signed up for kibbutz long before the application forms were even printed. My fascination with Israel stretched way back to 1973, when I first travelled there on holidays as a 3-year-old. It was just before the Yom Kippur War, when Syria and Egypt attacked Israel on the holiest day in the Jewish calendar, almost catching the Israel Defence Forces (IDF) unawares. The IDF won the war but lost over 2500 soldiers, causing then Prime Minister Golda Meir to resign over the near catastrophe.

According to my mother, I managed to spend most of that two-week holiday with my eyes shut, the glare of the sun unbearable. Small wonder when you grow up in rainy, drizzly Scotland, where summer has been indefinitely postponed and where autumn and spring have been hijacked by winter.

My sister, Ruth, was already living in Jerusalem, having immigrated to Israel the year before, and my parents, who had visited on countless occasions, had also lived there back in 1961 and 1962. So it was hardly a daring move. In fact, my departure for kibbutz barely raised an eyebrow.

But when my father told me that my great-grandfather had purchased a small plot of land in Rehovot, south of Tel Aviv, in the 1920s and had planted an orange orchard there, I realised that I was simply following a long family tradition.

The fact that the orchard had now been reduced to a traffic island in the middle of a busy intersection in a built-up neighbourhood with not an orange in sight was beside the point.

The road north from Nahariya hugs the Mediterranean coastline. Citrus orchards and banana plantations line either side of the road as it approaches the border with Lebanon. Just past the turnoff to the outposts of Shlomi and Sasa is Kibbutz Rosh HaNikra – the final frontier on Israel's northwestern border.

A cluster of villas dots the incline of the mountain that separates Israel from Lebanon. In the centre of the kibbutz is a huge dining room and kitchen. Underneath is the members social club. Adjacent is a set of offices where the CEO of the kibbutz and his or her committee administer the central planning of the farm. And peppered around the rest of the hillside, nestled between the villas and apartments, are gardens, children's nurseries, classrooms, a football pitch, basketball court and views beyond the cliff and out to the Mediterranean Sea that could qualify for *National Geographic*.

If it sounds like paradise revisited, it is. At least it was, back in 1988.

It later became clear why Sparky had barely said a word at the airport: he was smuggling an eighth of an ounce of hashish inside his cheek, and he was prepared to swallow it if he sensed trouble brewing. So he said after the event.

'Then what?' I asked him, as he produced the goods for viewing later that night in our rooms at the far end of the kibbutz.

'What d'you mean?'

'If you swallowed that hash, you'd spend the year tripping. You'd be fucked.'

He shook his head and rolled his eyes in that how-can-you-be-so-damn-naive kind of way. 'Bollocks Ben. I'd just crap it out from down under, fish it out the shitter, unravel the cellophane and . . . bingo!'

He made it sound as painless as knocking back a dram of scotch on a chilly night.

'Next time I smoke shite hash I'll know where it's been,' I said.

Sparky sniggered.

But I was out of his league. I had only recently paid £25 for a piece of hash that turned out to be compressed roof tar. Not to mention the time when I managed to procure a cocktail of oregano and thyme dressed up in marijuana leaves for an embarrassingly large sum of money.

The irony was that we were sitting on the border with Lebanon, one of the finest hashish-producing countries in the world. Sparky later admitted that the proximity of the kibbutz to Lebanon was one of the determining factors that swayed him to come along in the first place.

But it wasn't a factor in his decision to smuggle illicit drugs across international borders. His mission was to run the gauntlet of security personnel with a block of hash in his mouth. Not because he was worried he'd be dry upon arrival (though that was a fair point), but because he'd get a hit out of living on the edge. That was his fix.

Less than a kilometre farther up the coast from the kibbutz, the road ends abruptly at two huge, iron gates patrolled by a phalanx of IDF soldiers. A watchtower rises skyward. Armoured personnel carriers and UN jeeps hover in the area awaiting instructions. Tanks caterpillar across the border.

Beyond here is where Lebanon begins. Beyond here is where a war is being waged between the IDF (with its militia proxy, the predominantly Christian South Lebanese Army) and Hezbollah, an Iranian-backed Islamic militia hell-bent on jihad – holy war against the 'Zionist infidels'.*

Just before the gates is a lookout point on top of the white cliff. On a clear day, you can see down the coast, past Nahariya and ancient Akko and along the sweeping beaches as far south as the port of Haifa, over fifty kilometres away. In the other direction, to the north, you can see as far as the soldiers patrolling the gate – a distance of, at most, twenty metres.

To the south the view is serene; to the north it is submerged in blood and tears. Welcome to the beauty and barbarity of the Middle East.

* The IDF invaded Lebanon in 1982 on the pretext of driving out the PLO, which had been shelling Israel's northern communities. Hezbollah, literally 'party of God', was founded in Lebanon in 1982 and its name is derived from a tortured mullah (Muslim scholar) in Iran whose last words in 1973, allegedly, were: 'There is only one party, the party of God'.

CHAPTER TWO

LIVING IN A COMMUNE with twenty or so like-minded people was a marked departure from anything I'd ever experienced before. We picked fruit and drank beer, staying awake long after our eyes had retired. We shared our money and shared our souls. We learned about the meaning of compromise and community. And we learned about the troubles in this so-called Promised Land.

But mostly, we spent our days labouring in the fields and our nights drowning our livers in alcohol, suffocating our lungs with smoke and experiencing the emotion of love for the first time.

'When the siren sounds, the community hits the bomb shelters,' emphasised our guide on a tour of our new home several days after we arrived. As we strolled around the hillside farm, he'd stop every few minutes, mid-sentence, to identify another underground bomb shelter.

Like many other kibbutzim, he explained, Rosh HaNikra – one of some 250 across the country, accounting for around three per cent of Israel's population – was originally founded in 1949 as a border outpost to protect the fledgling state. When Israel was established in 1948, just over half of existing settlements were kibbutzim.

The pioneers of the kibbutz, immigrant Jews from Central and Eastern Europe, built it on the incline as opposed to the flat plain below because they realised that they stood a better chance of avoiding the missiles and katyusha rockets dispatched from Lebanon.

History has proved them right. The kibbutz itself has been spared from missiles or rockets landing inside its perimeter fence, although its banana plantations have been the recipient of wayward strikes.

But, our guide informed us, they had suffered one cross-border incursion. In the 1970s, Palestinian terrorists snuck across the border and broke into his house. He was shot in the back and, as a result, lost some of the mobility in his hands and neck. He raised his contorted palms as he told us that the terrorists were eventually surrounded by the army and killed.

The metal door and half staircase was all that remained above ground – a triangular-shaped structure surrounded by a huge bed of giant rocks held together inside iron caging that is usually used to prevent landslides.

The farther down the stairs we descended, the sharper the damp, dank stench became. At the foot of the stairs was a huge, half-metre-thick, steel-enforced door with a large, lever handle on the inside.

The shelter was not large, perhaps big enough for thirty people to sleep in. There was a dartboard on the wall and a toilet at the far end. Clusters of tables and chairs dotted the place. Graffiti was scrawled across the walls. Since it had been used sparingly over the years, and because it was adjacent to the dining room, this particular shelter now doubled as a pub.

I had never been inside a bomb shelter before. So, despite the stench, which I now figured was stale beer, there was something seductively cool about the prospect of spending a night underground. It had novelty value for one. And the chances of being woken up by rays of sunlight (my first visit to Israel was still scorched into my subconscious) were next to nil. Not to mention the fact that I'd be guaranteed to be alive, if a little smelly.

After a tentative first few days, we boys muscled in and dug ourselves a comfortable trench from which to lubricate our tonsils night after night. Soon we even forgot it was originally a bomb shelter.

We were introduced to Israeli Goldstar and Maccabi beers, as well as Araq, a local aniseed pinch-your nose-while-you-drink-it spirit that is high in alcohol content and low in pleasure. I could feel it stripping the mucous membranes off the inside of my throat as it trickled past my palate.

Our beer intake was recorded in a book and withdrawn from our collective work wages. And we had an allowance for free cigarettes each week, which were shared. Of course, as with most things free, they disappeared almost overnight, though you could bet on several packs lurking under mattresses, stuffed in dirty sock bags or wedged between the drainpipe and the cistern behind the toilets.

As the week dragged on and our supplies diminished, the hunt began to find where someone had stashed an emergency pack. Sparky, somehow, never ran out of smokes. He could always produce one, or at least a rusty half, in the midst of a drought.

Noblesse was the selected blend: it was cheap and, as a result, nasty – a dry, harsh smoke from hell that came in a soft green packet that would inevitably result in flat, squashed cigarettes. They were soon referred to as 'camel shit', and they were only marginally better than Time, another local brand, instantly recognisable by its nauseating chemical-like smell. 'Time' reminded me of some preposterous brand names I had seen on the black market. Like 'Hope', 'Eternity' and 'Heaven'. Twenty a day of these three would leave you with little hope in life, no chance of living anywhere close to eternity and every likelihood that heaven would be just around the corner. Time would not be on your side.

Friday nights were special for two reasons: Shabbat dinner welcomed in the day of rest, just as God had planned. At all other times, members, volunteers and kids would arrive to eat whenever they felt inclined within the two-hour session, sit wherever they wanted and dress as inappropriately as they desired.

Not on Friday nights. The whole community converged on the dining room. Most of the members arrived squeaky clean, hair brushed, dressed neatly, shoes on. And the kitchen would always dish up a special meal – chicken soup, shnitzel, roast potatoes – as opposed to the staple salad and leftovers from lunch.

Extended families sat together, while the kids played outside on the climbing frame. Even the dogs came along, running amok on the lawn just in front of the dining room.

But Friday nights were also synonymous with the pub. Because they preceded Saturdays, our only day of rest, they were long, torrid affairs that ended not long before sunrise and, for some, in black-outs. Saturday morning breakfast was a definite no-show. Lunch was a struggle; by dinner it was easy to discern who the casualties were.

CHAPTER THREE

SPARKY HAD ALREADY smoked two cigarettes by the time I reached the dining room. That was the story the ashtray told. But I knew him better. It was more of a probability than a possibility that he had had one in bed when he woke up (that's if he bothered going to sleep) and another on the way to the dining room.

Not a bad innings for 5.25 am.

He offered me a squashed Noblesse and we drank bitter coffee together as we braced for another day's work in the fields. He was working in the banana plantations; I was assigned to the citrus orchards, following in my great-grandfather's footsteps.

'You could've landed a missile next to me and it wouldn't have woken me up,' I said in between sips.

Sparky was rubbing his eyes with the palm of his hand. 'Tell me about it. I feel like I've been run over by a tank. I was in the pub until two.'

I barely blinked. I didn't need his confirmation or the stench of alcohol to tell me what I already knew.

Shuki arrived, bleary-eyed tiredness pasted all over the crusts that were still glued around his eye sockets. Born on the kibbutz, he was short and stocky, a guy whose width challenged his height. His biceps were almost as wide as my neck. But he was not embarrassed by his physique. On the contrary, he flaunted it because he had barely an ounce of fat on him.

He was a frogman, an elite subterranean soldier. His was a perilous task that required him to be submerged underwater for lengthy periods before surfacing to undertake military reconnaissance operations.

Sparky was mesmerised by some of Shuki's stories and spent much of his banana-picking time in his company, teasing battle tales from his memory bank. But right now, the pair were pulling cigarettes and sipping coffee, nursing the night before – and cursing the day ahead.

At 5.30 am the dining room was slowly filling as members arrived by foot or bicycle – there are neither roads nor cars within the residential part of the kibbutz – for a caffeine fix before venturing out into the fields.

Ever since the dawn of the Israeli kibbutz, the dining room has been the heart and soul of the community, where important decisions are taken and where equally unimportant gossip is exchanged. Its doors always remain open – day and night. Coffee, tea and bread are always available.

But the onslaught of capitalism coupled with the fall of communism has altered the reality on many kibbutzim. Self-interest, decentralisation and privatisation have seeped past the security fences and into the fabric of these socialist sanctuaries.

Some members want to eat privately with their families in their own homes. Others want to earn their own wages and pay their own gas and electricity bills.

As a result, some kibbutz kitchens are now locked for dinner. Others are only open on Friday evenings and festivals. And at Kibbutz Shfayim, not far north of Tel Aviv, members have to pay using a magnetic swipe card.

But, even though the vindication of capitalism has ravaged the original dream of the socialist founders, it has yet to quash the kibbutz as an Israeli institution.

We were oblivious to these political and economic issues. Ideology and all the highbrow philosophy that went with it were low on our list of priorities. We didn't come to sign up to be members of the Socialist Revolution. We barely even related to the fact that the Intifada, the Palestinian uprising which began in 1987, was burning in the West Bank and Gaza Strip or that there was a war being waged across the mountain in southern Lebanon. We were cocooned in our own blissful world, oblivious to the harsh realities of life – and death – in the Middle East.

Our wish list, like that of most youths our age, was threefold: sex, drugs and rock 'n' roll. In no particular order.

The most marked event surrounding our arrival on kibbutz was the departure, not long afterwards, of all of the 18-year-old boys and girls for the army, leaving all the 16- and 17-year-old girls in the lurch. To us, it was a God-given gift, like manna from heaven.

Throw in free cigarettes and subsidised beer and we were left with only one question on our minds: does life get any better?

Most of the boys in the group were recruited for the banana fields, one of the kibbutz's main crops. Others were in the citrus and avocado orchards; some were in the chicken houses, nursery, laundry, kitchen and dining room. A few of the girls even scored jobs in the scientific laboratory, where they researched how to produce weird and wonderful fruit hybrids like apple bananas.

And one bloke was stuck in the cowshed. Unsurprisingly, he permanently stank of cow dung. The rancid smell followed him like a lingering fart wherever he went, and it wasn't long before the group issued an edict prohibiting him from nearing our rooms until he stripped to his boxers.

In season, the banana boys chopped down huge bunches of ripe bananas, weighing up to fifty kilos each, and carried them on their shoulders to the loading cart. There, they passed them up to a couple of muscle-bursting guys like Shuki who attached the thick stems to nooses so that the bunches hung, like stuffed turkeys, upside down for their transport to the port. Then they set sail for world markets.

On the morning they received their long banana knives, the boys strutted through the dining room like kids who'd just discovered the art of wagging school. Though they were trying to be nonchalantly cool about their initiation, there was no mistaking their pride.

The dining room was their catwalk. Wearing a don't-fuck-with-us—we're-armed-and-dangerous look, they strolled through with their machetes in leather cases strapped to their belts.

Those of us lads in the orchards were suddenly overcome by a variation of penis envy. Miffed at missing out on the armour, we gaped at their weapons and, looking down at our small pairs of citrus clippers – no competition for a 40-centimetre banana knife – we felt insufficiently equipped.

The kibbutz car park is buzzing. Most people are dressed in navy-blue work shirts and shorts – the standard attire of a kibbutznik. Those wearing wellington boots are heading back from the grave-yard shift in the cowsheds. The midnight milk is over. The long machete knives make the banana boys unmistakable.

Our tractor drones into action, expelling plumes of black smoke from its vertical exhaust into the atmosphere. The trailer is half full. Eight of us are working in the orchards for the day.

One of them is Alan, an affable Englishman with a bushy moustache and a thick cockney accent, who came, like most travellers, to volunteer for a few months 'experience'. His claim to fame, according to the grapevine, is that he supplies the local sperm bank with his 'boys' in exchange for a handsome profit. That's why, three years later, he is still here, living for free while accruing a tidy profit from the 'bank'.

Most of us thought he was talking shite. But none of us would dare say so, although some of the boys thought they might nip down to Haifa, a half-hour drive away, to see what sort of return they would get from their 'investment'.

Two bangs on the outside of the trailer signal to the driver and orchard boss, Itzik, that we are all aboard. We descend the hill, passing a group of workers heading for the turkey houses near the entrance to the farm.

Rose, one of the girls in our group, is walking to the laundry where she works. I don't really know her well, but know that I want to get to know her. I catch her eye and manage to flash as good a smile as I can muster at 5.45 am on a Sunday morning.

As banal as picking fruit all day every day sounds, there is something delectably cool about being driven through the morn-ing mist by a tractor on the way to work. Long lines of fruit trees dominate the flat plain below the kibbutz, the morning wind teasing their palms.

Itzik is at the helm, driving slowly. Forty years on, he knows the pot-holed road like he knows each row of trees in his orchard. Hiding under a peaked cap and inside a wool jumper to keep out the biting wind washing up off the Mediterranean, he glides the tractor off the road and into the orchard.

He is a gentle, unassuming man whose skin reads like ancient parchment scribbled by the sun. As one of the pioneers of this kibbutz, he has lived most of his life here. When his day arrives, he will no doubt be buried here, too. Like other members of his generation, Itzik spends almost all of his life within the security fence of this self-sufficient community, barely venturing beyond its frontiers.

He feels safe. This is his home. But for Itzik, I soon discover, it is so much more than that. He arrived as a refugee from war-torn Europe, setting foot on these shores with barely an item to his name. He rebuilt his life from scratch. As a pioneer, he helped transform this rugged mountainside into the farm it is today. He fought in the 1948 and 1956 wars. He served as a reserve soldier in the 1967 and 1973 wars.

Since 1982, he has watched the legions of infantry and armoury pass by the kibbutz gate, his front door, on the way to Lebanon. And he has watched them return – some happy, some sad and some of them in body bags.

He is a man of few words. But the six-numbered tattoo burned onto his forearm speaks volumes about his life story: he survived Hitler's death camps, and I crave to walk through the pages of his memory.

CHAPTER FOUR

IN SUMMER, we drank freshly-squeezed citrus juice each morning, sitting on worn benches outside the small shed in a clearing in the middle of the orchard. It was still hot for a couple of months after we arrived in August, but when winter set in, we brewed a pot of hot Turkish coffee and huddled inside around a battered table surrounded by shelves piled high with tools, cans of engine oil and old boxes. The table, a relic of sorts, was engraved with carvings in Hebrew and English, reflecting the number of people who had worked here and then moved on.

We were only a small team, between six and eight people. Itzik maintained a silence that became increasingly noticeable. He answered when talked to, but he would be brief and to the point. Sometimes he would engage in a conversation and smile fleetingly before returning to his own private space.

The only thing I remember him telling me in any detail was an old story of a kibbutznik who travelled to Tel Aviv for the first time. He was not awestruck by the Shalom Tower, the highest building in the city, or the endless entertainment and shopping opportunities. No, Itzik relayed, he was dumbstruck at the sight of a beggar, a fellow human left to rot in the gutter.

It had never really occurred to me. A kibbutz is an island sanctuary where everyone – the weak and the meek, young and old, strong and sick – are looked after. While kibbutz life may have its restrictions, the community is devoid of the cut-throat nature of urban life, providing equally for its members – from the cradle to the grave. Which is why many people like Itzik don't bother leaving too often.

He and his wife – who was also a Holocaust survivor – do not return to those dark days. It's as if they had packaged those harrowing memories away in a box in the attic. All that remained was the tattoo on his forearm – the indelible stain of genocide.

All I knew of Itzik, which I learned on the grapevine, was that he had been born in a small village in Poland and was sent to Treblinka, one of six death camps established by the Nazis. Itzik survived, but he lost almost all of his extended family and friends. They say only three other Jews from his village were still alive at the end of the war. His silence tortured me. For the first few weeks I would return from work grappling to piece his puzzle together.

I didn't broach the subject with Sparky. He was too involved in Shuki's army antics. And the other lads were busy trying to work out a way of copying the key to the kitchen storeroom so they could satisfy their midnight munchies. Or working out how to pin a rat by its tail to the door of the girls' rooms so that it would swing into their faces when they entered. Just to scare them. Just for a laugh.

In the laundry, Rose would sit with the old ladies of the kibbutz and wash, iron and dry 400 people's clothes in industrial-sized machines that were large enough to consume her.

It was Rose who returned my underwear bag in the first week with what appeared to be lingerie belonging to an elderly woman along with a pair of kinky suspenders. This, despite the fact that all our clothes were clearly marked by number – mine was 724 – and all our underwear was washed inside a string sock bag. Sparky was quick to appropriate the suspenders and was spotted wearing them around his head at a bad taste party we organised when we got bored with the pub.

I was kind of hoping that maybe she planted them as her way of making a move.

Over the next few weeks, I became increasingly drawn to Rose. She had soft, caramel-coloured skin, almond eyes and two cute dimples that appeared with the slightest smile.

Her trademark was her blazing, orange-red hair; twists, tangles and curls, some of which stood on end, making her look like she was partially consumed by an electric shock. What she lacked in height, she more than made up for in beauty. But what attracted me most was that she was down to earth. She was a good listener too, but also willing to speak her mind if and when she felt strongly about something.

'Why do you portray him as a universal victim, without a personality?' she scolded me one night as I helped her fold our group's laundry and place it in the numbered pigeonholes. 'Maybe Itzik was always a quiet kind of guy, even before the war. You define everything about him through the prism of the Holocaust. How do you know what he was like before?'

I was left speechless. In one short, casual conversation, Rose had blasted my impression of Itzik to pieces.

'You see him first – and foremost – as a survivor, then as a human being. That's your problem, your guilt, your trap. That's your prejudice,' she said staring me straight in the eye. 'Me? I see him as a human being, an individual, a person who lives and loves.'

I gulped. I was humbled, almost embarrassed by my oversight, my labelling of someone who had suffered so much. But, somewhere between my humility and embarrassment, I was turned on.

We talked over dinner in the dining room. It was buffet style: uncut raw vegetables – lettuce, tomato, cucumber, onion and carrot – bread, hard-boiled eggs and the left-overs from lunch was as good, or bad, as it got. Every night, except Fridays and festivals.

We grabbed a table by the window and began chopping up an uninspiring salad. 'Maybe he is consumed by guilt, of having survived in place of his parents, brothers, sisters, family and friends,' I said.

Maybe. Maybe.

Rose waited patiently, twiddling a twist of curls.

'Maybe,' she said moving in to dice a cucumber, 'but maybe not. Perhaps in the process of building this kibbutz and planting his orchard, he began to rebuild his life, to heal his wounds. Now he has built a fortress around him. Inside his walls is his Garden of Eden – just because he has a tattoo does not mean he carries the burden of history on his shoulders day and night. Just because he has a tattoo doesn't mean he wants your pity.

'In any case, why do you have to analyse everything to the nth degree? Maybe he survived through pure luck, serendipity, fate or simply because he was in the right place at the right time.'

Jesus. I barely knew this girl, but I felt like she'd just plunged me into the Dead Sea with a foot full of cuts and grazes.

'Maybe,' I said reluctantly, as I squeezed a fresh lemon – quite possibly one that I had picked the day before – over my salad.

'To me,' said Rose, 'Itzik is a lighthouse and a fortress. To me, he must be an angel to have survived.'

I wanted to tell her it was she who was the angel. But it would have sounded too clichéd.

As days passed, I began to come to terms with the fact that it was impossible to try to stand in the shoes of a Holocaust survivor who had lost his whole family in the war. Here was a man who, as a teenager, had witnessed the end of his world.

I spent hours, days, weeks, months picking pink grapefruits, lemons, limes, tangerines and pomelos, filling my sack and emptying it into the huge tub between two fruit-laden lines of trees, trying to figure out how a survivor can forget the Holocaust despite the injunction to remember it. And when I wasn't thinking about Itzik, I was trying to work out how to summon up the courage to make a move on Rose.

Israel is not a place to forget about the Holocaust. Many argue that the state was built on the ashes of Auschwitz, the infamous icon that stands as the quintessential symbol of evil.

'Hitler made the dream come true,' writes Clive James in his book, *Flying Visits*. 'He set out to kill a race and ended up by creating a state.'

That would have been the irony to end all ironies. The truth, however, is that by the early 1940s a Jewish state was already, more or less, a *fait accompli*. But the annihilation of one-third of world Jewry no doubt accelerated its creation.

Whether Israel was created because of, or in spite of, the Holocaust, the two events are inextricably linked in the Jewish psyche. Two museums maintain permanent memorials to the tragedy: Yad Vashem, the national memorial in Jerusalem, and the lesser known Lochamei HaGeta'ot, the Ghetto Fighters' Museum, near Akko.

Emotion permeates the air that hangs heavy around these memorials: guilt that we did not do enough to prevent the slaughter; discomfort that we survived while our brothers, sisters, families did not; anger that the Allies in the West did not bomb the train tracks leading into Auschwitz when they could have; disbelief that our fellow human beings could stoop to such abominable depths.

What if Itzik did want to erase those memories but could find no place to hide? Barely a day passes here without some reference to the war in some form or other. Television, radio, films, books, magazines and newspapers flood the country with coverage on Holocaust-related issues.

Where was Itzik on 23 May 1960 when then Prime Minister David Ben-Gurion informed the nation that the Mossad, the Israeli secret service, had captured the architect of the Final Solution, Adolf Eichmann, in Argentina? No Jew, not least those who survived the camps, could not have been moved by the events that unfolded, day by day, for the next two years until Eichmann's execution in 1962; the first – and last – time Israel has used the death penalty.

And even if, on kibbutz, Itzik manages to avoid the past, there are two minutes every year where it is impossible to hide from the Holocaust. Each year on Holocaust Memorial Day, as Israel pays tribute to the six million Jews who perished, a siren hollers across every city and town, valley and field, kibbutz and moshav.*

It aches with pain, quakes with heartache and shudders with grief. The siren sends a bitter chill down the national spine, bringing the country to an immediate standstill in one life-defining moment.

---

* A moshav is a cooperative community like a kibbutz, except that the families do not share their profits. The first moshav was established in 1921 and after 1948 they became popular settlements for Sephardi Jews.

Then the siren becomes an echo, gently trailing into the distance. And, slowly, people pick themselves up, cradle their broken hearts and piece them back together again. On the one hand, it is incomprehensible that people can make such a sudden switch between death and life, life and death; on the other, it is a hallmark of our survival that we are able to straighten our backs and breathe life once again. The mere presence of Jews living in Israel is a poignant riposte to Hitler's Final Solution.

'Can you imagine what these two minutes are like for Itzik and other Holocaust survivors?' I asked Rose.

She shook her head. 'No. I can only imagine that it's like the pain of having six numbers tattooed onto bare skin.'

First came the deafening noise, a thunderous clap that sounded like a sonic boom triggered by IDF warplanes sprinting towards action in southern Lebanon. They were fairly common affairs here on the border, and after a while we became immune to them. But there were also shorter blasts, which sounded like missiles being detonated from beyond the mountaintop behind the kibbutz.

Then came what appeared to be fireworks, and soon the sky sparkled with light. The whirring sound of the siren, the call to descend underground, confirmed that they were not fireworks, but IDF flares illuminating the night to track down the enemy. The sound of distant gunfire was trailed by a window of silence.

At around 9 pm on a Friday night the war in Lebanon was threatening to spoil our party. I was in the courtyard between the two long, one-storey buildings containing our rooms when the siren sounded. Sparky showed little sense of panic. So I didn't bother to panic either.

Here we were on the border with Lebanon, salvos of katyusha rockets and flares collaborating in a pyrotechnic party in the sky, and we just stood there awestruck, necks craned skyward as if we had front row seats to Bob Marley & the Wailers.

Some of the kibbutz members began racing from their houses, submachine guns strapped across their shoulders.

I punched Sparky in the arm. 'Shit! Someone must have breached the kibbutz security fence. Why else would they be armed?'

'Let's make a break for it.'

We could have, should have, headed for our nearest shelter, about twenty metres away from our rooms. But it was Friday night and no Islamic guerrillas were about to lock us underground without beer. Or music. And definitely not without women. We headed for the pub.

For a minute or two we had to run for cover, scuttling to avoid being caught in the crossfire. We ran with our backs bent down like ostriches, our hands instinctively in front of our faces, protecting our heads in case of exploding shrapnel.

Clambering over the rock bed that insulated the bomb shelter, we descended into its tender warmth. The huge, cast-iron vault-like door was almost closed and it took both of us to drag it open. Inside, the music was blaring, the place jammed. Smoke swirled around looking for an exit that didn't exist.

We were under attack from guerrilla warfare overground and here, five metres underground, we proceeded to get blind drunk. When we crawled out several hours later, the sky was still. The air was calm. The battle was over.

The katyushas had missed the kibbutz.

CHAPTER FIVE

I USED TO think that the cost of travel was little. I invested my money in the university of life, not stocks and shares. Then I experienced the travel bug. That's when the real cost of travel began to bite: the more I travelled, the more I wanted to travel, the less money I had to travel.

But if a serious bug bites you, it can take the wind out of your sails and grind your travels to an immediate, and often unpleasant, halt. The bug that bit me almost knocked me overboard. For a moment there, back on kibbutz in 1989, it wasn't clear if I'd sink or swim.

We had spent a weekend at Kfar Yassif, a small Arab village just inland from the coast, not far from the northern border, meeting Arab youth.

The thing that strikes you as you enter this Arab town – and the neighbouring village of Abu Sinan, along with most other Arab towns and villages in Israel – is that it seems to be permanently under construction. Nothing feels complete. Work in progress appears to be the order of the day.

Just off the main highway, a pot-holed street splutters into the centre of town. Houses on stilts, still under construction, creep up the rocky hillside. Bare foundations erupt from the ground. Pipes lie overground awaiting a trench digger to bury them. A tangle of cables zigzags above the road, dangling perilously close to oncoming concrete mixers and tractors.

Part of this work-in-progress theme is cultural. The Arabs tend to build for the generations to come. They construct a floor to live on while they continue to build more floors for future generations. But it also has to do with a government funding issue that is clear to anyone who visits Jewish towns and then goes to neighbouring Arab villages. The lack of infrastructure and the dearth of basic amenities stick out in Arab villages as much as the trademark red roofs do in Jewish settlements.

Here, in Kfar Yassif, like many other Arab villages, the local Arabs – equal Israeli citizens in the eyes of the law – have been short-changed by the state.*

Israel's Arabs, numbering some 1.15 million people (about one-fifth of the Israeli population), are not conscripted to the army for obvious security reasons: they would be caught in a lose–lose trap if they had to fight for Israel against their Arab brethren.

Although the Palestinian Intifada was still raging in the West Bank and Gaza Strip, and although they empathised with the plight of their brethren across the Green Line, Israel's Arab sector never ventured into the Palestinian conflict.† Instead they live their lives treading a delicate tightrope between religion and nationality.

Several days after we returned from Kfar Yassif, my energy levels began waning. I felt nauseous. The more I slept the more I needed to sleep. I could barely walk, let alone work. I lost colour in my face, and my skin paled from off-white to fluorescent.

Eventually, Rose, whom I'd just managed to woo from friendship to relationship after weeks of Libran indecision, took me to the kibbutz clinic. The nurse thought I had a fever, so she gave me Akomol, the local version of paracetamol, and told me to rest.

---

* Israeli Arabs have made significant gains of late: thirteen Israeli Arabs were elected to the Knesset in 1999; the first Arab was elected to the Supreme Court in 1999; and in October 2000 the Barak government ratified a four-year NIS 4 billion development plan for seventy-four Arab communities in Israel.

† The Green Line is so named because during an earlier round of troubles, a British officer drew a line in green ink to divide the Cypriot capital, Nicosia, into two sectors. After Israel occupied the West Bank in 1967, the term 'Green Line' was used to refer to the 1949 cease-fire line in Palestine. Beirut acquired its own Green Line during the Lebanese civil war.

My condition deteriorated steadily. I went from slender to gaunt. My fever was a roller-coaster ride of highs and lows. But it was always there. Rose insisted I see the local doctor.

He visited the kibbutz from the nearby town of Nahariya twice a week. Examining me for a few minutes, he declared, 'Benjamin, you have fever,' and summarily dispensed antibiotics.

Days passed. No recovery of any sort was evident. Rose was far from happy that I was just lying there like a wilting flower. Nahariya hospital, some fifteen minutes' drive south from Rosh HaNikra, was the only remaining option, she decided.

'We'll need to do some tests,' the nurse said in Hebrew that I struggled to comprehend. She pulled the curtains around my bed and inserted an IV drip into one of my veins. It stood, like a soldier on guard duty, next to my bed.

The room was tiny. It consisted of four beds and four patients with just enough room for the doctor or nurse to squeeze between us. Next to me was a man who, though clearly sick, still wore his white turban in bed and was dressed in long white robes. He sported a thick, bushy, steely-grey moustache, and his forehead was ablaze with veins that looked on the verge of bursting.

He was, I soon discovered, a Druze, an offshoot of Islam that split from the mainstream in the eleventh century. There are around 75,000 Druze living in Israel, largely in villages in the Galilee and the Golan Heights. They consider themselves neither Muslim nor Christian, and their religion is steeped in mystery understood only by those who belong. They are a tight-knit community who, like ultra-Orthodox Jews, tend to keep themselves to themselves.

Most of them swear allegiance to whatever state they live in and, together with some of the Bedouin, are the only Arabs that serve in the Israeli army.

Two elderly Israeli Jews occupied the remaining two beds. I figured one may be Sephardi, of Middle Eastern or North African origin, and the other Ashkenazi, from European descent, but I wasn't sure and I didn't have the energy to befriend them.

One morning, not long after I was admitted, the matron – a large-breasted colossus of a woman from Russia – rolled up with a group of six other nurses. She pulled the curtain around my bed and all of a sudden there were seven women in a tiny space peering down at me. They all held clipboards and were desperately scribbling notes as the matron raced through what appeared to be an explanation of my condition.

I could barely make out what was being said since all of it was in Hebrew and much of it was in medical parlance.

She leaned over me, her breasts bulging out of her blouse through the sheer force of gravity, and began pulling my sheets back. She poked and probed, touched and felt, all the while addressing her students.

Petrified and unable to understand the gist of her spiel, I trawled her students for facial expressions that may have hinted at my predicament. There were plenty of frowners and several head-scratchers. The others looked simply bewildered or bemused. Except for one cute, black-haired nurse who seemed more intent on making eye contact with me than taking notes. Now was not the most appropriate time to start flirting, although, given the fact that I could not feel much worse, I did briefly entertain the notion.

All I wanted was my mum. Instead, all I had was some enormous babushka explaining to her students what a medical anomaly I was.

I cried when they left. There is little worse than being in hospital in a foreign country where the staff does not speak your language. But being experimented on by students for the pursuit of medical science, made me feel like a dissected rat in a biology laboratory. All I had for company was my loyal IV drip. And I barely had the energy to take it for a walk. My world had shrunk into breaks between bed baths and bad food.

A new doctor arrived one morning, greeting us with enough effervescence to fill a champagne bottle. He was a short man with a groomed moustache, and he stood there facing the four of us, clipboard under arm, spectacles folded in breast pocket, and delivered a speech that could have qualified for the Oscars. He spoke in English, jumping every so often to Hebrew and then, by instinct, to Arabic.

But, after a battery of tests, he was equally perplexed. He had never seen a case like it. By this time, I'd had enough. I wanted out. I summoned the strength to walk my IV drip to the toilet where I negotiated the sewerage system with all the delicacy of a nun. Then I went to phone Rose.

The hospital begrudgingly agreed to release me and packed me off with dozens of muscle-relaxing tablets to ease my pain.

Back on kibbutz, Rose nursed me and visitors greeted me day and night. She brought me chicken soup in an effort to activate its medicinal properties. It had a mild, short-lived effect.

The muscle-relaxing tablets had a much greater effect.

Sparky and some of the boys were quick on the scene. I knew they wanted to see me but I also knew that they had other business to attend to when they were not working.

It was on the third day after I returned to kibbutz that I began to suspect something. I had been taking the muscle-relaxing tablets and they had improved my ability to sleep and substantially eased my pain. But I was sure I hadn't consumed a whole packet already.

Then Sparky arrived.

'How you doin' Ben?'

'Bleak.'

'Those tablets not working?'

'Dunno. They feel good, but they don't seem to be making much of a long-term impact.'

Sparky was consulting the explanation on the package. 'Says here they work wonders for people with aching bodies, they pacify the pain, numb the muscles. Is this the stuff they use to tranquillise horses?'

Next thing I know he's popped a pill out of its container and thrown it down his throat.

'What the hell . . . ?'

'You don't mind mate, do you?' he asked as the pill bulged his Adam's apple on the way down. 'You got plenty. And the clinic will give you more. I borrowed some yesterday to test them out. They're quality.'

Then he was gone, a whole pack of twelve tablets peeking out of his pocket. That night all I could hear was incessant laughter as Sparky and a few of the boys hobbled about like jelly until the effect of the tablets wore off. Then they slept through their alarms.

Ruth, my sister who was living in Jerusalem, was *au fait* enough with kibbutz life to realise that it was not at the cutting edge of the medical fraternity. She raced up to the kibbutz as soon as she learned of my illness. I suspect Rose called her.

'We're going to Tel Aviv,' she announced, opening my cupboards and throwing some clothes in a bag.

I arrived at Ichilov Hospital in Tel Aviv and was put into a bed in the only space available: the corridor. The wards were all full so I was left out in the middle of the hallway, monitoring the swarm of passing people like a traffic warden.

Dr Topilsky was a specialist lung doctor with a reputation that preceded him like the letters that succeeded his surname. Within hours he diagnosed a lung abscess caused potentially, he cautioned, by a viral strain of pneumonia. It was a highly obscure illness for a 19-year-old to have contracted, he conceded, and I required immediate surgery to extract a ball of pus that was threatening to collapse my left lung under its weight.

'Don't worry,' he smirked unconvincingly. 'Why do you think God gave you two lungs?'

I awoke to find my parents, who had flown in from Scotland, sitting by my bed. I felt like a wall of water had just crushed me, knocking every ounce of everything out of me. I barely managed to keep my eyes open.

A week or so later, I was in a wheelchair being pushed through the hospital doors by my mother into the bright sunlight. I hadn't been exposed to the naked sun for so long that it felt like the rays were singeing my face. As she wheeled me along, I felt tears stream down my face. I was incapable of walking at the tender age of nineteen.

It became apparent there and then just how close I'd danced with death.

Six weeks later, having returned to Scotland to recuperate, I rejoined the group on kibbutz, needless to say against the will of my mother.

It was beautiful to see Rose again after so long. She still made me melt inside, though my intuition told me that something had changed. It had, and a couple of months later, she ditched me for another bloke. I was crushed, but when I got over my heartbreak, I realised how important it was to remain close friends. And we did.

Sparky pulled me aside not long after my return.

'How you feelin' mate?'

'Yeah. Not bad.'

'Sure?' he asked, as if my answer upset him.

'Yeah. Why?'

'I was worried about you. Glad to have you back on board mate.'

'Thanks mate.'

He paused, seemingly deep in thought. Then he turned, a smirk sweeping his face, and said: 'Hey, you wouldn't be able to get your hands on some more of those horse tranquillisers, would you?'

CHAPTER SIX

AFTER THE YEAR expired, Sparky and a few of the other lads decided to stay on in Israel. They loved life on the kibbutz, and felt at home in Israel. They saw no reason to return to the British pseudo-summers, and no college or university course could persuade them to trade their plough for a pen.

Changing their status meant that they would become Israeli citizens. And all 18-year-old Israelis are mandated to serve in the IDF as prescribed by the Defence Service Law. Men for three years; women for two. New immigrants, depending on their age, are required for less time. All men are also required for miluim (reserve duty) for up to one month a year, until the age of 41. This is the price you pay when you choose to live in a country that has existed under a state of emergency since its establishment in 1948.

Hard as it was to imagine Sparky being ordered around, I detected a certain patriotism (as well as a hint of machismo) in his attitude. Kibbutz life was tailor-made for him and he would make a good soldier, I reckoned.

I went to university in Manchester, along with Rose and several of my mates from kibbutz. I lived in a flat with seven not so like-minded students, none of whom I'd ever met before. One of them was an American called Matt who was struggling to suppress the acne erupting across his face. As we watched Israeli troops firing rubber bullets at stone-throwing Palestinian youths in the latest episode of the ensuing Intifada, he shook his head and turned to me: 'How is it that the Israeli army has become the modern-day SS?'

I bit my tongue, figuring silence was the only appropriate response to such a statement. But it troubled me no end. To him, it was black and white. Israel, the occupier, was using its military might against the Palestinians, the occupied. To Matt, and many others in my student flat, there were no shades of grey. To me, it was so grey that even I couldn't work out where to draw the line.

I got my first real job working in a wine bar to pay my rent. Last orders were at 11 pm, and by midnight the doors would be shut and we'd be corking some vintage *vin rouge*.

I also worked in a semi-pretentious French restaurant. One night a customer asked for his roast pheasant to be cooked rare (OK, the place was fully up itself). It arrived well done, so he asked me to take it back. The head chef, an Irish guy by the name of Paddy, was usually stoned and in good humour, except at rush hour. He took the plate, slit the meat with a knife and took one look at me.

'Yer foockin' kiddin' me awn,' he spat, his eyes apparently trying to exit their sockets.

I shrugged, and stared at my feet. There was no point in replying. If something got Paddy's back up, nothing could stand in his way.

The dead bird flew through the air and hit the wall; the plate smashed into smithereens. What was left of the pheasant landed on top of a freshly-baked chocolate mud cake.

'I'll tell them it's on its way,' I said, scampering out the door.

At university, I learned about politics and economics, history and philosophy. We studied Marxism and pluralism, Keynes and Friedman, Hobbes and Rousseau. I went to lectures when I felt like it, and bunked them when I didn't.

During those same formative years, between eighteen and twenty-one, my peers in Israel were conscripted to the army. And to make matters worse, they served at a time when the Palestinians were waging their Intifada, literally 'shaking off' twenty years of Israeli occupation since Israel's victory in the Six-Day War. The post-1967 generation of Palestinians had finally come of age. So, 20-year-old Israeli boys, armed with rubber bullets and tear gas, were chasing 20-year-old Palestinian youths, saddled with slingshots and rocks. It seemed agonisingly obvious that the IDF could win a war, but could never suppress a civilian uprising.

'Do you regret the fact that you had to serve in the army during those prime years of your life?' I asked an Israeli friend one afternoon on a bus up north. I was on a short trip to Israel and was going to visit a few friends, including Sparky, who was home for the weekend from the army.

'Yes and no. At the time, it was just something we all did and all knew we had to do since we were old enough to understand.'

Looking back, he said he had missed out on those years, tasting the bitter realities of war while most people his age were enjoying the sweet fruits of freedom. But he also said they were among the greatest years of his life. Apart from anything else, it was a new experience. And much of it was fun. Many other Israelis concur. They say that they learned about discipline, obedience and authority.

They learned about the meaning of responsibility. They went from being kids to being men when they became soldiers, leapfrogging their teens almost overnight. They began to understand the importance of brotherhood, nationality and identity.

They learned about life. And, tragically, when they buried their friends, they learned about death.

Israel was borne out of war and continues to live under the spectre of it. With 42 military cemeteries and 1400 memorials to the 20,000 or so Israelis who have been killed in battle since the 1947 UN Partition Plan, death is never very far away in this turbulent part of the Middle East.*

The kibbutz van sped past the orchards and the banana plantations as it approached the gate and began the steep incline to the car park. The kibbutz looked the same, but the faces had changed.

---

* The UN Partition Plan, which proposed a Jewish and an Arab state in Palestine with Jerusalem under international control, was voted on on 29 November 1947. The Arabs rejected the plan and violence erupted until the British left Palestine on 14 May 1948 and the state of Israel was declared, prompting the 1948 War of Independence. The Palestinians call this event Al-Naqba (the Catastrophe).

Some of the young men and women had returned from the army; others had been conscripted and were gone.

I didn't know whether to laugh or cry when I first saw Sparky, head shaved, dreadlock-less, in his olive fatigues: Laugh because he looked so hysterically different. Without his dreadlocks, he seemed unveiled. Denuded. Cry because it struck me then – aged twenty-three and working in London selling advertising space for two dodgy guys on a publication that didn't exist – that this was the price I would have to pay if I wanted to return to live in Israel, my homeland.

CHAPTER SEVEN

IT WAS ON that short trip to Israel in 1993 that my life changed in a way I could have never imagined. It had little to do with Sparky, Zionism or military service. It had everything to do with an Australian girl called Lucy, whose toffee-coloured hair and gentle blue eyes caught my attention across a jammed dining room on Bet Ha'Emek, a kibbutz just a ten-minute drive south of Rosh HaNikra.

I was passing through on my way to see Sparky; Lucy was revisiting the place where she had spent the year living in 1989. It soon transpired that we had left our footprints in the same places. Some of our friends had met. But our paths had never crossed. We had been on the same year-long program, and were members of the same international youth movement, only she had been with the Australian group, and I had been with the Brits.

She was magnificent – and I didn't think I stood a chance. Her clothes – part funky, part classy, part hippy – exuded style without being self-conscious about it. She didn't flirt and was almost stand-offish, which drove me mad. It felt like she had created a buffer zone around her that intimated that she was not interested in fool's play or one-night stands. I would later find out that she was an all-or-nothing girl.

After my visit to Sparky, I was planning to go down to the Sinai Desert to introduce my fluorescent Scottish skin to the sun. After doting around after Lucy for a few days, I summoned up the courage to ask her if she'd like to come with me, simply because I had to know for sure that I stood no chance.

I almost missed a heartbeat when she said yes.

A few days later we left for the Sinai, driving through the night, the rhythmic beats of Steely Dan blasting out of the sound system as we crossed the Negev Desert, heading south towards the border at Eilat.

I spent much of the journey tormented by brain-bending dilemmas about how on earth to make a move on Lucy without offending her, let alone losing her. I couldn't work her out. On the one hand here she was sitting in the passenger seat of the car, alone with me (whom she'd only met a few days earlier), driving into the wilderness for a few days. On the other hand, she wasn't exactly opening her door and inviting me inside. She remained aloof. And I have always been useless at crossing that first hurdle, expending endless amounts of energy worrying that I would receive that ego-shattering knock back.

Fortunately, nature has a way of dismantling the barriers, and we spent several romantic days camped in a bamboo hut on the Red Sea coast. We reminisced about our year on kibbutz. And we talked about living in Israel. I told her about my great-grandfather's orchard, that my parents had once lived here and that my sister was living in Jerusalem.

She told me that her grandparents were Jerusalemites, and that her father had been born there before the family moved to Australia in 1950.

'Eh? So . . . you're an Israeli?'

'Well . . . I'm mostly an Aussie. But here is where my soul feels at home. My heart, though, is with my family in Australia. But I have two passports because my father is Israeli and my mother Australian.'

I was amazed. We kept talking. And then we talked more. About each other, Israel, about us. And it soon became clear that, some day, she too planned to live in Israel.

For those few days in Sinai, the world stopped and we were flying sky high. But I was living in Britain and she was returning to Australia. Neither of us knew when, or even if, we would see each other again. All she left me were her aviator sunglasses and an aching heart.

I returned to London, where I was now living with two old mates from kibbutz days. We were addicted to *The Simpsons* and, since it was only available in those days on satellite television, we clubbed together to pay for a dish. Every Sunday afternoon at around six, a swarm of mates and mates of mates could be found lounging around our house, glued to the weekly, back-to-back episodes of *The Simpsons*.

They immediately sensed that something was different. They noticed the change in mindset, distracted concentration, the starry-eyed recollections I had of Lucy and the way I described each photograph with nauseating nostalgia.

The phone rang. The whole room erupted with a whopping 'Wooooooooooooo' when it was announced that it was Lucy on the other end.

She had just landed in Barcelona – her ticket to Australia allowed her one free trip anywhere in Europe before returning to the Antipodes.

'You're just around the corner.'

'I know.'

'What are your plans?'

'What are yours?'

'I'm here.'

'I'm here. But I'm going to France in two days and then I fly back to Australia from Italy.'

'France? FRA-AAAAANCE! That really *is* around the corner! It's one hour by boat from Calais to Dover. Come to London! Come!'

I cleaned my room up and sped down to Dover in the torrential rain to reunite with a girl who made me beam on the outside and melt on the inside. Predictably, while I was gone, the boys decided to make some minor adjustments to the house in honour of Lucy's arrival.

They didn't clean the oil-drenched piece of tin foil on the grill or throw out the crate of old milk bottles. Neither did they empty the overflowing ashtrays in the lounge. Nor did they clean the urine-splashed rim of the toilet. Or even put the seat down for that matter.

No, my mates decided to tinker with my bedroom. So, that night, I returned to London, introduced Lucy to the boys and took her upstairs to my room.

I turned on the light. It was red. Bright red. Cackles of laughter echoed up the staircase from the lounge. Fortunately, Lucy saw the funny side of it and, as I would later learn, Aussies are easily humoured. But it was only when we got into bed later that night that the filthy minds of my mates revealed themselves.

I pulled the blanket back and there, scrawled on my white sheet with a big black marker pen, was a giant diagram of the male genitalia. I cringed, winced and begged forgiveness. Then I realised that the only other sheet I owned was in the wash and so we'd have to sleep on the diagram or without a sheet at all.

By the time Lucy departed a few days later, I did not require Apollo 11 to launch myself to the moon. I was already there. And I sensed that it was mutual.

I didn't need my mates' approval to confirm Lucy was a rare find, though their endorsement was comforting all the same. But my intuition told me what I needed to know. Now all I had to do was work out a way of seeing her again.

Later that year, drama unfolded in Washington, on the White House lawn. On 13 September 1993, the Oslo Accords, named after the Norwegian capital where the secret agreement had been brokered, were officially signed by Israeli Prime Minister Yitzhak Rabin and Palestinian Authority Chairman Yasser Arafat under the gloating eye of President Bill Clinton.*

The accords outlined a road map to a final peace settlement, incorporating two main points: immediate Palestinian self-rule in Gaza and Jericho, and limited autonomy in the rest of the West

* Oslo II, as it became known, was signed on 28 September 1995 and called for Palestinian elections and further IDF redeployments, among other issues.

Bank. The accords, which assumed the eventual establishment of a Palestinian state, also outlined a timetable for the beginning of negotiations on final-status issues such as Palestinian refugees, borders, water, settlements and Jerusalem.

'Let me say to the Palestinians,' declared Rabin in his emotional speech that day. 'We are destined to live together on the same soil. We the soldiers who have returned from battle stained with blood . . . we who come from a land where parents bury children, we who have fought against you, the Palestinians – we say to you today: enough of blood and tears. Enough.'

Rabin could barely look Arafat in the eye. President Clinton was between them, arms outstretched, beaming like the Patriarch Abraham who had finally brought his bickering boys, Isaac and Ishmael, together to end their feud. Then, the two leaders' outstretched hands locked in a Nobel-prize-winning handshake in front of a swarm of media photographers and cameramen.

Arafat, dressed in his olive outfit with his black-and-white keffiyeh (Arab headscarf) draped in the shape of Greater Palestine, was smiling. Rabin was not. Arafat was Israel's public enemy number one. And here he was shaking hands with him.

Watching on television from London, I could understand Rabin's apprehension. And I could appreciate his reluctance to smile. He signed the Oslo Accords because he knew that the alternative – more bombs, more bullets, more bloodshed – was worse.

But he was not jubilant. I, on the other hand, was ecstatic.

CHAPTER EIGHT

I MADE A FEW more visits to Israel before landing in Jerusalem as a temporary resident in September 1994, sure of one thing: I didn't want to live in London, where I had been crawling in the fast lane since I'd graduated from university.

But I didn't know for sure if I wanted to live in Israel, let alone Jerusalem. So I became a temporary resident, a halfway house that afforded me the luxury of not committing either way. It also meant I would not have to worry, for the time being at least, about the army. But, most importantly, it was several thousand kilometres closer to Lucy.

The longer I stayed in Britain, the more I realised that my soul didn't feel connected in the same way as it did with Israel. When shit happens in Israel, it's happening to my people, and I care about it. When it happens in Britain, I can't honestly say that I care on the same scale.

And no matter how modern, Western, civilised and cultured Britain is, it lacks the soul and the effervescent, organised chaos of everyday life in Israel. Admittedly, Britain is a much easier place to reside. You don't have to push and shove to get on the bus, beg to withdraw your own money from your own bank account, have long-lost rabbis write letters to prove your Jewish line of descent or be verbally abused (at best) and stoned (at worst) just because you choose to drive on a particular street on Saturday.

Much as Israel isn't the easiest place to live, I felt a sense of belonging I didn't feel in Britain. Plus, my sister, Ruth, was still living in Jerusalem – a safety net to cushion my fall, if need be, and a welcoming open door.

Rose had also graduated from university and had already moved out to Israel the year before I arrived. She had no qualms about the army because women immigrants have the luxury of exemption.

She was ecstatic that I had arrived. Soon after catching up, however, I realised that Israel had become as much a launching pad as home base for her. She was forever renewing her passport. It was littered with Hebrew and Arabic entry and exit stamps.

In the last year, she had been to Giza in Egypt to marvel at Khufu's Great Pyramid, the last of the Seven Wonders of the Ancient World still standing. She had sailed from Haifa to Turkey through the Dardanelles and on to Istanbul to gawk at the Turkish delights of Ottoman architecture. And she had made countless journeys to the Sinai Desert. This, she said, was her true temple, the timeless charm of the Bedouin and the peaceful serenity of the wilderness luring her back time and again.

She, like me, dreamed of the day Jordan, Syria and Lebanon would open their doors to Israelis. Visa stamps for her were like football cards for me. The way she collected them reminded me of my school days collecting and trading cards, forever hoping the set would one day be complete. But there were always a few rare cards that eluded me. Likewise visas.

That altered unexpectedly one scorching afternoon in October 1994, several weeks after my arrival in Israel.

In the middle of no-man's land, deep in the Arava Valley, just shy of the southern tip of the country, Israel and Jordan finally dispensed with their 46-year-old war and declared a farewell to arms in an historic peace treaty.

The architects of the peace accord concerned themselves with conflict resolution and the art of diplomacy; we were more interested in travelling – open borders unlocked doors, behind which lay treasures that we had dreamed of for years.

Petra, the ancient lost city of the Nabataeans, was the jewel in the Middle East's crown; until now, closed to Israelis. Peace, for

Rose, meant Petra. For me, it meant that there might be a slightly greater chance the army would not require my services by the time my number was up.

No sooner had the border gates been flung open than a deluge of Israelis flooded into Jordan, desperately clambering to feast their eyes on Petra.

Rose had already begun packing her bag before the ink had dried on the peace treaty and the world's press had gaped in amazement as Israel's then Prime Minister, Yitzhak Rabin, signed his name using a dime-a-dozen biro as King Hussein's and Bill Clinton's gold-plated fountain pens flanked him on either side. Typically, Rabin was unmoved by the commotion.

Rose was beside herself with excitement. 'Come. Come to Petra.'

'No way. I need some time to sort my life out. Gimme a few weeks. I've only just arrived.'

'Come on. You'll be fine.'

'No chance. I need a job.'

'You'll get one. It can wait. Petra can't.'

She was fired up. Petra had cast its spell.

Deep down, I knew I was too. The lure of the red rock, lurking across the barbed-wire desert fence somewhere deep in the hills of Edom, was too compelling to resist. And the fact that I didn't have a job yet made it all the more sensible to go now. Or at least I managed to convince myself that it was.

'Sinai first,' said Rose, tossing a keffiyeh and some toilet paper – an indispensable commodity for travelling through the desert – in a bag.

'Sinai? What happened to Petra?'

'Petra later. First, I want to drop in on Sinai.'

'Drop in? You don't just drop in on a desert. In any case, the new border is in the Arava. We'd have to double back to Eilat. No way.'

'We'll sail across by boat.'

'It's official. You've lost the plot.'

But, to her credit, she had done her homework. A boat sails across the Red Sea from Nuweiba, Sinai, to Aqaba, Jordan.

'We'll arrive by sea,' she said enthusiastically. 'The Arava border will be teeming with tourists and Israelis. I'd prefer to avoid the crowd and slip in the back door. Wouldn't you?'

Rose was playing to my weak spot. And she knew it. I loathed the beaten track.

'OK,' I said. 'But if we don't see a single tourist or a traveller along the way, you have to put me up in Petra's finest hotel. That's the deal.'

'Deal,' she said.

'Ya'allah – let's go.'

CHAPTER NINE

DAWN EMBRACED the last remnants of night as we tumbled down the Arava Valley on a bus headed for Jordan, via Sinai. A milky blue light began to wash gently over the horizon.

We passed Be'er Menuha Junction, the site of two monuments, both in memory of Israelis who dared to cross the border fence on an illegal mission to reach the red rock at a time when Israel and Jordan were still engaged in a state of war.

One group of five youths left in 1953. Another group of four left in 1957. Petra, for these young, twenty-something, idealistic Israelis, was their Mecca. They could not conceive of the idea of dying without attempting their haj, their pilgrimage. For them, the adventure was both in the journey and the destination. They were willing to risk everything in pursuit of their dreams – even their lives.

They never returned. A Jordanian sergeant killed the 1953 group of five. But no one knows whether the 1957 group of four died content, having bathed in the beauty of the lost city or whether they were killed en route. The Hebrew inscription on their memorial simply states: 'They left for Petra from here, and met their death on the way'. The rest is steeped in local folklore.

The news of the failed missions aroused pangs of passion among young Israelis in those fledgling days of the state. Petra was a 2000-year-old secret, uncovered by Swiss explorer Johann Ludwig Burckhardt in 1812. Ever since Burckhardt's discovery, Petra lay there across the hills of Edom; a virgin, whom all of Israel wanted to penetrate.

The frenzy was uncontrollable; Petra hooked the younger generation. A song about the missions, 'HaSela Ha'Adom' ('The Red Rock'), was banned from Israel Radio for fear that it would inspire more cross-border expeditions.

The scandal even made it to the Knesset, the Israeli parliament, where then Prime Minister David Ben-Gurion warned Israeli youth against attempting to breach the border in their quest to reach Petra.

We also passed Masada, the site of the famous last stand of the Jews against a Roman siege. Here, on a mountaintop fortress in AD 73, Eliezer ben Yair convinced some 960 Jewish zealots to commit suicide rather than submit to slavery and conversion under the Romans, who had already conquered Jerusalem and destroyed the Second Temple.* They decided they would rather die as free Jews than as Roman slaves.

Masada has since become a symbol of Jewish resistance, and the incredible archaeological remains, uncovered here in 1963, are among Israel's most coveted ruins.

The morning light slowly stirred the passengers from their semi-slumber as the bus sprinted down the ruler-straight Arava Valley, the final furlong to Eilat. To our left, the towering mountains of Edom cast not red, but purple shadows across the desert floor.

Throughout the night we barely passed a settlement in the Negev Desert. But, at the southern apex of the country, just short of Eilat, lie several small kibbutzim on either side of the road. Most of these farms were originally established as army outposts, stationed here as vital strategic landmarks connecting the south to the rest of the country. From the bus window, they looked like anchorless ships, helplessly adrift in a sea of sand.

As we passed the turn-off to the new border crossing, the site where the peace deal was signed only days before, all the passengers gradually turned their heads to the left and looked down at the new tarmac road. A few hundred metres across, we could make out a large, sheltered station where border guards stood under an Israeli flag fluttering in the wind. Several hundred metres farther across the flat, parched desert floor was another

* The Second Temple was built by King Herod to replace the First Temple, built by King Solomon and destroyed by the Babylonians under Nebuchadnezzar in 586 BC.

shelter, this time under the Jordanian flag. Between the two was no-man's land, that geographical comfort zone that prevents two countries from rubbing shoulders.

We could have been in Jordan within an hour. Instead we would arrive days later, after a circuitous route via Sinai that made about as much geographical sense as Delhi to Kathmandu – via Bombay. But this was Rose's show. She, too, was staring across the valley, eyes locked beyond the towering cliffs of Edom.

Part of the Syrian–African Rift Valley – the longest valley in the world, stretching from East Africa to southern Turkey – runs along the line of symmetry that splits these geographically similar countries. The Jordanians call it Wadi Araba; the Israelis know it as the Arava Valley.

Here, at around 400 metres below sea level, lies the Dead Sea, the lowest point on earth where tourists come from all over the world to bathe in mineral mud, belly-up while salt stings every graze, scar and open wound. It is shared by both countries.

On the shores of the Red Sea, Israel's Eilat and Jordan's Aqaba are near duplicate resorts. What Israel calls the Gulf of Eilat, Jordan knows as the Gulf of Aqaba. They are two sides of the same coin. For us, like many Israelis, discovering Jordan was like being able to look behind the glass of a mirror.

Not far south of the Arava border crossing to Jordan is Taba, the border between Israel and Egypt. On the Israeli side, security agents and customs personnel whisk you through the usual array of checks: passport control, customs, exit duty. On the Egyptian side, the pace is slower, the queues longer and the bureaucratic red tape more frustrating. Crossing the threshold between the countries, I always feel a noticeable shift in gears: in Israel, it's all accelerator; in Sinai it's all clutch, and my engine slows to a gentle cruise almost immediately.

The match crackled, flickered, flashed. Finally, it flared alight. Rose's face glowed orange as she cradled the flame and nursed it to life inside our straw hut at Ras al-Satan (Arabic for Devil's

Head), where a cluster of huts on a headland straddles the coast-line north of Nuweiba, the nearest town of any size.

The hypnotic sound of waves crashing on the beach was no more than ten metres from us. Multi-coloured woven rugs, pinned to the straw walls, kept out the howling wind. Wax dribbled down the candle, creating a puddle soon absorbed by the sand. In the distance, music filtered in between the crashing of the waves. Some Bedouin were playing darboukas (Arab drums), the echo fading into the empty wilderness.

There's something seductive about candlelight and the romance it injects into the atmosphere. What it does to a person's face. How it softens the skin and produces a golden glow. The way it leaps, bends, buckles.

It felt liberating not being in love with Rose anymore. We had built such a strong friendship on kibbutz over five years ago and our relationship had threatened to destroy it. Now we were solid mates. With no regrets.

But Sinai was synonymous with the romantic adventure I'd had over a year before with Lucy. This was the first time I had been back since then, and as I lay there in the candle's shadows, I missed her, her smile, her presence, her softness. But I knew I would see her again. Somehow. Somewhere.

Rose listened to my stories of Lucy, and was soon so wound up in the romance that she began concocting ways of luring Lucy back.

Nuweiba port, south of Devil's Head on the Red Sea coast, is life-less. Tumbleweed spirals across the desert plain. A huge hangar rests beneath a corrugated roof that deep-fries under the midday sun. Inside, several hundred Arabs are crammed into fewer than several hundred seats. It could have been a theme party: keffiyehs and jelabiyehs (Arab ankle-length shirt-dresses). We stick out like butchers at a vegetarian convention. For Rose, it is worse. She is the only woman amid the throng of Arab men.

Most of them are wearing red-and-white chequered keffiyehs, largely associated with Saudi Arabian Arabs; some don white alone, traditionally sported by the apolitical Bedouin. And there are a few black-and-white keffiyehs, the colours of the Palestinian Al-Fatah movement, headed by Yasser Arafat. Though we were headed for Jordan there was every likelihood that we'd encounter as many Bedouin (the south of the country is largely populated by Bedouin tribes) and Palestinians (Jordan is 60 per cent Palestinian) as Jordanians.

There's little noise. It's too hot to talk. The boat is late arriving from Saudi Arabia. Agitation ferments. Flies zoom from nose to ear. Mosquitoes stalk the shadows, spying, I fret, on our tender, white skin. Roasting in the heat, it feels as though we are ceramic pots in a kiln. The corrugated roof looks like it's about to melt.

Then I spot her, making her way gingerly towards us. She looks frightened. And she has every right to feel so. She is staring at the ground, her eyes every so often darting either side and then straight ahead to ensure she is on track in our direction. Scores of pairs of eyes follow her shuffling across the hangar floor.

We sit aghast, watching as she approaches us.

'I don't believe it,' whispers Rose, elbowing me in the ribs.

'Far out,' I reply.

'How can she . . . ?'

'Dunno, but she sure as hell is in for a rough ride.'

We smile tentatively, welcoming her over. Amber is Irish. Freckles pepper her face. But the sole focus of all the attention is her long catwalk legs. She had chosen to parade herself in a miniskirt that barely qualifies for 'mini' or 'skirt'. She may as well have just strutted across the hangar in her underwear. In London, New York, Paris or Milan, her attire would have been acceptable, though she would still have invited an audience.

But this is Nuweiba, Egypt, home to the deeply-rooted conservatism that pervades much of the Middle East. I happened to be reading Lonely Planet's *Middle East on a Shoestring* at the time. The relevant passage on Society & Conduct states, 'Dress modestly. This means long skirts or pants (nothing too figure-hugging).'

I close the book, figuring that she didn't want to hear about her oversight.

Rose pulls a sarong from her bag and passes it to Amber. It isn't a gesture. Her eyes are communicating the strongest possible recommendation, just about ordering her to cover her legs. She looks at Rose sheepishly, and spreads the sarong over her bare legs. I am pissed off. Though I feel sorry for Amber, I can't figure out how anyone with half a brain could even consider an outfit like that in a place like this.

But what really irks me is not Amber's attire. It's just the presence of a traveller.

'Damn!' I murmur to Rose. 'Looks like I just lost my night in Petra's finest hotel.'

CHAPTER TEN

FOUR STEWING HOURS LATER, we edged our way across the Red Sea, the gentle breeze barely cooling our overheated bodies. The ship was colossal, and had it not been for the huge distance between deck and the water, we would have jumped into the sea.

Saudi Arabia was just a fingertip away. Mecca was not visible from here but there were no doubts about which way to face when it came to afternoon prayers. Virtually everyone aboard, the three of us excepted, was crouched on a prayer rug blessing Allah. It was mildly awkward, but not in any way threatening.

The last light of day was beginning to echo across the water as the reflection of the lights – Aqaba on one side, Eilat on the other – shimmered on the foreshore.

Although we had British passports, the pages were littered with Israeli stamps. Amber, by now aware of the fact that not only were we Jewish, but we had come via Israel, decided that we may be a liability and preferred to go alone. We geared up to enter what was once enemy territory.

A moustachioed immigration officer spotted Rose and me and beckoned us forward. He ushered us into a room.

I braced for a big frisk. But the officer, unexpectedly short and rotund, wanted to give us preferential treatment.

'First time?' he asked in broken English.

'Aiwa – yes,' we responded in duet.

'You speak Arabic?'

'Shwoie, shwoie – slowly, slowly.'

The sound of the rubber stamp marked our official entrance into the Hashemite Kingdom of Jordan. Rose greeted the new stamp, a welcome addition to her growing collection, with one of those yep-that's-another-one-in-the-bag smiles. Looking at my stamp, I thought briefly of Sparky and how he had always mused about a trip to Jordan.

He was not so interested in the romantic past of Petra, but believed there was a pharmacological reason behind the formal title of the kingdom: 'Why else would they call it the *Hash*emite Kingdom of Jordan?' he'd asked rhetorically on more than one occasion.

One of the most remarkable things about Aqaba was just being able to look across the border at the night-lights of Eilat. In the past, whenever we passed through Eilat on our way to Sinai, we used to gaze at Aqaba and wonder whether the felafel (balls of deep-fried spicy chickpeas in pita bread) was any good, the hummous (a chickpea, garlic and lemon dip) thick and lumpy or smooth and creamy, the people mellow – and when the day would come when we would be able to stand there and stare back across to Eilat. That day was today.

The first local Jordanian we met introduced us to his friend – a camel by the dubious name of Jack. While these ships of the desert abound in the region, there was a certain incongruity about Jack the Camel trotting down the main street of Aqaba.

Abdullah was the quintessential Bedouin. Draped in a white, ankle-length jelabiyeh, he seemed endlessly amused to be hauling Jack around the city streets on the end of a rope.

'You like felafel?' he asked. We nodded, having heard rumours of Aqaba's legendary felafel.

'I know where is best felafel. Jack hungry. He come too.'

Over dinner, Abdullah told us that he worked for his father in his shop.

'What do you sell?' asked Rose.

'Jelabiyeh,' he said, tugging at his white shirt-dress.

My ears perked up. Abdullah saw me take interest. It was easy to buy a keffiyeh, the only tricky part choosing a colour: non-partisan white was the safest option. But a jelabiyeh was a much greater commitment – and a much more serious statement. Yeah, I fancied finding out what life was like inside a jelabiyeh.

'You want?'

My face lit up. 'Aiwa.'

'Bukra – tomorrow, you come for jelabiyeh.'

By mid-morning the following day, I was standing inside Abdullah's father's shop, draped in an elephant-grey, ankle-length shirt-dress. A white keffiyeh was wrapped turban-like around my head and I was wearing the aviator sunglasses that Lucy had given me the year before.

Abdullah was doubled over in laughter. 'Inte Arabiya – you're Arabian.'

That brought on Rose's laugh. It was unmistakable. Truth is, she sounded more like a donkey braying. Her face imploded and she gasped for air and then heaved an enormous belching sound, like she was about to break water and give birth. You could hear her miles off. Her trademark dimples appeared in her cheeks.

When she finally gathered herself several minutes later, she said she thought it gave me a touch of *Lawrence of Arabia*.

Petra was our next stop, though Abdullah insisted that we pay a visit to Wadi Rum to see the unique rock formations. It was on the way, in any case, he said. And, according to Rose, some of *Lawrence of Arabia* was filmed there.

Our visit was short-lived.

My ludicrous costume confused the patrol guards at the entrance and we spent the following three hours trying to get out of the jam that Abdullah's jelabiyeh got me into.

Wadi Rum police station was nothing more than a Bedouin goatskin tent lined with palm tree logs draped with rugs. In the centre, a smouldering fire pouted and hissed under a dripping, charred-black teapot.

The chief looked me up and down and spluttered a mouthful of Arabic that sounded as though it were laden with expletives.

Maybe he thought I was some sort of Israeli undercover spy. A terrorist. Or a dissident. Or maybe he just reckoned I was one short of a six-pack.

I tried to break the ice. I put my two hands up, shoulder high, palms out, protesting my innocence. 'Scottish. Tourist. No trouble. No problem.'

It didn't wash. The other security guards looked on with what appeared to be bewilderment and amusement more than anger.

They were confused, and bemused, and sent us mixed signals, reprimanding us then embracing us. Coffee and tea soon flowed, glass after glass. Amid all the talking, passport checking, questioning and the like, there was never a hint of the possibility that I'd either be taken away, or that my jelabiyeh would be confiscated, leaving me, mid-desert, a Scotsman without his kilt.

When they finally agreed to release us, we were marched straight to the road and forbidden entry to Wadi Rum. Then they waved us goodbye. Very, very odd.

Rose wasn't too bothered. 'Perhaps it's fate that we head straight to Petra. But I'm not going with you in that dumb guise. I can't risk coming all this way and getting knocked back.'

I de-robed.

We caught a bus and wound our way across the mountains of Edom, arriving several hours later at Wadi Musa, the end of the road, where water is believed to have gushed out of the rock after Moses struck it.

Scaffolding lines the main street of Wadi Musa. Concrete mixers purr. Tractors grind. Bricklayers paste mortar upon brick. Bumper-to-bumper buses ferry eager tourists in and out.

The perpetual hum makes it hard to imagine that nearby lurks a hidden passageway to a romantic past.

Bab-es Siq, a narrow, winding gorge, leads from Wadi Musa down into the fabled lost city of Petra. Bare-footed Bedouin boys lead donkeys carrying elderly tourists; some horses and chariots race by. It's only a matter of days since the border has been opened and these kids are already saddled with suitable marketing skills: 'Shalom, habibi! Mah nishma? – Hello, my friend! How are you?' they cry in pidgin Hebrew before trying to peddle their wares: postcards, tours, drinks and bottles of coloured sand.

Some parts of the gorge are no wider than about three metres. Cliffs tower thirty metres high on either side, almost meeting in an arch overhead. They dwarf the legions of tourists who have made the pilgrimage.

The snake-like path dips and bends, teases and tantalises, for almost a kilometre. As we meander down, each bend feels like the final one that will open out to reveal Petra's secret.

But beyond each bend, we are denied. Finally, just visible between the narrow gap in the gorge is a slice of Al-Kazneh, the treasury. Then, rounding the last bend, the gorge fans out and unveils the contours of Petra's face. Words cannot come close to describing this masterpiece. Seeing it in that scene from *Indiana Jones and the Last Crusade* is one thing; gawking at it with a naked eye, quite another.

From a sheer face of red sandstone, the Nabataeans chiselled the most breathtaking temple facade, supported by six Corinthian columns. With delicacy and dexterity, they hewed mythological figures, Nabataean deities and ornate decorations. This was the keystone – and cornerstone – of Petra, where the profits from the spice trade were stored: jewels and precious stones, silver and gold, frankincense and myrrh.

Petra lay dormant for almost 2000 years, unknown to anyone but the local Bedouin, who lived in the caves. Then, in 1812, Johann Ludwig Burckhardt stumbled upon the ruins and unlocked the secrets of the ancient Nabataeans. It sat at the crossroads of the ancient spice route linking the Arabian Peninsula and the Mediterranean, thereby enabling the Nabataeans to maintain a monopoly over the trade of spices and silk from the East. From Petra, the spice route to Gaza, known as Darb el-Sultana, passed through the Nabataean town of Avdat (now in Israel), which they built as a key caravan station on the route to and from the Mediterranean coast.

Petra, rising 1000 metres high in a canyon set amid the rugged mountains of Edom, was an impregnable desert fortress. And Al-Kazneh is just the gateway to the treasures. Around the next bend lies a whole city, ten square kilometres, literally carved into the red rock. Over 800 tombs, huge temples, obelisks, places of sacrifice, a 6000-seat amphitheatre, a necropolis and numerous adorned facades.

Much like the ancient lost city of the Incas, Macchu Picchu in Peru, Petra is a spellbinding monument to humanity – a 2000-year-old testament to the engineering ability of the Nabataeans. It is intoxicating. The more you see the more you want to see. Wandering around the site, it's hard to grasp the scale of the place. A week would barely do it justice.

Late in the afternoon, we climbed up to the tombs on the Street of the Facades. Elaborate, vast steps, each some ten metres wide, have been carved into the sheer cliff face in five separate sections. From the top, we dangled our legs over the edge and scanned the panorama of this enchanted city.

'It's hard to believe it's real, eh? Last week we were at war with Jordan; this week we are sitting here gazing across what was enemy territory. Talk about the premium of peace.'

Rose was lost in romantic thought. 'How did the poet Burgon find the words?'

'What? A rose-red city half as old as time?'

'Yeah,' she said. 'If it's half as old as time, it's twice the beauty of any other place on earth.'

'No wonder those intrepid Israelis were willing to risk their lives to get here,' I said.

Rose nodded, her eyes fixed on the horizon. 'Yeah. If they reached here before their lives ended, they would have died content.'

CHAPTER ELEVEN

IT WAS NOT LONG after I arrived back from Petra that I met Mick and Charlie. You could spot they were dodgy a mile off. Here in Jerusalem, a city comprised of around 650,000 people – Jews, Arabs and Christians, among others – who are either largely ultra-Orthodox or ultra-Conservative, they stuck together, and stuck out, like hippies in a convent.*

They sported 70s flares, bushy sideburns, style-less hair and moustaches and beards at various stages of growth. If you didn't know they were Jewish, you wouldn't have suspected that they were members of the tribe. Though I was loath to engage in face-value judgments, it wasn't difficult to tell that mischief lurked behind their funky facades.

Mick had a penchant for talking (most of the time) and talking crap (the rest of the time). He was loud and outrageous and spent a large amount of his time bagging his old mate Charlie.

'If you had as many brains as teeth,' he jibed, 'then we'd be a force to be reckoned with. But you don't. So we're not.'

Charlie didn't offer a rebuttal. He was a man of few words. That's what made them such a dynamite duo. Mick's verbal diarrhoea was compensated for by Charlie's reticence.

Mick soon became known around town as 'the doctor', a nickname accorded to him after he opened a 'surgery' engaging in alternative therapy of the not-so-kosher variety.

With my sister Ruth, and only one really close friend, Shira, whom I'd met years back at camp before her family immigrated

---

* There are some 400,000 Jews and 200,000 Arabs in Jerusalem.

to Israel, I was eager to meet new people. Rose had stayed on in Petra and was planning to head up to the capital, Amman, for a while before returning to live in Tel Aviv. Sparky was in the army and a few of the other lads from kibbutz days were dotted around here and there. Essentially, though, Shira aside, I was on my own. I was glad to have come across Mick and Charlie.

Shira, who was almost as petite as Rose, was studying at university. We found an apartment together in Rechavia, a leafy neighbourhood near downtown West Jerusalem that was one of the last bastions of secularism in a city that was becoming increasingly Orthodox.

I enrolled in Ulpan, Hebrew language school, at Jerusalem's Hebrew University. Since I was planning to live and work here, I thought I'd better acquire fluency in the language. To blend into Israeli society, a command of the mother tongue is a crucial rite of passage, regardless of the fact that many locals speak English. I knew too many immigrants who had been here for years and who still didn't know how to avoid getting ripped off by a taxi driver. I wasn't about to become a frier – a sucker.

It'd been over two years since I'd left Manchester University in 1992 and, apart from being older than most of the other students in my class, I found my attention span had narrowed and my ability to concentrate was blunted. To add to my woes, my mind was still in Petra.

The most enjoyable part of university was the journey there. Walking to the bus stop each day, I took a shortcut down Rechov Al-Harizi, a tranquil, narrow sidestreet where a weeping willow sulked on the corner.

The bus took me through East Jerusalem then north to the university's curious location on Mount Scopus, from 1948 to 1967 an enclave isolated deep inside Jordanian-controlled Arab territory. It became a university in exile and, during those years, alternative campuses were established in Israeli-controlled West Jerusalem.

Travelling across the dividing line that separated the city for nineteen years, we passed Sheikh Jarrah every morning, stopping on Abu Obiedah ibn el-Jarrah Street, just outside Orient House, the unofficial headquarters of the Palestinian Authority in East Jerusalem. On my return, we passed the Arab village of Silwan in the Kidron Valley where potholed roads snake their way up the incline and stilt houses cling to the hillside.

Though the peace process with the Palestinians that began with the signing of the 1993 Oslo Accords was a year old, and the five-year Intifada had ended, tension was still palpable.

It was a fascinating journey across the former frontline of this conflict. Here, on the morning bus, Jews and Arabs, foreigners and immigrants, settlers and refugees, students and professors, were thrown across history's pages.

My first week of classes, in October 1994, coincided with the kidnapping of an Israeli soldier by Hamas terrorists.* Nachshon Wachsman was hitchhiking home from base when a car stopped to offer him a lift. Hitchhiking soldiers rarely have to wait long to be offered a ride home. It is – or a least it was – one of the unwritten rules of the road. After all, almost everyone has served in the army and everyone appreciates the desire to get home as quickly as possible to see family, eat a good meal and sleep. The news of the kidnapping was announced over the radio on the bus.

Wachsman was held for a week in the Palestinian village of Bir Nabala, not far from the West Bank town of Ramallah, and was used by his Hamas captors as a bargaining chip to obtain the release of 200 Palestinian prisoners held in Israeli jails.

His fate became that of the nation. Every hour, there would be an update of his situation, a comment from the prime minister or the IDF chief of staff. His mother made public pleas for her son's release. Hamas even produced a videotape of him with a balaclava-clad terrorist standing behind him, AK-47 machine gun at the

* Hamas, an acronym for Harakat al-Muqaama al-Islamiya (the Islamic Resistance Movement), was founded five days after the outbreak of the Intifada in December 1987, as an extremist opposition to Yasser Arafat's Al-Fatah organisation. Hamas promotes an Islamic state between the Mediterranean Sea and the Jordan River.

ready. His face, his character, his life story, was milked by the media so that, by day four or five of the abduction, Wachsman became known by his first name, Nachshon. We got to know him, his every detail, his childhood, his hobbies, likes, dislikes. Soon, he became everyone's son, grandson or brother.

Each morning, as the busload hung on every word of the latest news, it was possible to discern a certain amount of discomfort among the Arabs aboard. They, too, seemed moved by the human tragedy that was unfolding minute by minute as the Hamas ultimatum to release their prisoners drew to a close.

Ordinarily, fatalities in this bloody conflict are numbers, not stories. When Palestinians are killed in the West Bank, or when a suicide bomber blows up an Israeli bus, the dead are often counted and grouped as one. But this was different.

When it was announced that an army rescue attempt had failed, and that the terrorists had killed Nachshon, a veil of grief washed over the bus. Even the non-Jewish people aboard were touched by the plight of this kid in uniform, bound and gagged, blindfolded and abused before being murdered. He had become a symbol of the people, and the nation mourned as though each family had lost a member of their own.

So, by the time I arrived at university in that first week, I'd usually had my fix of education for the day. Facing a blackboard learning a new language from a colourless teacher was, to say the least, uninspiring. Which is why I found myself, aged twenty-four, crouching under a table in the cafeteria, hiding from my teacher because I was planning to bunk the rest of the day's classes.

That's where I met Mick and Charlie. They weren't hiding. They had no shame. They simply loped past their teacher, smiling nonchalantly, as they headed for the exit. I guess I was just too embarrassed to rub my apathy in my teacher's face. She may have been dry, but she seemed like a nice person, and I felt sorry for her.

We ended up in the Old City at a small coffee joint just inside the Damascus Gate in East Jerusalem where we sat, drank coffee, ordered a shisha smoke and whiled away the hours alongside a group of Arab elders playing cards, backgammon and dominoes as they counted their worry beads.

That's when they told me how they'd managed to con their London university into sponsoring them to go to Jerusalem for the year to 'undertake further research', as Mick put it.

We talked for hours and then wandered through the labyrinthine cobbled alleyways of the Old City's souk, purchasing laffa (large, round Arab pita bread) and fresh-pitted olives.

Within weeks we had joined forces and became a motley crew of non-compliance. In addition to our Hebrew classes, Mick and I enrolled in an Arabic course; Charlie studied Spanish because he was gung-ho about making it one day to Peru to follow the footsteps of the Incas. None of us lasted long, and the pidgin Arabic I speak now is largely due to my Israeli and Arab friends, not my Arabic teacher.

It soon became evident that Mick's 'research' project was located in the south, on the fringes of the Negev Desert. He travelled to a development town called Dimona once a week, where he would follow a friend of a friend into the sand dunes. There, his friend's friend would search for a stone marker as though he and Mick were about to embark on an archaeological excavation, a common activity here in the Holy Land. They would get out small spades and dig until they uncovered a large, sealed, air-tight bag of grass, which Mick would bring back to Jerusalem to sell, at not-so-mildly inflated prices, to students.

He managed to con a neck brace from the university clinic – along with a doctor's note relieving him from classes for an indefinite period due to a severe strain – and wore it as a decoy to smuggle his goods on the bus from Dimona to Jerusalem. Long after the pain had subsided and his neck had healed, Mick could be seen strutting the city streets, neck bound like an Egyptian mummy.

I needed work, and although Mick kept offering me a partnership in his medical practice, I preferred a less conspicuous trade, though I was more than happy to book in for an appointment from time to time. Needless to say, Charlie was a regular patient.

I soon found work at a tiny Italian joint, where, ironically, a short, stocky, Chinese man with the misfortune of being named Pong was the house chef. The kitchen was so small that the two of us could only work together if we remained in our respective corners. Movement out of my sphere would end in disaster, so I spent eight-hour shifts rooted to a corner, chopping vegetables, making fresh pasta and trying to communicate with a Chinese Jew in Hebrew, seasoned with Mandarin, in temperatures upwards of thirty degrees Celsius.

I didn't last long. When I was out of work, Mick would give me a wink and a nudge.

'The surgery offer is still open you know.'

Mick was so thrilled with his booming business that he started mouthing off about going to live down in Dimona on the fringes of the desert.

'Fish that don't keep moving get gobbled up by sharks,' he said, trying to justify his move to a desert town best known as the home of Israel's nuclear reactor and Mordechai Vanunu, the technician who sold the secret to the *Sunday Times* in 1986, was then captured by Mossad, tried for treason and espionage, and jailed for eighteen years.

I managed to find part-time work as an editor at the National Institute of Testing and Evaluation. It set entrance exam papers for the country's universities. The first thing I had to do on day one was sign a declaration swearing that I would not divulge any information for five years.

Because these exams are nationwide, and since the disclosure of any information could spark a national scandal, the offices were housed inside a massive vault, within which lay a chambered safe where the papers were stored. The building was littered with security codes and armed guards patrolled its perimeter twenty-four hours a day.

I went to work inside a fortress in West Jerusalem not far from the Knesset, the Israeli parliament, and the Israel Museum, which houses the Shrine of the Book, where some of the 2000-year-old Dead Sea Scrolls, arguably Israel's most prized archaeological discovery, are displayed.

True to form, Mick and Charlie soon hatched a new money-making scam. We were eating one evening at our favourite felafel stand, which was nothing more than a hole in a wall on Bezalel Street, when they told me their plan hinged on my co-operation.

On the ledge were about half-a-dozen glass bowls, each containing a different free salad: onion, mixed, green, pickled, tabouleh (cracked wheat, parsley and tomato), a bowl of tahina (sesame seed paste) and a smaller bowl of chilli sauce. Inside were a felafel machine and a spit, where a large shwarma was spinning. I was filling my pita bread with salads while listening to what I knew would be a harebrained idea.

Through their contacts at the university, they reckoned they could 'plant' examination clues in exchange for large amounts of shekels without anyone being able to trace them.

'Let's just say that our man on the inside, call 'im 'arry,' began Mick in typically confident fashion, 'is able to connect us to 10 per cent of all students taking the exam this summer. That's, say, around 600 people. So if we charge 'em 100 shekels for privileged "clues", we're looking at 6000 shekels.'

'That's 2000 each,' spluttered Charlie in a rare vocal moment.

Mick was grinning, parsley wedged between his teeth. I could already see dollar signs flashing inside his brain. 'We'd be minted mate.'

Both of them stood there, staring eagle-eyed at me as if they had just worked out the password to hack into the Pentagon's mainframe. Now all they required was for me to corrupt all the classified files.

'Two problems lads,' I began. 'First, I'm sworn to secrecy, signed a legal document and, if caught, would be bound, gagged and locked in the vault without clothes. Second, we prepare hundreds of papers for that very reason. They only choose the exact paper days before, so I ain't got no idea what the questions will be.'

The boys lost their 2000-shekel-grins in a flash. We munched down our felafels and walked home, through the backstreets of Nahla'ot, in silence.

CHAPTER TWELVE

I'M ABOUT TO DISCLOSE a piece of extremely classified information. It's a secret that may well be behind the IDF's miraculous victories against multiple Arab armies many times its size in the 1948, 1956, 1967 and 1973 wars.

The most powerful weapon in Israel's arsenal is not its revered air force or its powerful Merkava III tanks. In fact, it is not even part of the IDF. It is their other army: God's Army.

Aside from the Arabs (some Bedouin and Druze excepted), all Israelis, men and women, are conscripted for mandatory military service. With one glaring exception – those who subscribe to God's Army.

So, while most Israelis spend their late teens in army fatigues, there are growing legions whose training grounds are yeshivot, the Orthodox Jewish seminaries for Talmudic study. (The Talmud, comprising the Mishnah and Gemara, provides rabbinic commentaries and interpretations of the Torah.)

After the Holocaust and the creation of Israel, the rabbis argued that Hitler had taken their communities to the brink and back. They convinced then Prime Minister David Ben-Gurion that it was critical to rebuild the foundations of these communities. Ben-Gurion acquiesced, and issued a blanket draft deferment that is still in force to this day.

The result, though, has created a rift between the ultra-Orthodox and the rest of Israel. While their peers are off protecting the nation, these ultra-Orthodox youths are studying the Torah, pouring over commentaries, analysing every letter of the halachah (Jewish law), dissecting each argument between different schools of thought – and praying for peace.

Living in Jerusalem, it is almost impossible to avoid the flocks of haredim (God-fearing ultra-Orthodox Jews) who swarm this sacred city. The injunction 'Be fruitful and multiply' takes on new meaning here, and while the average number of ultra-Orthodox children per family is seven, families with a dozen or more children are not uncommon.

Part of the reason why it's hard to avoid them – aside from the fact that prams congest the pavements in certain ultra-Orthodox neighbourhoods – is due to their attire.

For men, beards and peyot (side locks) are almost universal. They wear a variation of black coats, white shirts (no tie), black shoes, wide-brimmed black felt hats on weekdays and a fur-rimmed one called a shtreimel on Shabbat and festivals. Women wear long skirts and blouses as well as a hair covering – either a scarf or a sheitel (wig) in keeping with religious law. The rubric is simple: modesty before God requires that barely a sliver of flesh is exposed in public.

To the uninitiated eye, they look like a homogenous group. They sound like one, too, preferring to speak Yiddish – the language spoken by their ancestors back in Eastern Europe – rather than Hebrew. But they are split into ultra-Orthodox sects according to their European shtetl (village) of origin. Each sect follows a separate rabbi, with varying nuances and customs.

Nevertheless, their common denominator is their unswerving commitment to live life abiding by each of the 613 commandments of the Torah.

On weekends off, Sparky usually went back to the kibbutz; occasionally he came to visit Shira and me, but the distance from the kibbutz and his unashamed abhorrence of the ultra-Orthodox were good enough reasons why he didn't come to Jerusalem more often.

'Dossim – scroungers!' he cursed, as soon as he walked through the front door of the flat on a rare visit not long before he was due to be released.

I still had to look twice when I saw him in uniform, head-shaved, big black commando boots on his feet, combat pants, olive shirt. When I looked at him the second time, I saw a mirror image of myself a few years down the track. And I freaked out. He shrugged his shoulders and offered a limp grin. He looked down at his boots and back up at me, and I knew he wanted to say that this is just the way life is in this mad country.

But he also seemed comfortable in his uniform, proud to be defending the country he loved, the place he called home. I respected that. We had both grown up, and those halcyon kibbutz days now seemed a world away.

I refrained from broaching my concerns about serving in the army. I figured there was no point since I was not yet a citizen and, in any case, he had already made it clear how he felt about the ultra-Orthodox 'scroungers'.

Even before his army days, Sparky was a dyed-in-the-wool secularist who felt no shame eating bread during Passover and who was absolutely orthodox about *not* fasting on Yom Kippur, the holiest day in the Jewish calendar when Jews avoid food and drink for twenty-five hours and pray for forgiveness for our sins.* That's partly why kibbutz, a secular sanctuary, was such a suitable home for him. But now that he was serving in the army, and most of the ultra-Orthodox youths were not, he was even more virulently opposed to them.

'The black hats are draft dodging while we protect the nation,' he spat. 'They're praying for our lives inside a comfortable room while we're risking our asses on the frontline.'

He was charged, angry as hell. 'Why should they be exempt? Why should they not pay the price? Why should there not be ultra-Orthodox kids among the soldiers buried in our military cemeteries?'

He had a point. Since when has God secured our frontline? Where was God during the Holocaust when the Nazis annihilated one-third of our people?

---

* Passover celebrates the Jews' exodus from slavery in Egypt and, to symbolise the fact that there was not enough time to let the yeast in the bread rise before they left Egypt, Jews eat matzah (unleavened bread).

'D'you know what I mean?' he asked rhetorically. 'In the army, your track record precedes you. These dossim have no track record. What they do have is a black record. God's Army ain't nothing but a draft-dodging scam if you ask me.'

But some of them do conscript. And, regardless of the security situation, they can be seen at daybreak, under their prayer shawls, eyes shut, swaying back and forth reciting the morning prayers – even as the enemy closes in. For they still believe that God will protect them.

The rabbis, however, believe that as God's Army they will protect the people through the power of their prayer. The Holy One, Blessed Be He, will protect us, they mutter in Hebrew. Israel's victories were divine miracles rather than military triumphs. And they don't seem to bow to the argument of discrimination – that there's one set of laws for secular kids and another for the ultra-Orthodox.

Riding the bus to university one day, an ultra-Orthodox youth who looked as though he should've been in the army sat down next to me. He began murmuring psalms, thumbing pages of his pocket-sized prayer book. That's when it occurred to me. If I were ever conscripted into the Israeli army, could I not subscribe to God's Army instead? After all, my father had once shown me that our family tree traces our line of descent back to one Ephraim Zalman Margolioth, a Galician rabbi who died in 1828. Technically speaking, then, I am the descendant of a rabbi.

I'd never heard of anyone becoming ultra-Orthodox just to avoid the army, but I'm sure that there must have been precedents. And even if there weren't, I thought to myself, I could always become the first, although I wondered whether it would cost me my friendship with Sparky.

CHAPTER THIRTEEN

I CONTINUED working part-time at the fortress, clocking into the vault for a few hours each day. Though I'd managed to free myself from Pong's Italiana, I was still searching for a full-time job that would nourish my soul.

I sent my résumé to dozens of organisations working to promote peace. With it, I included a pass-me-over-at-your-peril, self-glorifying cover letter that made me sound x times better and y times more qualified than I actually was. I mentioned my university studies in Middle Eastern politics, and I highlighted my limited encounters with Palestinians, such as Saida Nusseibeh, sister of the eminent West Bank leader Sari Nusseibeh, and London PLO chief Afif Safiyeh – both of whom I'd met during my university days.

Some never bothered to reply. Most sent me a standard, unfortunately-there-are-no-openings-at-this-time letter. They were near carbon copies of each other. First sentence: 'Thank you for . . . ' Second sentence: 'Unfortunately at present . . . ' or 'We regret to inform you . . . ' Finally: 'We have your CV on file . . . Wishing you luck in your career . . . '

Cold comfort for a guy who'd left the hustle and bustle of London, realising I didn't want to be a rat because even if I won the race, I'd still be a rat. Now I was at home in Jerusalem, but with barely enough work to sustain a stinking rodent.

I did get invited to an interview at Interns for Peace, an organisation that sends volunteers to far-flung parts of the country for a year or two to work at grass-roots level with Israeli Arabs.

The director was a liberal-minded American rabbi called Bruce Cohen, and I spent the first five minutes trying to work out what drove his parents to give the poor bloke a forename that couldn't be more antithetical to his surname.

Cohens – known as *Cohanim* in Hebrew – are the descendants of high priests, the highest 'rank' of Jews (followed by the Levites and then the rest of us Israelites) who were chosen to represent the people before God. In the days of the Temple, Bruce's ancestors and all the other male Cohens in town were the only people entitled to enter the Holy of Holies, the inner sanctum of the Temple, to pray to God on behalf of the rest of the Jewish people. And only once a year, on Yom Kippur, the holiest day in the Jewish calendar.

Jeremiah, Isaiah, Jacob or even Joseph. But Bruce?

He soon informed me that I'd be sent to work for a year in an Arab village, somewhere like Deir al-Assad or Majd al-Krum in the Galilee, teaching English to schoolkids.

'We provide bed and board,' he reassured me. 'But accommodation is basic and living conditions can be tough. Don't expect any luxuries.'

Though it was by no means lucrative, it wasn't a bad option and, given my recent work and study experiences, I didn't rule it out immediately. But it was the commitment to at least a year that finally persuaded me to turn it down, against what I thought was my better judgment.

Then, my boss at the fortress introduced me to her Dutch friend who worked at the Israel–Palestine Centre for Research and Information (IPCRI), a public policy think-tank of Israeli and Palestinian academics who write papers and hold round-table discussions in an attempt to influence government policy.

Having never heard of IPCRI, I was game to check it out. The offices – run by a pompous, pot-bellied Jew by the name of Dr Gershon Baskin and a gentle, unassuming but unfortunately named Palestinian called Dr Zakaria al-Qaq – straddled the dividing line between East and West Jerusalem.

'Once the . . . dome is in your . . . face,' spluttered the Palestinian secretary in a deep guttural voice, 'turn . . . left and then first left. Press the . . . buzzer at the garden . . . gate.'

The tree-lined road narrowed as I left the Russian Compound, a small enclave in West Jerusalem where my flatmate Shira worked at one of the dozen or so trendy bars in the area to pay off her student fees (and enable me to drink free Goldstar beer). Aside from the animated nightlife, the stunning Church of the Holy Trinity, with its eight Byzantine-style domes decorated with golden crosses, dominates the compound.

This area is not just known as the Russian Compound by chance. It is a remnant of the twilight years of the Ottoman Empire, when European nations raced to cement their grip on the Holy Land in their bid to acquire access to eastern Mediterranean ports. By the mid-nineteenth century, as boatloads of pilgrims arrived, the French, British and Russians were all ready to pounce when the Ottoman Empire crumbled.

The Russians bought this plot of land in 1860 and built a walled compound for a consulate, hospice, church and monastery to accommodate 2000 pilgrims annually. The place flourished until 1917, when the Russian Revolution deemed religion 'anti-revolutionary'. It then fell into the hands of the British who established their headquarters there, including a notorious prison, until 1948.

The most remarkable chapter in this compound's history took place in the 1964, when Israel wanted to purchase the tract of land back from the Russians. The price agreed was US$4.5 million – way beyond what the impoverished state coffers could finance. They brokered a deal. Russia was short of food; Israel was strapped for cash, but had an abundance of oranges. So, in what is arguably the greatest citrus barter of all time, boatloads of oranges departed from Jaffa port, headed for the Black Sea as Israel paid Russia for two-thirds of the cost in fruit.

Just down the road from the compound, along Heleni HaMalka Street, is the Old City. Before I knew it, and without warning, the golden cupola of the Dome of the Rock (the Mosque of Omar) was in my face.

I stopped dead in my tracks. I'd seen the dome many times before, but never from this vantage point and never in this light.

Damascus Gate was just below me to my left, but the dome took up most of my frame.

I realised then just how much I took my new home for granted. I'd been living here less than six months, and although I'd been here countless times before, this is one place in the world that continues to surprise with its beauty, day after day. Superlatives offer little insight at unparalleled moments like these.

I never could understand how Mark Twain, when he travelled here in the 1860s, found this place so uninspiring. 'Jerusalem is mournful, dreary and lifeless,' he wrote in his record of his expedition, *The Innocents Abroad*. 'I would not desire to live here.'

Jerusalem has changed dramatically over the years, but the Old City has not. Twain was even more scathing about Palestine (as it was called then), noting that it was 'desolate and unlovely'. True, compared to today's population, which has mushroomed to some six million, it was desolate back then.* But unlovely? I beg to differ: the olive-cloaked hills of the Galilee, the snow-capped Mount Hermon in the Golan Heights, the serenity of the Sea of Galilee, the sand dunes of the Negev Desert, the moon-like landscape of the Ramon Crater and the awe-inspiring sight of Jerusalem's Old City from almost any vantage point to name just a few prized spots.

The gentle wail of the muezzin's call to prayer began resonating from the mosque as I neared the walls of the Old City. I closed my eyes.

'Allahu akbar – God is great! La ilaha illa Allah – there is no God but God! Allahu akbar!'

The morning was so crisp and the dome so close I could almost smell the prayers of the faithful, crouched on their heels, kneeling simultaneously on prayer rugs following the muezzin's lead. Opening my eyes again, I made a mental note to carve this picture in my memory forever.

I did end up working there part-time for a while, but it wasn't long before I realised that the view of the dome of the Mosque of

* In 1914, fifty years after Twain's expedition, there were only around 800,000 people living in Palestine.

Omar was the real drawcard pulling me back, time and again. IPCRI was a think-tank that was devoid of any juice, as dry as a felafel with no tahina. There was too much mental masturbation going on. Apart from anything else, they were looking to employ academics, not guys like me looking to taste a slice of the peace pie.

I continued to chase one particular fund, an umbrella charity that raised money for its affiliates: charities that supported human rights, civil liberties, equal rights, women's rights and other egalitarian causes. I figured if I could get in there somehow, the door might open to any one of their affiliates.

Out of the blue, I got a call back from the fund's assistant coordinator one day.

'Ben, are you interested in a short-term job?' she asked.

'Definitely.'

'I should warn you that it's not an average 9-to-5 job.'

Nothing could have been less enticing than the predictability of a 9-to-5 job. If I wanted one of them I could've stayed in London. 'Sounds good,' I replied. 'What's the job?'

She sounded awkward. 'Perhaps . . . [silence] we can . . . like . . . discuss this away from the . . . [silence, muffled whispers] . . . phone if you know what I mean.'

The more she talked, the more intrigued I became.

'No problem. I was looking for something different.'

'No, no. You don't understand. There are things you need to know. You know what? I'll give the coordinator your number and he'll phone you.'

I was baffled. My intrigue was now upgraded to frustration. 'What's the job? What can be that secret that you can't just tell me?'

'Well . . . [silence] look, like I said . . . [more muffled voices in the background] I can't really talk right now. I have to go now. We'll be in touch. You'll get a call in the next few days.'

Click.

I was in cerebral overdrive. What? Who? Why? Where? Was it illegal? When would he call?

No name. No details. Nothing. Just the slightest inclination that it may be something secretive involving the Palestinians. I tried to put two and two together – but I had precious little to work on. No leads, no clues, barely even a hunch.

I moved the phone from the hall into my room, explaining to Shira that it was just a temporary measure.

Then the phone rang. I grabbed the receiver as though it were a life-threatening call. It was for Shira.

Days passed. I tried to forget about it. But I couldn't. I spent most of my hours at work in the fortress trying to unravel the conundrum of this seemingly once-in-a-lifetime opportunity; it rankled with me relentlessly.

When the phone finally did ring, and I heard the voice of a North American guy I did not recognise, I knew that this was it. My heart began racing; my brain was close behind, my palms were perspiring and I was breathing heavily.

All this exertion of emotions and the guy had barely said one word, let alone offered me a job.

'I've read your CV,' he said matter-of-factly. 'I'm looking for someone I can trust.'

What was I supposed to say? I'm your man? No worries? Trust me pal, I'm a rock?

Instead, I tried to calm my heavy breathing. So I lit a cigarette.

'Look, I'm about to start talking about an extremely sensitive, classified matter. If, at any stage over the next few minutes, you feel uncomfortable or uneasy, just say so and I will hang up and pretend we never spoke. OK?'

This was driving me nuts. Jesus, just spit it out, I felt like yelling. What the hell do you want me to do? Plant a wire in Hezbollah leader Sheikh Hassan Nasrallah's telephone? Befriend Yasser Arafat's wife Suha?

'OK. No problem,' I lied.

'You've heard of Bir Zeit University, right?' he asked.

'Yes. It's the main Palestinian university near the West Bank town of Ramallah.'

'Right. But there are also other, less well-known universities. I have been doing some work with one of them. But I can't do it overtly from the offices of the fund because the university is known as a breeding ground for militant Palestinian nationalism and I can't mention the name of it over the phone for security reasons.

'So I'm working covertly but I need help. It's no secret that some of the directives during the Intifada came straight out of Bir Zeit University. They also came from the students at this particular place. That's why this project I'm involved in has major ethical dilemmas and is why the fund cannot overtly support my work.'

'What exactly do you want me to do?' I said, cutting through his long-winded background detail.

'At this stage, all I want to know is whether you have a moral or ethical problem being involved in aiding and abetting the Palestinians of this university.'

'Without knowing the exact details of the mission, I can't really comment,' I said, trying to avoid committing myself.

'OK, I understand. Are you interested in hearing more?'

'Yes.'

'Then meet me tomorrow at 8 pm at the fund's offices. I have to work there at night after everyone has gone home so as not to create political problems for them. It's the fourth floor. You've been before, no?'

'Yes.'

'Good. I'll see you tomorrow then.'

'Yeah. Thanks.'

'Oh, not a word by the way. This is totally confidential.'

'No problem. You have my word.'

I hung up and tried to compose myself. This was my break. All the energy I had put into finding a job with meaning had finally surfaced. I could barely hide the smile erupting across my face. I wanted to talk, to tell someone, but I was sworn to secrecy.

I returned the phone to the hallway and lay down to sleep. My brain was buzzing like a computer processor trying to search its hard drive for a file. It was hours before I managed to log off and shut it down.

CHAPTER FOURTEEN

I SPENT MOST of the following day ploughing through every possible permutation I could think of. I had a hunch it was the university in Hebron, although there may have been other smaller campuses in Jenin or Jericho, Bethlehem or Nablus. But I'd heard of Hebron University and couldn't confirm that there were others anywhere else.

I wanted to try and ascertain in advance where I would draw my own line. Without knowing exact details, I knew enough to know that I would be forced to decide just how far I was willing to go in the quest for peace.

What would I consider beyond the pale? What if those I was to help wanted to take revenge for the years they have suffered under Israeli occupation? Could this kind of work be considered treasonous to some Israelis?

And if he asked me to go to Hebron, would I?

I had been there once before, back in 1987, just before the Intifada ignited a fuse in the hearts and minds of the Palestinians, leading to a full-scale uprising against the Israelis, and a year before we arrived to live on Kibbutz Rosh HaNikra.

I had spent the summer hitchhiking around the country with two old mates I'd first met at various camps over the years: Freddy, a fanatical Manchester United supporter who would go the extra yard to grab the limelight, and Frankie, a Londoner who followed Arsenal.

'Want to visit the Judean Desert, go on a jeep tour and climb Masada for sunrise?' coaxed a 20-something bearded American chap as we were waiting in Jerusalem bus station to catch a bus to Tel Aviv.

He handed us a glossy pamphlet and talked up the tour.

'D'you go to the Dead Sea too?' asked Freddy, whose full-time occupation was trying to get his arse out of first gear.

It was an inexpensive three-day tour, and although we'd planned to go to all these places, it would not only have cost us about the same amount, but it would have taken much longer. This was a hassle-free alternative and since we were short on time and money, it seemed like a good idea.

'Fuck it,' slammed Frankie, sporting a peroxide quiff and a freshly sunburnt nose. 'Let's do it. We'll have a crack, and if we don't . . . we'll hijack the jeep. In any case, going alone with you two is a liability. By the time you both get your shit together, we could already be floating in the Dead Sea.'

I agreed. Travelling with Freddy was worse than trying to hitchhike with a shopping trolley for a backpack. It'd been a tough few weeks up north, and I was into parking my posterior in a jeep for a few days with someone else navigating.

Freddy was nonplussed. 'What? I thought we agreed to stick on our own. No tours. No guides. No groups. You wanna go in a jeep? Let's hire our own jeep. I didn't come over here to have some weirdo beardo babysit me.'

Frankie and I ignored him and began filling out forms.

Hebron, like Jerusalem, is another Jewish–Muslim flashpoint on the Middle-Eastern fault line. Here in Hebron, the patriarchs Abraham, Isaac and Jacob – along with their wives, Sarah, Rebecca and Leah – are entombed in the Cave of the Machpelah, the Tomb of the Patriarchs, Judaism's second holiest site after the Western Wall. But it is also holy to Islam, since Abraham, according to the Koran, was the first Muslim.

Just to complicate matters, the Cave of the Patriarchs was first a synagogue, then a church and, during the seventh-century Islamic occupation, it became the Ibrahimi Mosque, known locally as Haram el-Khalil. And although the 120,000-strong town is largely populated by Arabs, a colony of several hundred Orthodox Right-wing Jews, protected by several thousand IDF soldiers, have entrenched themselves here, desperate to cling on to this holy shrine. Suffice to say, it is a disputed site deep in the disputed territory of the West Bank. Not the kind of place you go for a Sunday picnic.

Since 25 February 1994, the synagogue and the mosque have been segregated, courtesy of Baruch Goldstein, a Jewish extremist who murdered twenty-nine Palestinians as they knelt in prayer. But, back in 1987, we entered the huge, Herodion, fort-like structure alongside Muslims.

It was only when we arrived later that day in Kiryat Arba, a barbed-wire, fenced-in satellite town adjacent to Hebron, that I began to suspect something was awry. We passed the fortified security gate and were waved through by an armed guard. The first thing we had to do was fill out a questionnaire, which asked suspicious questions like, 'Why do you think the Jews are the "Chosen People"?' We looked at each other and pulled faces. After dinner, when the group broke out into a rendition of 'Grace After Meals', I began to suspect that things really were not quite as they seemed.

Unofficial but unequivocal confirmation that we were sequestered in an extremist Right-wing West Bank settlement on a tour run by a bunch of bearded brainwashing American settler messianists who believed that this land was their birthright came the following morning.

We were woken at dawn. Needless to say we refused to rise. Frankie suddenly caught a serious fever and was rolling around in his bed. Freddy pretended to have died during the night, and lay there comatose (a regular pose). Soon we were forcefully removed.

We were each handed a bag of tefillin (phylacteries), two small black boxes containing pieces of parchment with portions of the Torah inscribed on them. The boxes are attached to straps that religious Jewish men wear for morning prayers six days a week, the Sabbath excepted. One box sits on the head; the other on the upper arm. The leather arm strap is wound on the forearm and then over the hand in the form of a Hebrew letter that stands for God.

Freddy was livid. He had never wanted to come in the first place. Now he was scowling as he wrapped phylacteries around his arm before breakfast, surrounded by a bunch of strange-looking men, swaying to and fro while muttering prayers at what seemed like the speed of light. And it was not even 6 am.

We survived the ordeal – just. As soon as we departed Kiryat Arba, heading on a jeep tour of the Judean Desert en route to Masada, we knew we had escaped being either chained down to a yeshivah in a West Bank settlement or being held hostage in the Casbah, Hebron's Arab market.

I hadn't been back since, and didn't intend to. I guess the brainwashing didn't have any effect. Baruch Goldstein is now enshrined at the entrance to Kiryat Arba in a park named after Meir Kahane, another Jewish extremist, whose political party, Kach, stood on a platform that demanded the expulsion of Arabs from Israel's birthright.

I had no desire to return to such a bastion of Right-wing, rabble-rousing messianism. Unless the fund sent me there.

Surely not. I discarded the idea that I'd be sent back to Hebron as preposterous. Darkness had fallen, drawing a conspicuous curtain on the city, behind which myself and a guy whose name I did not even know would discuss classified information. I braced myself for my meeting and called a cab.

'Alo! Alo!'

'Yes, I'm going to Baka'a . . . '

'Shesh dakot – six minutes!'

Click. There are no formalities on the phone to taxi companies here.

Baka'a is a suburb in southern Jerusalem, just off the road that runs down to Bethlehem and on to Hebron. It's a short ride and, as usual, the radio was on in the background. Three bleeps signalled the headlines.

'Kol Yisrael. Erev tov. Hinei hahadashot – This is The Voice of Israel. Good evening. Here is the news . . . '

Usually, the driver turns up the volume. But, my driver decided to turn it down.

'How much worse can it get? I've had enough of the news. All news is bad news. First Nachshon's murder, then the shooting here in Nachlat Shiva.'*

'I know what you mean. Seems like the peace process is more fragile than ever.'

'It's the peace process that *is* the bad news, habibi. When Rabin shook hands with Arafat, he sold our birthright.'

I was more than a trifle sceptical. 'Without the peace process, we'd have another Intifada, another war. With the peace process, at least we've got a chance that our children may inherit a life in a land worth living in.'

'Shtuyot – nonsense. Before you know it we'll be giving away Tel Aviv, Jaffa and then Jerusalem.'

'So, you'd prefer the alternative? To live in a state of war?'

'Ata meshugah – are you crazy? I don't want war but what choice do I have? We've survived for almost fifty years, and we'll continue to survive. The Arabs will never defeat us on the battle-field. Sheva shekel – seven shekels,' he snapped, screeching to a halt.

And on that abrupt note my taxi ride ended. Had I told him that I was about to meet a guy to discuss a clandestine mission involving Palestinians in the West Bank, would he still have given me a ride? I feared not. And had he deemed my work treasonous, he may have stripped me naked, bound me by the hands, driven me to Hebron and dumped me unceremoniously in the middle of the Casbah with an Israeli flag wrapped around me. Just to corroborate his argument that peace with the Palestinians is an illusion. Just to prove his point.

* On 9 October 1994 two Israelis – one soldier and one Israeli Arab – were killed and fourteen were injured when a Hamas terrorist opened fire in this popular pedestrianised street in downtown Jerusalem.

CHAPTER FIFTEEN

I RODE THE ELEVATOR up to the fourth floor, staring in the mirror. Pathetic, I thought to myself. My attempt at 'smart casual' had, as usual, backfired. What the hell is 'smart casual' in any case if it isn't an oxymoron?

He was waiting outside the office door. Tall, dark, lean, unshaven. His hair was scruffy and his fingernails were chewed almost down to the cuticles. He talked softly.

We shook hands.

'There are still a couple of people inside so we can't really talk.'

'Shall I come back later?'

'No. No. Come in. I have some background information for you to read.'

We entered a small office weighed down with books, pamphlets, files, folders, magazines and mission statements. He passed me a thick wad of papers, put his forefinger to his lips and disappeared, closing the door behind him.

It struck me that maybe this was a test. After all, it had all the trappings of a stitch-up. Could it be? Why? What was the motive? Who was behind it? Then I realised that it was the neurotic inside me playing mind games. Still, it threw me off-centre and, for a few minutes, all the words on the pages merged into one illegible scribble.

By the time he returned, fifteen minutes later, I had barely read a word.

'So what do you think?' he began.

'I think I need to hear more. Just give me the black-and-white picture. What exactly do you want me to do?'

'Simple. I'm working with the students of Hebron University.'

I smiled, my hunch confirmed.

'They have no money, their coffers are empty and if they can't get any money, then fewer and fewer will be able to enter higher education. They are desperate for cash and there's one fund that I'm trying to get money from, but they are not organised in the way we are. They have no idea how to fill out this twenty-page application form or how to write themselves up as a worthwhile charity case.

'When it comes to getting cash out of donors, they are novices, useless. I'm Israeli, although my mother is American. I speak fluent Hebrew, Arabic and English, but my writing isn't up to scratch and I can't find anyone willing to undertake the project. That's where you come in.'

'What? All I have to do is write up this proposal?'

'In a nutshell, yes.'

'I don't actually have to go to Hebron myself?'

'No.' I smiled again, kissing goodbye to the vision of bumping into my bearded acquaintances from Kiryat Arba.

'So how am I supposed to "dress" them up when I have never seen the place, let alone met any of the real people affected by the lack of funding?'

I vaguely knew what I was talking about because one of my most recent freelance jobs had been writing mundane project proposals for poor . kibbutzim deep in the southern Arava Valley, comprising two cows, three families and four chickens, who were desperate for funds to build a childcare centre, music hall, youth club or swimming pool. But I had to schlep down there with a photographer to see the site for myself and interview people whose lives would be adversely affected without the funds.

'I go to Hebron twice a week to meet with them. The situation is too risky. The Intifada may be over, but embers are still burning and they don't know you, let alone trust you. Building their trust has taken me years.'

'OK, so you go, feed me the information and I write it up. No drama. So what's with the secrecy, classified information, undercover working conditions?'

'Look,' he said, edging his bottom into a more comfortable position on his chair, 'half of me doesn't even want to enter into this discussion because I just need you to trust me and do the job. The application must be sent in five days. We're talking up to US$10,000 at stake here. But the other half of me understands that it would be irresponsible and unfair for you to walk into this minefield blindfolded.'

'So the Palestinians of Hebron University, like those at Bir Zeit, fuelled much of the discontent during the early days of the Intifada? Does that mean they don't have a right to education?'

He smiled. 'Precisely. But appreciate that those who seek to condemn my work argue that the money, if received, may never find its way into education.'

'That's like saying that you're unprepared to teach them chemistry in case they discover how to prepare explosives. Or build bombs.'

He eased back in his chair, and swung on its two hind legs. 'Exactly. Their right to higher education should never be compromised by their political persuasion. They have lost enough. To lose education would be like losing the freedom to think.

'But, the main reason why I do this without any scruples is that the most important building block in the bridge between Israelis and Palestinians is education. What fuels the war is not just deepseated enmity, religious animosity or national prejudice. It is ignorance. And education is the potion of peace. The more Palestinians that are well educated, the better the chance of the next generation of Israelis and Palestinians living in peace.'

He was convincing. I was bought and sold, twice over.

'Ancient Chinese wisdom tells us that one who wants to plan for a year should plant rice; one who wants to plan for ten years should plant trees; but one who wants to plan for future generations should work in education. This is my contribution.'

I was somewhat surprised at how innocuous my role was. Basically, I just had to sit in an office and type out an extensive charity proposal. For all the secrecy and hush-hush surrounding the job, it was hardly a contentious task.

We parted on a handshake of goodwill. There was no contract or formalities. It was a cash-in-hand job. The background material was in my bag. I had to immerse myself in it before tomorrow evening when we would begin in earnest. We would work every night for four nights, all night if need be, to get the proposal out before deadline. The remuneration was modest; the satisfaction, I figured, would more than make up for the hole in my pocket. And, apart from anything else, it was a short-term project, which, I hoped, would have a long-term impact.

I left content that I didn't have to go to Hebron and felt, for the first time, that I would be contributing, albeit it in a minor way, towards peace.

Ray, my sister's husband, was a paid-up Israel Labour Party supporter who had his finger on the pulse of the peace process. Although he had been born in England, his parents were both Israeli. So he knew what he was talking about and was a resolute analyst who could assess both sides of a coin. When I mentioned my new job to my sister that evening as I was scouring the fridge for whatever was lurking at the back of the bottom shelf, she insisted that I talk it over with Ray.

I explained the mission to him on the balcony of their flat. He sat there, in typical fashion, listening, absorbing, thinking. His silence was the first thing that struck me. I could almost hear his brain ticking over.

'So, what do I have to lose?' I concluded.

Ray remained silent for a few more seconds. Then he looked at me, stern as a military commander-in-chief.

'Everything,' he said. 'You could lose everything.'

'What? How? Give me an example of what I stand to lose. It's the Palestinians at Hebron University who will lose the right to education.'

'Ben, calm down.' He could see I was seething with stress. 'In principle I agree with you entirely. But there are two implications that you must be 100 per cent aware of. Why? Because they could seriously alter your life here in Israel.'

'Keep talking,' I said.

'First is the issue of working with the Palestinians of Hebron. Remember whom we are talking about here. You can't classify all Palestinians in one boat, much like you can't stereotype all Israelis, let alone Jews. These Palestinians are not your Haifa Arabs, neither are they Umm al-Fahm youth. In fact, most are paid-up subscribers of George Habash's PFLP.* They are widely known as being among the most militant supporters of jihad – holy war.

'When a bomb goes off in downtown Jerusalem, for example, the Shin Bet is pretty sure that the students in Hebron are not that far away from the eye of the storm.† Sometimes they are the iris of the eye themselves. So, when you go delivering them a cheque for $10,000, think about where that money will go. Are you naive enough to believe that it will build new classrooms, fund new scholarships or create a new computer centre? Or will some, if not all, of it be siphoned off and shunted down a pipeline to the militant wing of an organisation bent on bombing innocent Israelis in their quest to blow up the peace process?

'And if, or rather when, the next bomb blast rocks this country and they suspect that the bomb factory was in Hebron, will you be able to sleep at night?

'And when the tiny, half-sized coffins of innocent Israeli children are laid to rest, their mothers grieving uncontrollably, will you be able to look at yourself in the mirror without breaking down, without . . . ?'

Ray paused. I choked. I blinked. And then blinked again and again, trying desperately to dam the flood of tears. They streamed down my cheeks in any case.

---

* Haifa's Arabs have managed to co-exist with the Jewish community; Umm al-Fahm, the second largest Arab town in Israel, is an Islamic stronghold. George Habash's Popular Front for the Liberation of Palestine (PFLP) is a radical guerrilla organisation that opposes the PLO's leadership of the Palestinians.

† The Shin Bet is Israel's internal secret service; it is the sister organisation of the Mossad, which operates overseas.

'I'm sorry,' he said. 'I didn't mean to hit on you that hard. It just all came out. The situation is so tense; it's too hard to call. I just want to make sure you know the implications. That's all. In the end it's your decision, but you've got to know what you're getting involved with.'

'What was the second thing?' I asked, really not wanting to know.

He sighed, and rubbed his forehead. I could read between the lines that I wasn't going to like what he was about to tell me.

'Well, you are involving yourself in a procedure that could be frowned upon by the authorities if you are detected. You see, right now at this very minute, there are 18- to 21-year-old boys staking out potential terrorists in Hebron, risking their lives to pre-empt the next suicide bombers from murdering innocent Israelis. The army's anti-terror unit is one of the most sophisticated wings of the military.

'In their eyes, it is possible you would be considered an accomplice to the Palestinians. The penalty for such a crime could be imprisonment, though it is doubtful you would be incarcerated for merely writing a proposal. The point is you cannot predict what will happen, whose hands the money will land in, what they will do with it and who may suffer as a result.

'But, say that the worst-case scenario did evolve, not only would the paper trail lead back to you, but you could be involved in a legal case. The arm of the law could, if it decides, reel you in and lock you up.'

'Is that all?' My cynicism was bursting to be let loose.

'Yeah. Actually . . . no. Thinking about it, I guess there's one other thing: if you do go ahead with it, and you are detected, I guess they may "use" you when you get conscripted.'

'Eh?'

'Well, you'll be privy to inside information. You may have contacts with Palestinians in Hebron that the army is trailing. They may need your assistance to carry out missions.'

'No chance. I'm not planning on going to the army, let alone betraying my work.'

Ruth had listened to the whole conversation. She hugged me.

She knew how badly I wanted to do this and how much Ray had just bulldozed my dreams. I was cracking. I needed out.

I left my sister's flat and wandered home on foot. The West Jerusalem pavements were sparsely populated; even the roads were tame, save for the just-passed-my-driving-test-youths who screeched past, blaring techno tunes from daddy's car. A few old-timers were walking their dogs.

I decided against going straight home and headed down Ben Yehuda Street, a pedestrianised hub of restaurants and shops that acts as a magnet for tourists and travellers alike. I slouched into an outdoor seat at a café, ordered a cappuccino and watched the human traffic pass by. Three coffees and four cigarettes later, I trudged home, stopping on the way to empty my change into a rusty can belonging to a old, bearded guy with one leg and a crutch, with whom I'd come to empathise over the last few months.

I spent the next twenty hours in a crisis of conscience. My moral code felt as though it'd just gone fifteen rounds with Mike Tyson. Aside from the fact that my brother-in-law had, in not so many words, equated me with Islamic fundamentalists, I was still perplexed at his blanket correlation between Hebron students and militant Palestinians. Wasn't that a generalisation? Because some of them had established a notorious name for themselves, did that make them all terrorists?

And, in any case, whatever happened to innocent until proven guilty? What about the benefit of the doubt? I for one was willing to give them that. It had been over a year since Rabin and Arafat swore an end to this war on the lawn of the White House. Sure, after half a century of blood, the enmity was still deeply rooted, but give them a chance. And if you deny a people education, what does that leave them with?

I didn't speak to anyone else that night. The following day I walked around the Old City's streets peering behind keffiyehs, standing in queues for Arab buses in East Jerusalem that I didn't want to catch and hanging around souk stalls talking to Arab merchants from whom I had no intention of purchasing anything.

I had no real purpose at all, just a longing to debunk the myth that all people can be categorised as one. Or that those who shout loudest smear the silent with their tarnished brush.

By sundown, I had made up my mind.

It was too hot to handle. Being active in promoting peace was one thing; but supporting a project that could be sabotaged by militant Palestinians who oppose the peace process was quite another. There was a plethora of legitimate pro-peace organisations within the Israeli body politic. Hebron University was not one of them.

Although I felt guilty, I comforted myself with the fact that the guilt I was feeling would be a fraction of the guilt I would have to live with for the rest of my life if Ray's worst-case scenario unfolded.

I called the number I was given and explained my ideological rift. My contact sounded bitterly disappointed and began to try to talk me around when I said that I felt I was betraying the Palestinians' basic human right to education. But he stopped short when I said that, morally, I could not be party to something that could backfire on my people. And, as a result, on the peace process.

I'll never know if I did the right thing. Or if the thing I thought was right turned out to be wrong. Or even if, by not doing it, the next generation's chances of living in peace would be diminished.

Several weeks later, two Palestinian suicide bombers detonated themselves at Bet Lid, a junction where dozens of soldiers were waiting at a bus stop. They killed twenty-one Israelis and injured sixty-nine others. As the nation mourned this latest attack, I felt relieved that I was not a potential accomplice.

I thought of my partner in crime. What would he be thinking right now? Where would he hide his shame if the bombers were found to come from Hebron? How would he be able to live with himself? And how would he be able to face his so-called 'friends' in Hebron again?

CHAPTER SIXTEEN

IT TOOK ME more than a few weeks to shake off the emotional burden of my Hebron encounter. By that time winter had already set in, and at an elevation of more than 800 metres, snowflakes were beginning to coat Jerusalem in white flecks, making it look like the wind had lightly dusted the Holy City with icing sugar.

Winter in Israel means Hanukkah, the Festival of Lights. Eight-branched candelabras dapple naked candlelight, inside on windowsills, for eight consecutive nights to celebrate the victory of the Maccabees over the Greeks in 165 BC. The eight candles recall the miracle of the single flask of oil found in the Temple after the Greeks had ransacked it. The flask lasted for eight days; enough time to prepare a new supply.

But for Israel's 150,000 mainly Arab Christians, winter means Christmas. And, for them, Christmas is synonymous with Bethlehem, the birthplace of Jesus Christ.

Israeli Jews don't hang out in Bethlehem. Even before the stone-throwing, tyre-burning days of the Intifada, there was little to lure them to this West Bank Arab town just ten kilometres south of Jerusalem.

Beyond the Church of the Nativity there's little else to Bethlehem, except kitsch shops selling Jesus paraphernalia to busloads of tourists, next to snack bars and restaurants procuring profits from pilgrims.

Having never been before, and a little intrigued by Christ's birthplace, I decided on a day trip. After all, it was only down the road and the festive season seemed an appropriate time to visit. But I didn't want to go alone.

I asked an Israeli friend from work if he was interested.

'Bethlehem? Mah, ata meshugah – what, are you crazy? What do you want to go there for?'

'I dunno. I guess I'm interested to see where Jesus was born.'

'If you're unlucky you'll end up there in the army. That's the only reason I'd ever go there.'

I asked a couple of others who showed similar disdain for my proposal. I figured the only two guys in town I knew who weren't working, and could be persuaded to come, were Mick and Charlie.

Charlie wasn't answering. But I knew he was in. It was only one in the afternoon, and there wasn't a shred of doubt that he would be anywhere but horizontal, lying comatose after another heavy dose of Mick's 'medication'.

Mick was flat out supplying the student population of Jerusalem with 'loaded' Christmas stockings. Demand always peaked at this time of year, and his mobile phone was on 24-hour call.

'No time dude. Sorry. All of a sudden, everyone needs an appointment at the surgery.'

'It's not as if I'm going overseas or anything. It's down the road. Half an hour away, tops. Your phone will still work in the West Bank you know and it's not like you have to close down the surgery or anything.'

It was not difficult to convince Mick to do anything that sounded remotely intriguing. 'You sure my phone will work?'

'You really are on drugs. Course it will. Where do you think we're going? Baghdad?'

'Yeah, OK. I can probably squeeze a few hours this afternoon.'

We meet at Damascus Gate to catch a sherut – a stretch taxi – to Bethlehem. Mick, to my horror, is wearing his neck brace and, along with his pinstripe flares, goatee beard and long, scraggy hair, looks like he is about to audition for the cast of *Jesus Christ Superstar*. He is yapping away on his mobile phone when I arrive.

The sherut soon fills up and heads out, trading suburbs for rugged olive groves and barren hills as we make our way south towards Bethlehem.

Most travellers enter Jerusalem from the west, up the mountain from Tel Aviv. In all other directions, military checkpoints block the entrance to the city: near Ramallah in the north, Beit Haninah in the east and Bethlehem in the south.

These checkpoints are positioned at the crossing of the Green Line into the West Bank, where the border used to run between Israel and Jordan from 1948 to 1967. Today, the IDF monitors everyone entering and leaving the capital, in an attempt to prevent suicide bombers and terrorists from wreaking havoc.

The traffic slows to a near standstill as soldiers trawl vehicles for suspects. On the other side of the road, a car has been pulled over; one soldier is searching inside, another is questioning the driver while checking his documents. The car in question, like all cars from the West Bank and Gaza Strip, has a blue registration plate – as opposed to the yellow licence plates of Israeli cars. The Hebrew letter at the beginning of the plate, preceding the numbers, refers to the town of residence: 'R' for Ramallah, 'H' for Hebron, 'N' for Nablus and 'B' for Bethlehem.

Though the soldiers are on the lookout for terrorist suspects, the fact that Mick's neck brace is lined with marijuana makes me nervous.

'You're an eejit,' I mumble to him.

'Why?'

'You know exactly why. You could've left it at home.'

'Never like to be caught with my pants down. And in case you hadn't noticed, this is a tight ship I'm running here. I'm on call 24/7, assisting the weak and the meek in their hour of need.'

Mick scratches his neck, strokes his goatee and flashes a cheesy grin in my direction just to provoke me.

He loves standing out from the crowd. Not the greatest attribute when you're smuggling illicit substances across a military checkpoint.

We inch our way towards what is formally known as the 'Occupied Territories'. A soldier peers into our sherut. Barely pubescent, he takes one look at Mick and stops. If he had the time or the energy, he could nail his ass to the floor and have him begging for mercy while his comrades, armed with rubber gloves, threaten to investigate his rectum. He frowns at Mick and then waves the driver through. Mick is in raptures. I am not.

Soon we are in Bethlehem's main plaza, Manger Square, dominated by the Israeli police headquarters, a mammoth fortress barricaded behind a high, barbed-wire fence.

On one side of the police station is the impressive Church of the Nativity, Christianity's oldest working church; on the other is Omar ibn al-Khatab Mosque. Bethlehem's 30,000 Arab residents are fairly evenly split between Christians and Muslims; minarets and spires tussle for supremacy on the skyline.

The imminence of the festive season is palpable. Tinsel and lights surround the square's perimeter. Municipal workers balance on ladders as they string decorations along the streetlamps in preparation for the annual Midnight Mass on Christmas Eve, pictures of which are beamed around the world.

We walk to the Church of the Nativity – a stunning fourth-century house of worship built under the aegis of Emperor Constantine. Underneath it lies the cave in which Jesus was born. The entrance to the church is through a tiny door, allegedly narrowed by the Crusaders in an attempt to prevent enemies from being able to ride their horses inside. Mick makes a mental note to copy this idea so that his house cannot be raided easily – either by the police or a gang.

We stoop to enter. Inside, a golden glow hovers around the church's large main nave, which is lined with Corinthian columns painted with frescoes of the saints. At the far end lies the Greek Orthodox High Altar surrounded by golden lamps and lanterns, candelabras and dripping candles. This is where Jesus was circumcised.

Mick is prattling on about his brit milah (circumcision) when he was eight days old. I ignore his obtuse remarks and tune into a tour guide who is telling his group of American pilgrims, all clearly identifiable by their oversized nametags, that Christian factions dispute the ownership of the site.

It transpires that the Greek Orthodox, Roman Catholics and the Armenians all vie for control over Jesus' birthplace and crises can erupt over anything as innocuous as a proposal to move a pew.

The tour guide then discloses that the denominations even celebrate Christmas on different days: Catholics and Protestants on 24 and 25 December; Greek Orthodox in early January; and Armenians in mid January.

The Greek Orthodox Church, the most powerful patriarchate in Israel, controls the Grotto of the Nativity, down two flights of steps adjacent to the High Altar. On the floor at the bottom of the stairs is a star accompanied by the Latin inscription, 'Here Jesus was born of the Virgin Mary'.

The guide explains that Roman Catholics made the inscription in 1717, but the Greek Orthodox removed it in 1847. Then the Turks ordered them to put it back in 1853. This, he says, led to a dispute that sparked the outbreak of the Crimean War.

That's when I begin to suspect more than a hint of hyperbole. Surely there is no historical basis to the outbreak of a war over an inscription in a church. 'Caused the Crimean War? You're kidding me on,' I mutter to Mick. 'I mean what on earth would a Russian town on the Black Sea have to do with a church in Bethlehem, eh?'

'I wouldn't rule it out mate. This is Israel, the Middle East, where wars have been waged for far less controversial reasons.'

Unusual though it seems, he does have a point. 'Yeah. I guess so. Actually, now that I think of it, an inscription in a grotto underneath a church in the Holy Land is actually a highly plausible pretext for war. Why not?'

'I reckon it's a damn fine excuse. Very imaginative indeed. Without it the Crimean War would have been a footnote in history. Instead it's a major landmark.'

'There you go again. Talking shite.'

We walk up Milk Grotto Street to visit Milk Grotto Chapel where, so the story goes, Mary spilt breast milk on the floor, turning the rock in the cavern chalky white. Women come here to pray for fertility because this is where Mary lactated.

Mick is perplexed by the whole notion of lactation. Unfortunately, I am unable to shed any light on the issue and, suspecting that he may embarrass us both in front of two nuns, I make a swift exit.

Leaving the chapel, we amble down the narrow street back to Manger Square when we hear a crowd approaching. It doesn't sound like a violent demonstration, more like a prayer ritual.

The noise begins to increase in volume and although we can't see anyone down the winding sidestreet, it is clear there is a crowd in the area. Suddenly, around the corner a sea of people, dressed in black garb, is marching towards us.

'We're shafted,' splutters Mick.

I look around. There is no place to go. Our only option is to head back in the direction we have come from. But that is also the direction the crowd is headed. We are snookered. By the time we have weighed up our options, the wall-to-wall mob is about to wash over us. Their chant reaches a deafening crescendo as they approach.

We become increasingly anxious. There aren't many, if any, fellow Jews around Bethlehem that day – except for the Israeli police. And they are barricaded behind barbed wire – which is exactly where I wanted to be right now.

I can't work out if the mob are Christians or Muslims because both speak Arabic.

Mick tightens his neck brace. 'This could be trouble.'

'What are they carrying?'

'I've no flippin' idea. And I don't really care either. I'd rather not be here to find out.'

We press ourselves tight against the wall, instinctively breathing in as if it may, somehow, help them pass.

'It's a coffin!'

The neurotic inside me wonders whether they are coming to collect me. Then, as it passes, I see what I've never before seen. It has no lid. The deceased is lying there, dressed neatly in black, hair brushed, moustache groomed, mouth closed. It is an Arab funeral procession heading for the cemetery beyond Milk Grotto Street.

We stand there gawking as we watch the coffin disappear up the road while hundreds upon hundreds of mourners brush past, chanting prayers. It seems like an eternity before the crowd thins and the sidestreet once again opens out. Breathing a sigh of relief, we head back to Manger Square, where we swap funeral notes while sipping over-priced coffees.

Mick is shocked to hear that I have been to a cremation.

'You're winding me up. Why would you go to a cremation?'

'My mate's grandma was a Jewish communist who emigrated from Russia to England. She wanted to be cremated.'

Never before have I been so bemused or perplexed as I was watching her coffin make its way ever so slowly along a conveyor belt before being subsumed in a furnace – all to the tune of a bizarre hymn as my mate's family and friends watched with pallid, uneasy faces.

'You think that's bad?' I continue. 'I went to my first funeral in Jerusalem the other week. A mate from work's father died. We all went along to support him. The guy was buried without a coffin.'

Mick almost chokes with laughter on his coffee. 'What? Stark bollocks naked?'

'Yeah, right. Can you imagine the rabbis dealing with that? He was just wrapped in a tallith (prayer shawl). I think it's to return man to earth in the same state as Adam arose from it.'

Mick pulls a face that makes him look as though he could have been sitting on a toilet, attempting to evacuate his bowels.

Our appetites suddenly evaporate and we head back to Jerusalem.

At Damascus Gate we are about to return home to West Jerusalem when I get an urge to close the circle. I have been to Jesus' birthplace. Now I want to visit his deathbed.

Nazareth, where he grew up, would have been the next logical stop on the pilgrim path, but it's in Galilee, several hours north of Jerusalem.

'Fancy heading up the Via Dolorosa?'

'What? You ain't had enough of Jesus for one day?'

'Nah. I fancy checking out the Church of the Holy Sepulchre.'

'Next you'll be inviting me to your baptism. OK, I guess my phone works in the Old City. But I've got deliveries to make, so let's not mess around, eh.'

'Ya'allah – let's go!'

CHAPTER SEVENTEEN

DAMASCUS GATE, with its Ottoman arch and ornate crenellations, is, without doubt, the most impressive of the eight gates to the Old City.* It is also the liveliest. In the small plaza in front of the gate, Arab traders flog everything from fresh fruit and vegetables to dated bootleg cassettes in a makeshift marketplace.

We are bombarded by kids trying to offload anything and everything. Their repertoire is, by now, familiar.

'Wallah! Chai . . . wahad shekel – tea . . . one shekel . . . Wallah! . . . achla baklawah – very tasty baklawah. You like music? Cheap. Cheap. Wallah! Very good. You need guide? Wallah! Make very nice tour. Wallah! No problem.'

An elderly Arab man stands behind a glass display unit perched on two wheels, selling freshly baked bagels coated in sesame seeds, which he trades along with a pinch of za'atar, a local spice belonging to the oregano family, wrapped in an old page of the Palestinian *Al-Fajr* (*The Dawn*) newspaper.

Mick buys one and we tear it open.

We fend off the ubiquitous moneychangers under the arch of the gate and shoulder our way past postcard sellers and through the sweet smell of shisha smoke into the Old City itself.

Two youths muscling a wheelbarrow of vegetables almost run us over as we watch a young Arab boy meander past, carrying a bronze tray with at least eight glasses of Turkish coffee. He holds it from above by a tripod-like handle making it swing

* The eight gates are: Jaffa Gate, Dung Gate, Zion Gate, St Stephen's Gate, New Gate, Herod's Gate, Damascus Gate and the Golden Gate (the only one which is blocked – by the Turks in 1530 – and remains closed to this day). Both Christians and Jews believe that the Messiah will enter Jerusalem from the Golden Gate and resurrect the dead.

as he delicately dances his way through the throng without spilling a single drop.

Above the gate, IDF soldiers, barely old enough to understand the meaning of love, perch themselves on the ramparts, eyeing the crowd for any signs of unrest.

We turn onto the Via Dolorosa, the Way of the Sorrows, where Jesus carried his cross to Calvary. Here, every Friday afternoon, the Franciscan Fathers carry a cross from the spot Jesus was tried all the way down the fourteen Stations of the Cross, ending up at the site of the crucifixion, the Church of the Holy Sepulchre. It wasn't Friday, but other tourists and pilgrims are retracing Jesus' steps. Joining them, it feels as though we are walking through the pages of someone else's history.

Mick is bemused by the sight of pilgrims carrying a giant cross down this ancient street.

'Can you imagine if we re-enacted the binding of Isaac?' he asks.*

'Not exactly. Can you imagine if Muslims re-enacted Allah's ascent to heaven?'

'Not exactly.'

'Well, there you go then. You're talking crap again. Every Passover we re-enact the Exodus from Egypt. Every Sukkot, we build palm-frond huts to simulate our journey through the desert wilderness for forty years. And, yeah, by the way, the ram's horn we blow to herald in the New Year originates from the animal that was slaughtered in place of Isaac.'

Mick offered no retort. It was a rare moment of silence.

In the courtyard outside the door, a crowd is mingling. Several nuns hide under the hoods of their habits, Japanese tourists peer behind their video cameras, Evangelicals harmonise psalms, a Greek Orthodox priest, cloaked head-to-toe in black, sways back

---

* The binding of Isaac was when God tested Abraham's will to see if he would slaughter his own son as commanded by the Lord. When God saw that Abraham's loyalty was undisputed, he substituted a ram in place of Isaac.

and forth with his eyes shut and an old Ethiopian sits on a low stool thumbing pages of the New Testament.

We enter and wander through the frankincense-fragranced, incense-laden, candle-lit chambers. It is a vast, dark space and the acoustics reverberate under the rotunda. Groups of pilgrims are huddled around guides and the murmur of psalms echoes from dark recesses, lending an eerie, but spiritual, edge to the place.

We had become experts in joining other tour groups for free. Our latest tour guide is explaining that here, at *the* shrine of Christianity, Christian factions also dispute ownership of the site. This time, however, there are not just three sects that stake their claim: the Greek Orthodox, Armenians, Syrians, Egyptian Copts and Roman Catholics all co-exist in a bizarre truce that perennially simmers on the edge of explosion.

Just for good measure, it transpires that the gatekeeper, a man by the name of Wajeeh Nusseibeh, whose family has been opening and closing the Sepulchre's gates since the twelfth century, is not a Christian, but a Muslim. And there's more. The gatekeeper is not the key holder. That honour goes to Jawad Joudeh, another Muslim. So here you have the entrance to the holiest shrine in Christianity in the golden hands of two Muslim families. The origin of this religious conundrum dates back to the end of the Crusader rule in the Holy Land and their defeat by Saladin in 1187. He was concerned that the Crusaders would return disguised as pilgrims, so he issued the chore of administering the church gates and keys to Muslims. And it has remained that way for more than 800 years.

Downstairs in the Sepulchre is where Jesus was laid to rest. Under the dome of the rotunda is the tomb, a tiny, dark space that holds no more than three people at a time. Eight ornate lamps are suspended above a marble slab, the empty burial site of the Son of God.

Mick is baffled. 'Not much of a shrine, eh?' he whispers, forehead fraught with frown lines.

I scowl at him. There's a time and a place to bag someone else's shrine. And it is not now.

Back on the Via Dolorosa, Mick is still bewildered.

'What's the big deal?' I ask. 'Man, we pray to a wall of stones covered in emerging moss.'

'True. I guess so. I just expected it to be much more lavish. It's the Muslims, I guess, who have the elaborate golden dome.'

'Yeah, but the beauty of the Sepulchre, like the Western Wall, is its humility. In any case, it's not about the architecture, it's about the history of the place. It may not be Notre Dame, but then Jesus wasn't Parisian.'

'Fair point.'

Here in Jerusalem, a city whose soul is saturated by religion, it is easy to forget that not only are there inter-religious conflicts, but there are also intra-religious disputes.

We were exhausted. We'd been walking all afternoon, so we hailed a cab.

'Rechavia please,' I said in Hebrew.

We sped off on the short trip from the Old City.

'Can you put the meter on please?'

'Fifteen shekels.'

Mick hated nothing more than being treated like a tourist (which is effectively what he was). 'What? You're joking! I live here habibi. I'm no tourist. Put the meter on or drop us off.'

'Twelve shekels.'

This guy was now pissing me off too. But I didn't have the energy to argue with him.

'Stop! Stop! If you don't put the meter on we're getting out. It's your call,' ordered Mick.

'OK. OK. Ten shekels. The meter's broken.'

By now I couldn't hold off. 'You guys always try to pull that stunt on us. Come on man. Stick it on. It's no more than seven shekels and you know it.'

Mick started opening his door and the driver, furious that he'd been caught out by two guys who looked like foreigners but lived locally and spoke the language, slid on the anchors and pulled in.

We traded expletives and hand gesticulations before trudging home along Jaffa Road and up Ben Yehuda Street.

CHAPTER EIGHTEEN

IT HAD BEEN a couple of years since I had romanced Lucy, my Australian sweetheart, on the shores of the Sinai. Time only served to stoke my fire. Even though I was living in Jerusalem, my heart was in Australia.

Love letters crossed the Indian Ocean between the Middle East and Australia at least once a fortnight and I soon realised I could hold off no longer. In mid 1995, a few months after my sojourn on Christianity's pilgrim path, I bought a ticket to Melbourne, Australia, gambling that an expensive trans-Pacific trip would work out.

We planned to cross the Australian outback in a third-hand Russian-built four-wheel-drive that we would buy after Lucy had finished her studies in rehabilitation with blind and vision impaired people. We wanted to travel from Melbourne to Sydney via the red centre: the Simpson Desert, Alice Springs, the Northern Territory and the Queensland coast.

In Melbourne, desperate to earn money for the trip, I managed to get a job in a Middle Eastern joint. Ironically, I wound up working with a Druze called A'di from Daliat al-Carmel in the north of Israel and a Palestinian called Moussa from Ramallah in the West Bank. At around 5.30 on ice-cold Melbourne mornings, a Druze, a Palestinian and a Jew would collaborate in the recesses of a small shop in St Kilda to bake fresh pita bread, fry hundreds of felafel balls, mix hummous and prepare an absurd amount of meat drenched in cumin and other spices for shwarma.

Moussa, A'di and I had an amicable relationship, conversing in English, Hebrew and Arabic. We frequently found ourselves sitting around drinking Turkish coffee and discussing the peculiarity of our dislocation here down under. As well as our longing to return to our roots. Moussa and I never broached the fact that we both believed our roots came from the same tree, which was planted on the same hallowed ground. Or that the ownership of that ground was bitterly disputed between our people.

We felt a certain empathy for each other; it was strange that here, just about as far away from the Middle East as you can get, we could co-exist quite amicably while there our families were feuding.

Lucy and I set off from Melbourne and headed down the stunning Great Ocean Road, which hugs the cliff face along the southern edge of Australia. We were weighed down with jerry cans of water, litres of spare fuel, two extra tyres and enough spare parts to register as collectors.

The jeep's manual boasted of its ability to start in freezing conditions of minus fifty degrees. But it said nothing of plus fifty degrees.

We took the Oodnadatta Track from the one-pub township of Maree and headed deep into *terra incognita*. The Simpson Desert is an inhospitable destination in northern South Australia, not far from the border with the Northern Territory. Signposts warned us not to enter this remote desert without sufficient spares: fuel, water and food. We felt confident. We had everything we could possibly require. Or so we thought.

Our jeep had been built for the Arctic tundra and was ill equipped for sub-Saharan climes. Several days down the track, the jeep began backfiring, letting off blasts that sounded like they'd erupted from an elephant's posterior.

It was with great relief that we emerged from the dust of the desert to find the outback town of William Creek. To define this place as a town is an exercise in hyperbole. Even to label it a village is an exaggeration. William Creek is little more than a single roadhouse in the middle of a vast desert. And although William Creek has an official population of ten, there was only one human being visible on 6 November 1995 – the day we rolled into town.

The landlord of the William Creek Hotel, it transpired, was also the publican, chef, travel agent, mechanic and petrol attendant. As well as the local pilot and air traffic controller.

Without even looking at our jeep, he pointed north and said one word: 'Oodnadatta'. We had already suspected that one man mid-desert could do little to help us. Instead, we perched on two dusty stools at the bar and lubricated our arid palates.

CNN was buzzing in the background on the cable television. My right ear picked up a nonchalant comment about the 'arrival in Israel of hundreds of foreign dignitaries for what would be an emotionally charged funeral'. Suddenly, we both spun around and tuned in. It took us several minutes to catch wind of what had happened. And then several days to absorb the totality of the assassination of Prime Minister Yitzhak Rabin.

At 11.14 pm on 4 November 1995, we soon learned, Eitan Haber, Rabin's chief aide, had announced: 'With horror, grave sorrow and deep grief, the Government of Israel announces the death of Prime Minister and Minister of Defence Yitzhak Rabin, murdered by an assassin'.

More than 100,000 people had demonstrated in Tel Aviv that night along with Rabin and his erstwhile brother in peace, Shimon Peres, in support of a peace deal with the Palestinians.

But one man, and a few of his friends, had other ideas. At the end of the demonstration, after Rabin and Peres had led the people in 'Shir l'Shalom' ('Song of Peace'), Rabin exited down the back steps of Tel Aviv's main square.

In the shadows stood 27-year-old avowed Right-wing extremist Yigal Amir on what he later said was an 'order from heaven'.* No one, not even the Shin Bet secret service, had predicted a Trojan Horse – that Rabin's assassin would be a Jew. While everyone else was focusing on restricting terror from outside Israel, an internal cancer was allowed to inflict terminal damage on the nation.

* Yigal Amir was a member of a group called Eyal, which was associated with the virulently Right-wing Kahane movement. Kahane supporters celebrated the Rabin assassination by visiting the grave of Meir Kahane.

Because of the antagonistic climate that had been brewing among the Right-wing settler movement, including effigies of Rabin dressed in SS Gestapo garb, he had been advised to wear a bullet-proof vest that night. But he refused, saying he felt 'safe and secure' among his own people.

Two bullets were enough to kill him. Rabin paid the same price as Egyptian President Anwar Sadat, another great leader who strove to take his people toward a new future. Muslim extremists assassinated him in 1981 for what they considered his treasonous Camp David peace treaty with Israel.

Rabin was the man who, reluctantly albeit, had had the courage to sign the historic Oslo Accords in September 1993. For him, it had been a heart-wrenching moment, the greatest turning point in the conflict. A year later he had shaken hands with Jordan's King Hussein and ended a 46-year war along the eastern flank, bringing the Israeli–Arab conflict one step closer to conclusion.

No other prime minister had walked so far along the tightrope to peace. Rabin was able to do so because he garnered support from both Left and Right. He was a hawkish dove who, as defence minister during the Palestinian Intifada, ordered his troops to 'break their bones' if need be to suppress the uprising. And then he became the man who made great overtures towards peace.

In the late 1950s, Rabin, then head of the IDF's manpower branch, had a sign above his desk at the military headquarters where he worked. It read: 'If you want peace, prepare for war'.

It was Rabin who was IDF chief-of-staff in the miraculous 1967 victory. For over forty years, he waged war against the Arabs. That's why, when he became prime minister again in 1992, he enjoyed the support of a large majority of Israelis.* He had the vision and the courage to grasp the historic opportunity,

* Rabin was previously prime minister once before in 1974, after Golda Meir resigned over the Yom Kippur debacle (when Israel was almost defeated by Egypt and Syria). He resigned in 1977 and Shimon Peres replaced him before he was defeated by Likud's Menachem Begin.

to herald the beginning of the end of this conflict, and his legacy remains deeply tattooed on the Israeli psyche.

In the same way that all Americans remember where they were in November 1963 when John F. Kennedy was assassinated, all Israelis recall their whereabouts when they first heard that Rabin had been assassinated in November 1995. Including Lucy and me. Most people on the Oodnadatta Track blink and miss William Creek. Lucy and I will never forget it.

We huffed and puffed our way towards Oodnadatta knowing all the while that we were driving the jeep to the wall.

As we passed Lake Eyre, a moon-like expanse of crusty, dry salt, where Donald Campbell made land speed history in 1964 by driving at 648.6 km/h, our jeep began protesting again. Then came the final *coup de grâce*: the head gasket exploded. Left with no other choice than to sizzle under the searing sun, we ploughed on to Oodnadatta, praying that we'd arrive alive.

Eventually we rolled into town – dusty, ramshackle, corrugated-iron shacks housing a 200-strong, mainly Aboriginal, community. The local policeman advised us to move on down the track because the local Aborigines, who owned the pub, became a touch boisterous when inebriated. We advised him that our Siberian jeep was about to hyperventilate. He pointed us in the direction of the town's landmark: the unmistakable and unremarkable pink roadhouse – a one-stop café-cum-petrol-station-cum-library-cum-local store-cum-bank-cum-post-office. And local garage.

It took us nine hours from Oodnadatta, winched onto the back of a truck, to reach the closest form of civilisation. That's just how far we were from anywhere. And Alice Springs, with a population of 25,000, is next to nowhere. From here it's thousands of kilometres to a metropolis of any size or significance.

The jeep required immediate hospitalisation. The nearest accident and emergency centre was in Adelaide.

'Call me in three weeks – minimum,' barked an Alice mechanic above the purring of a drill.

The mechanical damage was substantial. But the financial

damage was going to be far more painful. With only just enough money to make it around Australia, we were faced with an uncompromising choice: abort our trip and take the bus home – or find work to pay for the damage.

We chose the latter and ended up in Ntaria, the Aboriginal name for the township of Hermannsburg, a remote village in Australia's Northern Territory about 130 kilometres west of Alice Springs, deep in territory belonging to the Aboriginal Land Trust. Surrounded by river gum trees, date palms, honey ants and colonies of termite mounds, it is home to several hundred Aborigines of the Arrernte Tribe.

The Lutherans, who built a mission here dating back to 1882, renamed it Hermannsburg. It was home to the famed artist Albert Namatjira, the first Aborigine to be granted Australian citizenship in 1957. An irony that some 40,000 years after Namatjira's ancestors first occupied the area, the new European settlers decided to confer citizenship upon him. As a result, he was allowed to purchase alcohol at a time when it was prohibited to Aborigines, but a year later he was jailed for six months for supplying the locals with liquor. He died soon after, aged fifty-seven.

Our job was to look after the gallery of his work and show passing visitors around. 'No worries,' as they say in the vernacular.

Tourist brochures trumpet this neck of the woods as the Red Centre of Australia. Others, however, know it as the 'dead' centre. Next to nothing survives in this desolate empty expanse.

After living in Israel, a minute country with an exploding population, the first thing one senses when entering the Australian outback is the eternal space. In all four directions only one thing remains constant: flat, red earth.

Except for the occasional mass of stone, like Uluru (Ayers Rock), sprouting up almost in defiance of the surrounding flat plains.

In Israel, it is possible to be skiing on the slopes of Mount Hermon in the Golan Heights in the morning and, by evening, be snorkelling in the Red Sea, off the coast of Eilat. To drive across the width of the country takes about one hour; and it doesn't take much longer to fly the total length of the country.

Lucy and I spent four months driving around Australia, clocking up almost 20,000 kilometres, and didn't even get halfway around the island continent. Just flying from coast to coast, a distance of around 3000 kilometres, takes over four hours – the same time as a flight from Tel Aviv to London.

It was here, on my first experience of living with Aborigines, a people who have existed in these parts for millennia, that I began to understand the nature of the problem when modern civilisation tries to impose its Western prescription on indigenous people. And it wasn't long before I saw the similarity between the Aborigines and the Bedouin.

Both people have suffered from the doctrine of *terra nullius*: when the British colonised Australia at the end of the eighteenth century, they deemed it unoccupied, despite the presence of around 300,000 Aborigines; when the Jews immigrated to Palestine in large numbers at the beginning of the twentieth century, they considered it a land without a people for a people without a land, despite the fact they only comprised one-tenth of the largely Arab population of 800,000 in 1914.

Ntaria reminded me of Rahat, just south of Be'er Sheva – one of seven Bedouin towns in the Negev Desert, replete with schools, medical centres and modern amenities – built by the Israeli government over the last two decades.

There used to be close to 100,000 Bedouin dwelling in the wilderness of the Negev Desert. They belonged largely to the Azazma tribe and roamed from wadi to oasis, their camels, goats and families in tow.

No more. They, like other indigenous people, have drawn society's short straw. In Israel – despite the fact that many serve in the Israeli army as adept trackers – the Bedouin are being slowly ushered out of their nomadic existence.

First came a cluster of remote kibbutzim. In order to safeguard its desert borders, and to help sow seeds to make the desert bloom, Israel established a number of cooperative farms in the Negev Desert and the Arava Valley.

Then came the 1982 IDF withdrawal from Sinai. The 1979 peace agreement with Egypt included the return of the Sinai, where the IDF had built airstrips, firing zones and training grounds for military manoeuvres. The Negev was the only open space large enough in the country and, since the government did not officially recognise the land the Bedouin lived on, there was no legal obstacle to removing them from vast tracts of desert land in order to relocate the army. Even though some Bedouin have title deeds dating back to the Ottoman era, they never registered them with the authorities and they are now considered virtually null and void. Other parts of the desert were sanctioned for nature reserves in order to protect the fragile ecosystems.

In the incessant race for space, the Bedouin were losers, time and again. Today, only a fraction of the Bedouin population, perhaps 10 per cent, still lives a nomadic existence. The rest have been shepherded into brick towns and urban villages, in a similar fashion to Australia's Aborigines.

Both peoples are members of tribes whose homes have no fixed address. The Aborigines call it walkabout, following their song lines back through history to their Dreamtime. The Bedouin are more nomadic.

In an attempt to 'help' them out of antiquity and into modernity, the Australians and the Israelis, among other modern nations, have tried to impose their worldview on people who have lived by the laws of nature for millennia.

They may live side by side geographically, but their cultural norms are worlds apart mentally. Urbanisation is anathema to the Bedouin and the Aborigines. And because their history and culture is not inscribed in legal constitutions, charters and documents, but passed down by the elders, generation to generation, they have little sway when land disputes are taken to court. As a result, the ancient customs and traditions of the Aborigines and the Bedouin nomads are slowly vanishing from the desert wildernesses. Aborigines, unlike the Bedouin, however, have reclaimed large tracts of land, most notably as a result of the historic High

Court's 1992 rejection of the concept of *terra nullius* in the Mabo Land Rights Case.

And the irony of the situation is that we soothe our consciences by ushering them into purpose-built villages like Rahat or Hermannsburg, offering government subsidies, medical centres and education to boot. It's a bandaid solution that doesn't stick. The Bedouin and the Israeli, like the Aborigine and the white Australian, do not speak the same language; they do not live by the same value system.

At great expense our jeep received triple bypass surgery in Adelaide and we were soon on the road again, leaving Ntaria in a blaze of red dust. We collected our permit to travel through Aboriginal land and headed down the Mereenie Loop Road, a dirt track through the bush that leads to Uluru via Kings Canyon.

Lucy found the experience of living and working in an Aboriginal community enlightening, but emotionally draining. It was the old black-and-white photographs of the Aboriginal community, taken at the turn of the twentieth century, that disturbed her most. Almost every member of the Arrernte Tribe had once been tall and lean. Nowadays, their faces are bloated, their spines bowed and their stomachs swollen.

For generations, they lived off the land eating 'bush tucker', like snakes, kangaroo meat, berries and shrubs. Now they gorge themselves on chips, sweets, sugar, processed food and alcohol. As a result, they suffer from obesity, diabetes, trachoma. Their bodies simply cannot cope.

'I can't believe they're members of the same tribe,' she mused as we bumped down the dusty track. 'It's not just the fact that they were once tall and lean. They also looked proud. Now most of them are obese. And they don't look proud. They look timid.'

I too was appalled by the way they had become addicted to Western food and drink. Alcohol, especially, was poisoning them, although the elders of some communities, Ntaria included, had made it illegal to possess or consume alcohol on their land. But what alarmed me most was their seeming indifference to money.

'Many of them don't even wait to collect their change. It's incredible.'

'Why?' asked Lucy. 'They managed to survive without money for 40,000 years. What makes you think they have any idea about the notion of savings?'

She was right. But it was another example of how Western society has imposed its norms on an indigenous people and expected them to conform to something so alien to their culture.

The result, sadly, is that the rich culture and heritage of the Aborigines is being slowly sapped.

'Soon, all that will remain of their culture will be preserved in museums like Namatjira's Art Gallery in Ntaria,' said Lucy, staring out at the colony of termite mounds that lined the dirt track.

I nodded. 'Yeah. Just like the Bedouin. All their remnants will eventually be housed behind glass caskets at the Bedouin Heritage Centre in Rahat.'

CHAPTER NINETEEN

AT FOUR O'CLOCK on a winter's morning in January 1996, I made aliyah, invoking the Law of Return, which enables any Jew anywhere to return home and automatically become a citizen of the Jewish state.*

Having already lived in Jerusalem, I decided to join the secular trend by moving to Tel Aviv. After all, the Orthodox and the ultra-Orthodox had already overrun many secular neighbourhoods and were beginning to impose their iron grip on the municipality. Secular life there would only get harder.

I was met at the airport by a representative of the Jewish Agency and went through a barrage of bureaucracy in order to receive a temporary immigrant's passport, which enabled me to claim certain benefits, such as rent subsidy, Hebrew lessons, health care and tax relief.

I was issued with my temporary passport. Next to my name and passport number was an ID number. That number would be fed into a computer and picked up by the Israeli army, who would log my details on a file until such time as they decided to conscript me.

I had just become a citizen of Israel, and I was overcome by the emotion of returning home. It was a strange feeling, both invigorating and unnerving, exciting and nerve-wracking. But, mostly, it felt reassuring to know that the soil under my feet was mine. And, although I was alone, I knew that Lucy would be joining me in a few months after she finished her studies.

My arrival in Israel was greeted by news of one of the most bizarre undercover security operations in the history of Israel.

* Aliyah literally means 'ascent', but is used to describe Jewish immigration to Israel.

Hamas has been a thorn in Israel's side since its founding on the impoverished streets of the Gaza Strip in 1987. An extremist organisation, its mission is to derail the peace process. As the Intifada gathered pace, Hamas' support swelled in Gaza and the West Bank as young, impressionable Palestinians, born under occupation, decided to take their fate into their own hands.

But the military wing of Hamas, Izz al-Din al-Qassam, is the extreme end of this extreme organisation. It is a much smaller, independent battalion whose members believe that martyrdom will bring them redemption. They are trained in guerrilla camps in the Sudan and southern Lebanon (with the aid of Hezbollah) and are willing to sacrifice themselves to torpedo the diplomatic negotiations. Hamas' suicide bombers are members of Izz al-Din al-Qassam.

Their martyrdom, they believe, will result in the destruction of Israel and, in its place, the creation of an Islamic state of Palestine based on the Koran.

Thirty-year-old Yehiye Ayash was the brains behind the bombs. Known locally as 'The Engineer' for his ability to construct deadly explosives, he spearheaded the Izz al-Din al-Qassam bomb factory and was therefore indirectly responsible for the deaths of countless Israeli civilians.

The Shin Bet, the internal Israeli secret service, had been trailing him for four years without success. So, when they learned that Ayash's mobile phone was broken, they hatched a plan to nail him. Allegedly, they paid a Gaza businessman one million dollars (and provided him with a false passport as well as an escape plan) to deliver a 'new' mobile phone to Ayash, who was getting his own phone repaired.

A simple telephone call to his new mobile phone number from the heart of Tel Aviv was all that was required. Ayash answered the phone in Gaza City and immediately detonated the booby-trapped device, ripping his head off.

That was the end of 'The Engineer'. But it was not the end of the jihad that Hamas pledged to wage on the streets of Israel. Far from it. Ayash was finally dead, but in those four years, he had prepared his legacy, teaching dozens of disciples the art of constructing suicide bombs.

If I thought I'd need some time to find my feet, I was wrong. I was immediately grounded within days of my arrival back in Israel. By contrast, during the six months I had been in Australia, I had barely encountered any form of civil unrest, let alone riots.

The largest protest I recall was over the testing of a nuclear bomb on a French island in the South Pacific near Australia. But it hardly registered a ripple on the consciousness of the country and it had no effect whatsoever on day-to-day life.

The contrast was striking. Australia's political pulse seems sub-normal in comparison with Israel's racing heartbeat. The Israeli rollercoaster ride of life is fast and furious, exhilarating and exasperating, pulsating and petrifying. But it is never dull.

Life in Israel – whether it is good, bad or even ugly (and it can be all three in one day) – is vibrant. People wear their emotions on their sleeve. Ask someone how they are and they'll tell you their whole life story. Don't ask anybody anything and you'll still have your neighbours offering their opinions. Israelis are a semi-dysfunctional people hung up on neurosis, driven by guilt and consumed by history and memory in a country where normality knows no home.

But they are my family. And, after 2000 years living in exile as strangers in other people's lands, we are once again writing our own story into the chronicles of history.

Sparky had completed his military service and had returned to live on Kibbutz Rosh HaNikra. Shira was still studying in Jerusalem and, apart from Rose, the only other person I was really close to in Tel Aviv was Hannah, an old friend I had met years back on the beach in Israel.

She was originally from England but had immigrated with

her kid brother and parents at the age of fifteen. I remember cooing with envy when she told me her tale: her family sold their house, bought a ten-metre yacht and sailed via the southern Mediterranean to Israel. She told me how they got caught in a terrible storm off Majorca, which almost took their lives. And how they sang the national anthem, 'Hatikva – The Hope', as they approached the Israeli coastline.

Three years later she received her draft papers, like all other 18-year-old Israeli girls. But her Israeli friends had had eighteen years to get used to the idea. And her English friends were all preparing to start university. Psychologically and ideologically, she was not ready to become a soldier. Just before she was due to enlist, she went to England – and never returned.

She studied at Nottingham University, and we met up several times over that period. A few years later, she returned to Israel.

Although I had a few other friends dotted about the country, I was closest to Rose. She lived in an old neighbourhood on the fringe between Tel Aviv and Jaffa, and I spent my first few weeks at her place until I found a flat for Lucy and me.

One of my first missions was to score some wheels. Tel Aviv lies on the coastal plain and is largely flat, lending itself to bicycle transport. More importantly, the city streets are generally clogged with traffic and I soon realised that two wheels would be more practical than four.

Uzi, a friend of Hannah's boyfriend, Rami, was a motorbike dealer. He thrived on the rush of speed and, it seemed, the thrill of staring death in the face. His partner posted – and then boasted – a record time of eighteen minutes between Jerusalem and Tel Aviv. Ordinarily, the trip takes forty-five minutes. So they opened up a motorbike sales outlet in the seediest part of Florentine, an old industrial neighbourhood south of the city that was becoming increasingly populated by the city's young and trendy.

Their business card put me off before I even entered their shop: 'If you're crazy enough to drive a motorbike in Israel, come to us'. When I read the card, realised that Uzi's name was also the make of an IDF submachine gun and saw a bottle of Araq liqueur propping up the till, I began to think twice about my inquiry.

'Ahalan achi – hey brother, what are you after? A 650 cc Suzuki? We've got a top deal on a Kawasaki 950.'

'Habibi, the only bike I've ever driven in my life had pedals, and no engine. I'm not a biker. I just want a scooter, you know, to get around ... '

'Aaaaaaaaaah. You need ladies' transport. Sorry, we don't stock anything under 500 cc.'

I thanked him and was halfway out the door when he yelled back at me.

'Hey, achi. You know what? I've got this banged up Vespa out the back. It's old – a 1988 model. It's only 49 cc. I don't know what to do with it. Want to have a look?'

'How much do you want for it?'

'I think you should check it out first.'

'Why?'

'You'll see.'

It was the ultimate in uncool. Not only did it call into question the point of having an engine, but it required bicycle pedals in order to jump-start it.

I test drove it around the block and quickly became the not-so-proud owner of a scooter in a country where motorbikes seem to fuel testosterone levels, lubricate libidos and massage the machismo of the locals.

Its greatest asset was the independence it afforded me. I could be studying at university in Ramat Aviv, just north of the city, and eating a bowl of fine hummous in Ajami, an old neighbourhood of Jaffa, south of the city, inside half an hour. They were my limits. It was too dangerous to go anywhere near a highway. Which, given the way Israelis drive, was probably a blessing.

But its biggest drawback was its bicycle pedals. Whenever I wanted to go anywhere I had to peddle away, frantically trying to get the engine to kick in. And even when the engine did finally spark, my humiliation soon gave way to desperation as I opened the throttle to unleash all 49 ccs – and struggled to overtake pedestrians travelling by foot.

CHAPTER TWENTY

I HAVE HAD the honour and great fortune of meeting Moses. And I can confirm he is a salt-and-pepper bearded Old Testament specimen. A man with vision, a true leader. He is of average build, sports round spectacles and has a balding scalp save for two bushy, greying segments of curly hair on either side of his crown.

But, unlike his biblical namesake, who was left on the fringes of the Promised Land, this particular Moses, known in Hebrew as Moshe, is alive and kicking living in Israel.

He is a kibbutznik – a husband, father, head teacher and, in his spare time, he acts as my mentor. The more he ages, the more affable and astute he becomes. The two tablets of stone carved with the Ten Commandments have long since given way to a worn leather satchel, slung casually across his shoulder. But the depth of his wisdom remains. He is my reluctant Messiah.

I was working in London when I first met him back in 1993. He had just arrived to promote the ideals of kibbutz, and his English was a bit rough around the edges. I helped him out. Ever since, he has wanted to return the favour, begging me to visit his kibbutz.

Over the years he kept reinforcing the invitation. Each time, he would add, almost as a teaser, 'Habibi, you must to come; there's something I must to show you. You must to come. You must.'

A few weeks after I returned from the Australian outback, I finally made it to his kibbutz. I took a bus up the north coast, got off at a junction just beyond Netanya and hitched a short ride inland on the back of a tractor.

For some unknown reason he always greets me in Arabic. 'Shalom, habibi. Kif . . . ?'

I reply in part Arabic, part Hebrew. 'Sababa, mah nishma? – great, you?'

'Nuuuuuuu?' he asks me, invoking one of the most commonly used Israeli expressions, which defies translation. Right now, he is using this single word, together with a twist of his left wrist, to indicate that he wants to hear my latest news.

Kibbutz Magal lies in the fertile centre of the north of the country. Here, the distance between the Mediterranean Sea and the Green Line is approximately fifteen kilometres. That's no more than a twenty-minute drive. This is where Israel is at one of its narrowest junctures, a slender sliver of land along the Mediterranean.

Whenever we talked about the Palestinians, Moses, a staunch Labour Party supporter and an advocate of 'land for peace', always brought the reality on the ground into the equation. For him, 'land for peace' meant much more than an empty slogan. When Israelis talk about exchanging land in return for a peace deal, they are talking about trading his doorstep for a piece of peace.

Moshe shares his home with some 230 members, though the community, including kids, parents and partners, numbers close to 500. It is also one of the most successful kibbutzim in the country.

While many other kibbutzim were sinking deep into debt (because they took out massive loans in the early 1980s as the new Likud government's free market policy was implemented just before hyperinflation reached a staggering 445 per cent and interest rates rose to 88 per cent), Magal was reeling in profits. Much of that financial success was, in part, down to Moshe (though, being modest, he won't admit as much). He was the CEO, the general secretary of the kibbutz, between 1989 and 1992.

'We realised that if we didn't change, we'd end up like Kibbutz Bet Oren, which went . . . you know . . . kaboom,' he tells me sitting on a rocking couch in his back garden.

'Bankrupt?'

'Yeah.'

'We realised that we have to take the initiative. Even slaughter sacred cows.'

I noticed that his years abroad had improved his English.

So he did. He led his community down the capitalist road towards privatisation. 'We moved a high percentage of the . . . taxiff . . . the budget from the community to the individual. This enabled much greater freedom and responsibility.'

He cites the example of electricity. Before his elected term of office, there was no accountability. Even if you went on sabbatical for a year and left a light on in your house, the kibbutz would foot the bill. The notion of a bottomless vault ended under Moshe's tutelage. Meters were installed in each household and individual families were charged for their electricity. Receiving a bill of any sort on a kibbutz was a novelty for most members, he admits.

'The result? Bills almost halved.'

'Has the original vision of the founding fathers altered then?' I ask.

'Look, there is no pope, guru or chief rabbi of kibbutz, nor is there one book that defines what we should be.

'In the job market, every job was given its alternative value so that members could be more aware of their income and expenditure,' he notes, inviting me to eat lunch in the communal dining room.

We walk through the manicured gardens of the kibbutz to the dining room, the silence and tranquillity a trademark of life in these rural oases. Over lunch he explains that while he instituted radical changes, putting the onus on the individual not the community, the kibbutz already had a firm financial base to begin with.

'Together with two other kibbutzim, we have built up an international drip irrigation company, Netafim, with factories in the USA and Australia. Local sales are around the US$100 million mark; export sales are almost ten times that.'

This is big business – especially for a kibbutz.

Despite the crises on other kibbutzim, this is one communal settlement where financial woes are not a part of the local lexicon. Magal is one of the wealthiest spots in the country, and its members are living within sight of the lap of luxury. Even if you want to jump on the bandwagon, you can't. Not even if you're a volunteer.

'Come,' he beckons me with his forefinger. 'I want to show you the view.'

We take our plates into the dishwashing room and stack them in huge trays that roll along a conveyor belt, like a car wash, awaiting a high-powered jet wash and rinse. Moshe opens a slim metal door adjacent to the kitchen and begins to scale the solitary ladder. He pushes open a trap door onto the roof and yanks me up by the arm.

'Look,' he says, pointing to the sea on the horizon. 'This is Israel.' It's a picture postcard: green fertile fields sprouting fresh crops belonging to the kibbutzim of Magal, Ein Hachoresh and Giv'at Hayim run down the Hefer Valley; the houses of the small religious community of Kfar Haro'eh rise beyond them before the land ends at Mikhmoret beach. Dangling like a red-and-yellow lollipop on the horizon is the sun, readying for its evening dip in the water.

He swivels around 180 degrees, from west to east. 'Now, look here.'

Below our noses, just beyond the border fence of the kibbutz, lies the Arab village of Zeita. 'It was part of Jordan before 1967,' says Moshe, implying that the border, the Green Line, is the narrow strip of land between the village and us. Magal was a front-line kibbutz during those six desperate June days in 1967.

He points slightly left to a village no more than 200 metres from the kibbutz fence. The minaret rising from the cluster of houses tells the story. This is the Arab village of Ja'at. Then he swivels right: the Arab village of Yama reveals itself.

Kibbutz Magal sits just inside the Green Line. But it is surrounded on three sides by Arab villages, one of which, Zeita, is hostile. 'Some days,' says Moshe, 'like on Land Day, we don't use our eastern gate.* But we can go to Ja'at and Yama to walk and shop, though we have better relations with another Arab village – Baq'a al-Gharbiya.'

'So,' I ask him bluntly, pointing down just beyond the kibbutz fence, 'could this be the future border of Palestine?'

* Land Day dates back to 30 March 1976 when six Arabs were killed protesting Israeli expropriation of land in the Galilee. Nowadays it's a national Arab day of protest against Israeli land reclamation.

He remains silent and strokes his beard. Then he nods his head ever so gingerly, raises his eyebrows and lifts the palms of his two hands skyward in a this-is-what-appears-to-be-the-case kind of way. 'We're talking about a matter of metres, not kilometres,' he says finally.

Here, on a dining room roof in the heart of middle Israel, the Israeli–Palestinian conflict suddenly takes on an agonizingly geographic dimension.

It's easy for me to be a bleeding heart, paid-up member of the peace camp living in Tel Aviv, and even, for that matter, in West Jerusalem, let alone London, Manchester or Glasgow. But when you see the proximity of the situation here on the frontline, all moral, ethical and philosophical arguments dissolve into a haze of geographical reality.

Though he has built his life on this kibbutz, and the farm's industry has flourished into an international company, Moshe knows, deep down, that he may be bracing for a volatile future, depending on the final-status negotiations with the Palestinians. He is not too happy about the border road being parallel to the kibbutz, but he remains eternally optimistic.

'Habibi, I am excited by the prospects of real peace,' he tells me as we watch the sun to sink into the Mediterranean.

Back in his house, I ask him if living in such an affluent community is really as great as it sounds. 'We are a very rich kibbutz,' he admits with aplomb. 'Nobody leaves – it would be a stupid move – young kids are coming back, the place looks beautiful and we are building lovely new houses.

'Can I say that the members are happy? I'm sorry to disappoint you. People are people are people. They want more commodities and less change, and they suffer from the normal human instincts of jealousy and suspicion.'

The truth, so it seems, even in this paradise oasis straddling the frontline between Israel and Palestine, is not as rosy as it looks at face value. But it is not so bad either. Last I heard of Moshe, he was living in temporary accommodation while the kibbutz rebuilds his house – bigger, more beautiful, more luxurious.

The members, he told me recently by email, had voted by a 75.3 per cent majority in favour of owning their own homes and their own cars (among other things) – concepts that, once, would have been contradictory to the original principles of the founding fathers of the kibbutz movement.

They still exist as a united community, however, an island sanctuary where the rules that govern them are equal for everyone. And, it seems, the dividend is equally profitable.

CHAPTER TWENTY-ONE

IT WAS LATE in the day. The sun was beginning to burn on the horizon. Soon, it began melting into the Mediterranean, ripples of crimson shimmering across the water where huge ships, bobbing gently up and down on the horizon, looked like rubber ducks in a bath.

Motti, a swashbuckling, high-flying real estate agent, intent on soaking up yet more commission dollars from super-inflated prices, was beaming. For him, it was postcard-perfect conditions to nail down a deal.

He spoke Hebrish, a hybrid of Hebrew and English, which allowed him to rely on Hebrew whenever his English failed him. 'Here you can live . . . c'mo melech (like a king),' he touted, offering me an influential cigarette to maximise the moment.

We were leaning against the wall of the roof, four-and-a-half floors up in downtown Tel Aviv, facing the now blood-red sky, *sans* sun. He had barely shown me inside, preferring to 'sell' me the view. It soon became apparent why.

Though it was a roof flat, it was more roof than flat. In fact, it would almost be fair to say it was virtually all roof, almost no flat. It was bigger than a basketball court and commanded a view on all four sides. The truth, though, was that only one direction was worth the look. The other three sides were carbon copy, back-to-back roofs of apartment blocks littered with television aerials and solar-powered water heaters. Here and there, the green of the trees tried to break through the monotony of the concrete.

But, to the west, beyond the tangle of aerials and water heaters, lay the Mediterranean Sea. Although it was about half a kilometre away and only comprised perhaps ten centimetres on the horizon, the sunset was spectacular enough to captivate me until it melted into the water.

Motti was the consummate salesman. His jet black hair was swept back with gel; he carried a file in one hand and his mobile phone in the other. The orange lenses in his sunglasses were clearly a fashion accessory. He was dapper, in a sleazy sort of way.

Being ripped off is never pleasant, though it is marginally more palatable when you know about it in advance. And I knew I was being ripped off – big time. But I also knew that here on Balfour Street, slap-bang in the middle of downtown Tel Aviv, people would be queuing to snap up this piece of prime real estate.

Motti kept harping on his real estate mantra while pointing at the horizon. 'Location this . . . location that . . . and the other.'

'Achi (my brother), you know how many people I have queuing for this roof? One block from Sheinkin, the ladies who walk past your door,' he put his fingers to his lips and blew a kiss, 'oh, slicha (sorry), you have girlfriend . . . OK . . . lo mishaneh (it doesn't matter) . . . Allenby is here, Rothschild Street is up there, Shuk HaCarmel is just across the street . . . and the beach, achi, is no more than a ten-minute walk . . . Melech (king) . . . You be melech . . . parties . . . ahhhhhhhh . . . Mah ze kef (How much fun)? . . . You can build here a sukkah (shack) . . . no rain for six months you can to sit here under the . . . cochavim (stars). Mah od ata tzarich (What else do you need)? Ein. Pashut ein – there is simply no other place like this.'

His mobile phone rang.

'Ken – Yes.

Ahalan – Hi.

Ken, ani po – Yes I'm here.

Lo, hoo ohev – No, he likes it.

Lo batuach – I'm not sure.

Tismoch alay – Trust me.

Yihiye beseder – It'll be OK.

Al tidag – Don't worry.

Lehit – Bye.'

The cynic in me reckoned it was a staged call. In any case, he was sure working the hard yards. But what tipped the scales was not Motti's sales finesse.

It was February. Lucy was due to arrive from Australia in April and we had both ranked outdoor space marginally ahead of sanitary facilities as a top priority. March signalled spring, which meant that summer was around the corner. May brings Independence Day, heralding the official beginning of summer. And summer in Israel means four long, hot months, virtually devoid of rain.

Even the weather forecasters forget the formalities and cut to the chase: 'Hot and getting hotter' becomes the monotone message on the news. It remains that way through June, July and August.

Only the arrival of a hamseen – a stretch of swelteringly hot days when the wind blows a burning breeze in from the desert – alters their script. Living in Tel Aviv during a hamseen is like having a hairdryer held a few centimetres in front of your face. Power on Level Three. Heat on High. Nasty, brutish and long. Hot, harsh and unrelenting.

Tempers overheat. Nerves fray. Anxieties explode. Road rage victims increase exponentially. Hamseen, meaning fifty in Arabic, is supposed to be the number of days the hot winds last for. Forget the Israeli–Arab conflict, there'd be all out civil war if a hamseen ever lasted fifty days here. When the hot winds finally subside, the nation breathes a collective sigh of relief, much like the farmers when the first autumn rains save their harvests – and their livelihoods.

This seemed like a reasonable place to sweat it out. Facing the sea, eighty-eight steps up in downtown Tel Aviv, I figured we'd have an even chance of surviving the summer sweat.

'Done!' I said in Hebrew, and Lucy (though she did not know anything about it) and I proceeded to become the unenviable tenants of a janitor's cupboard, comprising a tiny kitchenette that doubled as a bathroom, and a bedroom the size of a double mattress.

Inside, paint was peeling off the walls. A fan, coated in layers of dust, dangled ominously from the low bedroom ceiling. Mosquitoes whizzed through the holes in the fly nets. The sticky vinyl floor felt like it had had a can of Coca-Cola emptied onto it. The toilet, notably, was a box that could have asphyxiated anyone who chose to empty his or her bowels with the door closed. Underneath the sink, dead insects were gathered in a funeral pyre for the invading cockroaches to prey on.

The only saving grace was the bathroom/kitchen arrangement that afforded me the singular hedonistic pleasure of being able to grab a bottle of beer from the fridge while in the bathtub, though that luxurious notion soon evaporated when I realised the tub was too small and the supply of hot water too short.

All up, it would be a great place to house some mops, hoses, buckets, disinfectant and dirty rubber gloves. But what attracted me was the roof that came, de facto, with the flat. It was no more and no less than a view with a room. All for US$500 per month.

Daylight robbery, to be sure. But here, in this sliver of the Middle East, six million people clamour for homes and most of them live – and more want to live – within the triangle of Jerusalem, Haifa and Tel Aviv. This particular part of downtown Tel Aviv is considered the hub of the nation, one of the most densely populated parts of the country. Next to nobody owns a house; almost everybody lives in flats and many have nothing but a makeshift balcony for outdoor space. No wonder the rage rises with the heat.

February was tough. The dribs and drabs of winter still hung around like bad breath, wreaking havoc on anything stored outside. Inside, I managed to drill fifteen shelves into the bedroom walls. It was harsh, tough living indoors – I could feel the neighbours pointing at me and whispering to each other as I passed them on the stairs. They thought I was mad. Or, perhaps, brave. No, mad.

The rains soon abated and I began to convert my janitor's cupboard into a penthouse apartment for Lucy's arrival. I built an outdoor extension onto the roof using shade cloth and two poles concreted into large garbage bins, transforming the area into an outdoor lounge room. Throwing soil on top of the concrete I planted herbs: mint, sage, basil surrounded by snapdragons and a few petunias to add a hint of colour.

Next, I built a kitchen bench, hooked up a gas stove and re-plumbed a sink. The renovations caught on and friends began to arrive with whatever junk they found on the street: couches, carpets, trinkets and trash.

Soon, the flat had tripled in size. The outdoor lounge looked endearing if not attractive. Even Ziggy the dog, a lean, black border collie with a patch of white on her neck and spotted black-and-white socks, had a purpose-built penthouse suite all of her own.

Tel Aviv labels itself the 'Big Orange' – but the only similarity between Tel Aviv and New York is that both cities are the pulse of their respective nations. Regardless of the fact that Israel has undergone massive Americanisation – including the advent of GMCs, mega-malls, cable television, mobile phones, Pizza Hut, McDonald's and, of course, McDavid's (the kosher version) – Tel Aviv is a far cry from Manhattan.

Sheinkin Street, one block away from Balfour Street, is Israel's answer to SoHo – a place where the ultra-hip rub shoulders with the ultra-Orthodox, beggars meet babushkas, soldiers cross paths with supermodels and new immigrants from Eastern Europe busk Yiddish folk tunes while record stores thrash out the latest techno tunes. Tattoo artists and body piercers are *en vogue*. Gays and lesbians indulge the straight and narrow while the locals gawk in awe and wonder at the eclecticism on display in their backyard.

Running from the entanglement of Magen David junction, where the Carmel Market intersects with Allenby and King George streets, Sheinkin Street runs up to Rothschild Boulevard, where the city's founders first gathered on the sand dune in 1909 and picked lots from shells to decide where they would live.

Israelis come from all over the country to comb Sheinkin's shops, lounge in its cafés and flirt with its fashion. But for us locals who live around Sheinkin Street, its life and soul are the ordinary traders.

The fresh juice man parks his old, battered VW Beetle, plastered with stickers of Jaffa oranges, outside his stall; the baker, affectionately known as the 'soft cake man', adds an extra boreka pastry to whatever I buy; the nut vendor, an icon on almost every Israeli street corner, warms his wares on a low heat: almonds, cashews, peanuts, salted nuts, sunflower seeds, caramel-coated cashews, fried nuts – and pistachio nuts. Nuts are to Israel what bubble gum is to the US.

Farther up is the egg shop. The first and last egg shop I have ever seen in my life. Eggs – nothing more, nothing less. Just eggs. Dozens, stacked in their cardboard containers, one on top of the other. They sit there, cradled in their corrugated cardboard trays awaiting cholesterol-crazed consumers. Strange it may seem, but this is Israel. Eggs are a fairly staple part of the Jewish diet: hard-boiled eggs often accompany hummous, malawach and jachnoon, among other dishes. And mourners who have just buried their loved ones begin the seven-day shiva (week-long mourning period) with an egg because it symbolises the continuance of the life cycle.

But then this is Sheinkin Street, home to eccentrics. Take Café Ke'ilu, as an example. It is Israel's first pseudo-café replete with menu and waiter – but no kitchen or food. Customers simply pay to see and be seen.

It offers everything. And delivers nothing. To the city's high-flyers, it is seductive and alluring; to me, it's upmarket and downright pretentious.

When you stand on Rothschild Boulevard, at the top end of Sheinkin Street, it's hard to imagine that less than 100 years ago this was a sand dune, stretching down to the beach barely half a kilometre away. Now, the poinciana trees that line the boulevard create a river of green through the concrete jungle. Modern glass and metal buildings of the city's financial heart clash with old

Bauhaus International architecture as the area becomes modernised and more money is pumped through its veins. On the pavement, the poincianas' flat, woody pods carpet the concrete.

And in the middle of it all lies the Chabad Lubavitch headquarters, an ultra-Orthodox seminary attracting the pious from the neighbourhood. Almost daily I'd encounter them brushing past their ultra-secular neighbours. Though they would look away, or cross the street if I was with the dog (strangely, many of them seem to be petrified by dogs), there was never a hint of animosity. In my small street, neighbours adjacent to me, below and across the way were members of ultra-Orthodox sects.

Not once did I experience any problems. In fact, their presence served as an alarm call: I could tell that Shabbat was approaching when their weekend wardrobes – long black coats, white shirts, white prayer shawls and fringed undergarments (tzitzit, which remind the Orthodox of the 613 commandments) – were hanging on the washing line.

I knew that Rosh Hashanah, New Year, was on its way as soon as I heard the sound of the shofar (ram's horn) every morning for the whole month prior to the New Year. Or that Sukkot, the Festival of Tabernacles, was around the corner when they began constructing booths of bamboo and palm fronds on the fire escape landing or on their tiny balconies. I couldn't help but notice the irony as they squashed into a bamboo cubicle on a half-landing in one of the most densely populated parts of the country in order to symbolise the Israelites' exodus through the empty wilderness of the Sinai Desert.

No one in Israel, however, needs any warning of Yom Kippur. During the 25-hour fast, the country closes down, there's barely a car on the streets and calm descends upon the country from dusk until one hour after dusk as Jews repent and ask God to seal the people of the world in the Book of Life for another year – even in Tel Aviv, the secular capital.

Though I never really communicated with my Orthodox neighbours, we didn't ex-communicate each other either. That sometimes happens in Jerusalem. But rarely in Tel Aviv.

CHAPTER TWENTY-TWO

THERE WAS nothing particularly unusual about the morning of 4 March 1996. Except, perhaps, that it ushered in spring, a three-month paradise wedged between the dank deluge of winter and the stifling heat of summer.

All along Tel Aviv beach, people frolic in the water, the waves licking the shoreline and receding again in a graceful, almost meditative, manner.

Children run, laugh, fall. Guys and girls play matkot, a beach ball game with two bats and a squash ball that drives sunworshippers mad. Wedges of watermelon served with squares of Bulgarian feta cheese, a bizarre but beautiful concoction of savoury and sweet, is the rage.

The marinas burst with activity; fishermen's vessels cram the harbours. The masts of boats dot the horizon.

Like caterpillars-cum-butterflies the people come alive, shedding their clothes to flirt with the sun.

On the city's dirty streets, shops and malls overflow with consumers. Mobile phones ring simultaneously. A crowd of pedestrians crosses Dizengoff Street, the most chic street in Tel Aviv in the 1970s. Egged buses, expelling big, black clouds of exhaust fumes, wend their way downtown, passengers either on their way to the hub of the city or to the respite of the seaside. Not-so-white cars jam the main intersections, horns hooting, tempers fraying, patience expired long ago.

The country is, literally, abuzz. The annual migration of birds from Europe to Africa – storks, pelicans, kingfishers, among others – pass over, stopping en route for a drink and a rest. Red and yellow poppies begin to blaze across green pastures. Like a shot in the arm, the spring sunshine injects a contagious warmth into the atmosphere.

The pseudo-air pumping out the air-conditioning vents cooled the temperature inside the blue-chip hi-tech company on the fringe of the city's Silicon Wadi where I was working that day. I landed there by default, working on the mind-numbing job of de-bugging CD-ROMs, thanks to Hannah.

I spent most of the morning gazing into forever, my eyes subconsciously locked onto nothing in particular, just a vague area of unbridled beauty somewhere on the Tel Aviv horizon. Freedom was here. Peace was near.

The echo reverberated across the city, tremoring like an earthquake that registered eight on the Richter Scale. It jolted the metropolis into shock mode, as if struck by a sudden heart seizure, trailing total silence in its wake. People around me jerked, their eyes rolling from side to side.

Radios suddenly bellowed into action. News reports started flooding in. Telephones began ringing simultaneously. Panic, of the most inordinate scale, ensued. From a nanosecond of absolute silence, life had once again been breathed back into the office.

It was almost as if, at the sound of the blast, we all took a collective deep breath. One that felt like it lasted a lifetime. Then we exhaled. We were alive.

But such was the random nature of suicide bombs, any of our loved ones could be among the dead. Immediately, news filtered through that one, maybe two suicide bombers, who were members of either Hamas or Islamic Jihad, were dead. But, amid the chaos, no one could ascertain what the exact civilian death toll was.

The office was by now submerged with noise, tears, crying, people desperately clamouring to ascertain the whereabouts of their families, friends, loved ones. How ridiculous has life become? In most countries, people phone their partners to tell them they miss them, love them, can't wait to see them. Here in Israel, the phones are jammed with people screaming, 'Ani beseder . . . ken . . . ani chai – I'm OK . . . yes . . . I'm alive.'

All of a sudden, the lines overloaded and the network crashed.

Everyone turned to the television in the boardroom. Television crews were already swarming the site of the blast like bees to pollen, policemen trying to usher them back, winding safety tape around the zone.

The panic was ingrained in the reporter's voice. He was as shocked as the public. He was just one of us and, in these rare instances, it is impossible for him to maintain his composure. This is Israel. These people, whose flesh is lying in pieces strewn all over the junction, are brethren. They are one family. We are one family. The chances of knowing someone who knew someone whose sibling was now dead are fair.

Israel is a small place, home to one big family.

The death toll mounts. Eight, no nine, ten, according to Channel One. Channel Two reports the count at twelve. Fresh reports keep coming in. No one is sure. No one can be sure. The bomber detonated such massive amounts of explosives that it may take some time before the official death count is released. Images, harrowing images, of limbs scattered across the pavement open the floodgates of those who had, until now, managed to control their emotions.

On the television, crowds of onlookers and passersby begin to swell the intersection at the heart of Tel Aviv, where King George and Dizengoff Streets meet – one of the busiest junctions in the metropolis.

My flat is a stone's throw from there. Hannah's is even closer. I have crossed that junction more times than I care to remember. That bomb may have blasted me or her into nothingness in the same instant as it did to so many others.

Hannah was in a rage. She couldn't get through to her boyfriend, Rami, by now a good mate of mine, or her mother because the network had crashed.

She continued punching numbers on the phone. 'The fucking network's still down! Where is he? He could be anywhere . . . Turn the radio up! What channel are you on? Did the television identify any of the victims' names yet? Have you searched the news on the Net?'

How the hell do you console someone who can't reach their loved ones to confirm that they are alive? What goes through someone's mind during those few minutes when they simply have no way of knowing if this time is their time?

But for Hannah, those few minutes of living in limbo must have been infinitely more excruciating than most. Her time had already been. And gone. Her brother, Alex, had been injured while on patrol in southern Lebanon in 1993. He and a group of soldiers were on a reconnaissance mission to rescue their comrades who were under siege by Hezbollah in its guerrilla war against Israel's occupation. A roadside bomb exploded near his tank. Alex had his head out of the top of the vehicle. Shrapnel lodged in his brain. His friends carried him on a stretcher to a helicopter, which evacuated him back into Israel.

He lay in hospital for sixteen days, suffering from severe brain injury, before he died at the age of nineteen. Hannah, who was in England studying at university at the time, got the call that changed her life from her aunt in London. She raced out to Israel to be with him as he slid slowly away.

For Hannah and her family, those days must have felt like a lifetime doubled. Imagine the torture of the waiting and, when it finally came, the pain of the truth: Alex never made it past his teens.

And now, here she is, less than three years on, unable to contact her most beloved.

We hugged. We cried. No words were exchanged. None were necessary. We were close enough to know what each other was thinking. And to appreciate that any words would simply be a contrived quick fix, like a bandaid to a broken heart.

Work was over. Everyone knew the drill. There was no official announcement from the boss. When a tragedy of this nature rips through the heart of downtown Tel Aviv, spilling innocent civilians' blood and guts on your very doorstep, you don't wait around to be told to go on home. The protocol, tragically, is no longer in

its infancy. Israel instinctively plunges into a week of mourning. The following days would be low-key, the headlines dominated by the funerals of the victims – or what was left of them.
The office quickly emptied, only the pained cries echoing in the corridors. I got on a bus to go home; my blood was pumping and a headache was hitting hard. It was hot. What began as a brisk spring morning had boiled over.

It took me several minutes to grasp the irony of the situation. And by then it was too late.

There were about twenty of us on board. The three beeps, the clarion call for the news at the top of the hour, were barely audible. The driver pumped up the volume, as is customary on all Israeli buses. But it was nowhere near the top of the hour.

The voice was cold, quaking, solemn. The death toll, it was reported, had increased to sixteen, though it was neither final nor official. Ultra-Orthodox paramedics, members of the Hesed Shel Emet (True Benevolence) organisation were combing the site for body parts, fulfilling the religious obligation to return every part of human flesh to the earth. In the background, crowds could be heard, chanting their catch cry: 'Mavet l'Aravim – Death to the Arabs! Death to the Arabs!' The reporter could barely be heard over the deafening din of the protesters.

I was angry, furious, livid. These bastard terrorists were attempting to hold us to ransom in our own homes. They think they can destroy the peace process by destroying themselves and some of us. And all they are actually doing is fuelling the Right, giving them yet more evidence that we can never, ever trust the Arabs. And, by deduction, therefore, we should not give up one inch of land. What a mess!

The old woman next to me began to cry. My throat locked, as if a key had suddenly turned inside, blocking the passages to my lungs. A young mother squeezed her baby into her chest. Behind me people were snivelling. No one talked. No one even murmured.

Then it occurred to me. A bus bomb. Hamas were renowned for double strikes. Just for good measure. Strike twice, three times the impact. That was their theory. Their message would be loud and clear: we will torpedo this peace process, derail this peace train, do whatever it takes to jettison the treason of peace.

Only the previous day, 3 March, another suicide bomber had detonated explosives inside a Jerusalem bus on Jaffa Road, not far from where I used to live, killing nineteen and injuring six. Yesterday Jerusalem, today Tel Aviv. I shuddered to think where tomorrow's casualties would be from. Only last week, on 25 February, yet another suicide bomber had blown up yet another bus in Jerusalem, this time killing twenty-six and injuring eighty. Another strike made sense. It also made me sick with fear.

My bag was being eyed, like an infrared laser gun injecting rays onto it. Instantly, I was infected by the same bug. I trawled each and every person, looking deep into their eyes in the hope that they would expose honest, ordinary people who couldn't harm an ant on a whitewashed windowsill.

We were all at it. Eyes were crisscrossing the length and breadth of the bus. Ordinarily, we would have been travelling as innocent civilians. Now, we were all potential terrorists in each other's eyes. How sad, how terrible, how pathetic that we were reduced to thinking this way about one another, judging on face value if there was a terrorist in our midst.

Stuck in a traffic jam, each of us scanned everyone, hoping no one had a two-kilogram detonator attached to their rib cage.

The police roadblock began up at Rothschild Boulevard. The driver ordered everyone off the bus. It was the end of the line. Most were going a lot further, but everyone gave a collective sigh of relief. The imminent danger was over.

The streets down to the fateful junction were, by now, pedestrianised. Police car and ambulance horns wailed in the background; the streets seethed with people heading towards the site of the explosion. King George Street was jammed. The bomb site was gridlocked.

Reciprocity was tangible in the air. You could almost smell it. The knee-jerk reaction had already been jolted into action and crowds of knitted yarmulke-wearing youths, the trademark of the national religious movement, were chanting their death curse on the Arabs. Others were calling for Acting Prime Minister Shimon Peres, who became Prime Minister after Rabin's assassination, to activate a permanent closure of the West Bank and Gaza Strip. Others still were cursing and swearing. More were crying and weeping and a few had collapsed from the shock. Paramedics knelt around them, treating them with oxygen, IV drips and the like.

I headed home, empty, nauseous. The light on the answer machine was blinking. I had one message. Mum and Dad, I figured, although the news was probably only just filtering across the world by now. Still, if they had already heard, they would be worried sick. They knew where I lived. They knew where the blast went off. They understood the proximity.

'Ben, we want you to come and stay with us,' said the broken woman's voice in Hebrew, getting straight to the point.

'Arik will pick you up. Phone him immediately.'

Click. The answer machine bleeped as the tape rewound. Click.

The message was from my surrogate parents, old friends of my folks whose kid happened to be living in Britain. So, my parents looked after their kid; they looked after me. In the depths of despair, there was no time for pleasantries. They felt responsible for me. This was no time to pretend to be OK. It was also not a courteous offer. This was the next closest thing to an order.

I grabbed a bottle of Goldstar beer and managed to empty a quarter of it down my shirt before choking on the fizz. On the roof adjacent to my flat, I thought for a moment I could smell fresh flesh, so I lit a cigarette and drew heavily on the filter, closing my eyes.

Questions, and question marks, appeared in my mind's eye. Unanswerable questions, endless questions, meaningless questions.

I felt weak. I hadn't eaten. I had barely had anything to drink, except the beer. And I was burning this cigarette like my number was up.

The silence scared me more than anything. The empty, vacuous, sound of nothingness, like the morning after the night before. Even the normally tranquil horizon of the Mediterranean seemed unattractive that afternoon. I returned inside without my cigarette or my beer.

I turned the television on. The sound hit me before I saw the picture. It was a familiar sound. All Israelis recognise it instinctively. It's part of the Israeli psyche. You hear it throughout Holocaust Remembrance Day. And Memorial Day for Israel's Fallen Soldiers. It's a distinctive sound that you hear. And you understand immediately what it means. Here it was again. That sombre music, those humble ballads, that mourning melody imbued with pain, tears, sorrow.

I slouched into the sofa and cried. I cried because my body knew no other recourse, no other means of expression. I cried because everything was so foreign to me. Even the spectre of an IRA bomb on the British mainland, which I'd only ever seen on television, had not prepared me for this.

In hindsight, though, I cried for the victims whose number, by now, had risen to twenty with some seventy-five injured. Perhaps more for their families. For the parents who would have to go through the harrowing experience of burying their children. For the country which had, again, suffered another scar on its battered, war-torn body.

In just one horrific week, three suicide bombs – which had killed sixty-five and injured 161 innocent civilians – had seemingly blown any hopes of peace.

But most of all I cried for the children. Jewish and Palestinian. I cried because here, yet again, was seemingly conclusive evidence that the children of today would remain bound to the barbarity of war tomorrow.

I cried because when I had returned to Israel in 1994, when peace was more than just a hollow slogan, I had believed that tomorrow would bring hope. But today was all about despair. I cried because I no longer knew, or even believed, that tomorrow would exist.

And even if it did, I no longer believed it would be worth living.

It was only several days later that I read newspaper analysts and political commentators suggesting the reason for this spate of suicide bombs: to remind Israel that although they may have assassinated 'The Engineer', Yehiye Ayash, they had not eliminated his disciples.

CHAPTER TWENTY-THREE

MIKE WAS a self-proclaimed hummous aficionado. He was also the only guy I knew in the Middle East who was as fanatical about football as I was. He had come to volunteer on a kibbutz fifteen years ago – and never left the country.

I was the young pretender, the new immigrant; he was the veteran. Since I had only recently discovered the lure of hummous, served traditionally in a bowl drenched in olive oil, lemon juice and herbs, he decided to offer me an induction course: lunch became a tour of Tel Aviv and Jaffa's finest hummous parlours.

'What a week, eh?' I said to him as we braced for a bowl in Tel Aviv's Yemenite Quarter, one afternoon soon after the blast. 'I haven't gone near a bus or a crowded intersection since.'

'You've got to move on,' he said, pinning his Lennon glasses up on the bridge of his nose.

'Easier said than done. You can feel the country mourning, the funeral parades haven't even ended. People can't stop talking about it. Everyone knows someone who knew someone who was killed in the blast. You can barely breathe without a mention of it. It's suffocating. There's nowhere to hide.'

'Look. You're not a veteran here, though neither am I. But I can tell you this: for you, it's like having your heart and soul ripped to shreds; it's the same for many Israelis, with one difference: most of them were born into this world of bullets and bombs. So they become immune to it. You will too. It's sad, but true.'

'You reckon?'

'Mate, this is Israel. Open your eyes. There's a war going on.'

'Really? I thought that we were on the cusp of peace.'

'OK. So this is the war for peace. I don't know any more. After a while here you begin to become cynical about all the fanfare over the peace process. Reality bites mate. You know what I mean?'

'Yeah. I think I know exactly what you mean.'

'The families of those bastard bombers should be held responsible. Their houses should be razed.'

Our heads turned simultaneously in the direction of the voice. The only people there were two men busy playing shesh besh (backgammon).

After a while in Israel you become used to people joining your conversations, offering their opinion uninvited when the opportunity beckons. It's derived from a familiarity of feeling at home and although it can be frustrating to find yourself conversing in private with the rest of the nation, it's also strangely comforting. Even the minutiae of daily life are up for public discussion. Money is not taboo. Your salary, mortgage and overdraft are all legitimate statistics for public consumption. Bizarre though it may sound, my personal laundry – clean and dirty – is available for public perusal.

There's no menu. In fact, I'm not even convinced that this particular parlour even has a name. There are a dozen or so small tables, mostly on the pedestrianised sidestreet underneath a makeshift shade cloth canopy. Inside, there's no kitchen, just a gas burner with one huge vat of hummous, a fridge with drinks, a sink and a stack of bowls. The place is three-quarters full. Locals playing shesh besh in between cups of Turkish coffee frequent some of the tables.

They may be friends but you can smell the satisfaction they get from the sound of a double six as they slam the wooden pieces down on the board. Alongside them, an elderly man watches, patiently pulling on his nargilleh (water pipe) and sending wafts of fragrant sweet smoke billowing around us. Ofra Haza, the queen diva of Israeli pop, is pouring her heart out to an oriental beat on a nearby radio. A Yemenite immigrant, she is a rags-to-riches story, managing to fuse her Yemenite oriental rhythms with a dance beat that propelled her to number one in the Euro charts in 1985. She gave hope to the impoverished Sephardi community, many of whom live in the Yemenite Quarter and who feel short-changed by the ruling Ashkenazi elite.*

There are no frills. Even the waitress spares no spoils. This is a no-nonsense establishment. Though the nouveau riche dining on Sheinkin Street are a stone's throw away, we have chosen to dine in the insalubrious but very authentic Yemenite Quarter in a joint that shuts up shop when the daily vat of hummous is finished. Unlike Sheinkin Street, you don't come here to see or be seen. You come to eat hummous, and while away the afternoon playing shesh besh.

The proprietress spills a plate of raw onion and naked chilli onto our table, followed by a basket of hot pita bread and a bowl of green olives. I immediately pop a few in and suck on their juicy flesh. 'Two?' she asks, cutting to the chase.

'Yeah. One with fuul,' says Mike, ordering his bowl layered with a thick, slimy fava bean paste mixed with garlic and lemon that guarantees complementary colonic irrigation.

'Just regular for me,' I stress. I've not been in the country long enough for the lining on my stomach to fend off an avalanche of pureed spicy beans. After my last attempt, I could barely feel the muscle movement.

Mike is giggling. 'You'll get used to it. Once you can handle fuul, you'll be able to master most things.'

We burn a cigarette each. Mike shifts back in his seat, placing his mobile phone on the table. I shift back in my seat too, though I have no mobile phone – a sign that I haven't been around these parts too long. Anyone who is anyone and almost everyone who is no one has a mobile phone here.

After all, families need to stay in touch. Jewish mothers worry about their children, especially if they are in the army, day and night. Mobile phones pacify them.

Our bowls arrive. My hummous seems to be swimming in a sea of olive oil, topped by finely chopped parsley and sprinkled

* Ofra Haza died from the AIDS virus in 2000.

with some paprika. The onion is cut into quarters enabling each layer to be used as a spoon with which to scoop up a mouthful of hummous. The crunch of the onion slowly subsides, compensated by the smoothness of the hummous.

Mike begins mixing a small dish of a green slimy substance. 'What's that?'

'Schug. It's hard core. Go easy.'

Schug, I soon learn from experience, is to Yemenis what vindaloo is to Indians. It has the capacity to wreak havoc on your throat. It burns your eyes just looking at it but a smidgen of it on top of the hummous on top of a wedge of onion makes for a gastronomical *ménage a trois*.

The man at the adjacent table slams down a backgammon piece triumphantly. His partner, a Sephardi Jew probably of Yemenite or Iraqi descent, whispers a lewd Arabic curse in his direction comparing him to a private part of his mother's anatomy.

More pita bread arrives without request. I delicately open it up like a pocket and gently paste some hummous to the sides with the back of a spoon, close it up and begin eating my sandwich. I soon learn, however, that this is a Western interpretation of a Middle Eastern ritual. The locals simply break off a corner and scoop up the hummous. Here, in Israel, there's no time for such Western pleasantries. This is a country in a rush.

I'm not entirely sure why. Is it rushing from war? Or towards peace? Or simply because the uncertainty of the situation causes people to rush around doing things that they may not get a chance to do if they hang around and wait? Perhaps people's impatience is a function of the stress that blows in the wind around this contested piece of land.

We wash a Marlboro Red down with some Turkish coffee and amble back from the Yemenite Quarter, through its narrow, potholed alleyways. The houses front directly onto the road, some without even a pavement. They look tired and worn. The paint is peeling off their facades. The din of workmen drilling trenches nearby disturbs the afternoon peace. Here and there, a few houses have been renovated; the gentrification of the nearby neighbourhood of Neve Tzedek seems to have started spilling over into the Yemenite Quarter as this seaside area of downtown Tel Aviv slowly becomes eyed by real estate entrepreneurs.

Mike is a national anomaly. That's the only way I can describe him. He's been living here for fifteen years and he's never once received his army conscription papers. He is, as far as I can understand, a statistical error, a one-in-a-million mistake. Maybe he was accidentally deleted from the system. Whatever the reason, he hasn't served and has never been asked to. So, he hasn't broken the law.

Though I have yet to receive my draft papers, I figure that they will arrive one day soon. I envy him. And he knows it.

'I still don't understand how you got out scot-free.'

'Just ignore anything they send you,' he says. 'Maybe they'll ignore you too.'

Weeks pass. Somehow, life returns to normal quicker than I expected. The funerals come and go, passengers gingerly return to the shopping malls and buses and, for the average Israeli, the only lasting reminder of the Dizengoff bomb is the flickering vigil of candles near the junction where the blast took place – a silent sentinel to that explosive March morning.

A few weeks later, I borrowed Hannah and Rami's car and drove out to Ben-Gurion airport at around 6 am to meet my match. I had stayed up half the night putting the finishing touches to the roof flat before Lucy arrived.

Exhausted, I bought a bunch of flowers – Australian natives – and sat down opposite the giant video screen so I could spot Lucy coming into the arrivals hall.

Next thing I knew Lucy was standing there, arms crossed, smiling, but unamused that I had fallen fast asleep at such a monumental moment. Dazed and unsure of whether I was dreaming or not, it took me a few moments to gather myself before I realised the enormity of my gaffe.

I had no time to feel nervous or anxious, vain or self-conscious. I must have looked the way most people look on three hour's sleep, and there were blotches of paint all over my arms that had managed to evade the turpentine. But Lucy knew me inside out, and we were excited to be together again – in Israel.

I had played the flat down over the phone, so Lucy was pleasantly surprised when she reached the roof. She is an old soul, a queen of markets and second-hand shops and a romantic who prefers old and antiquated surroundings to modern and sterile. Our décor was certainly old and although it wasn't antiquated (recycled would be a more appropriate term), it was far from sterile.

The smell of rotting fruit and vegetables stewing in the drains hung heavy in the air around the Shuk HaCarmel, Tel Aviv's main fruit and vegetable market, during summer. This place, five minutes walk from our flat, soon became Lucy's home from home. She got to know the intricate network of alleyways and lanes, every nook and cranny, where to find the best and cheapest, the most elusive and unique.

She knew where to buy the freshest flowers and the finest hummous in the market – a tiny corner stall which always had a fresh mountain of creamy hummous ready to tantalise passersby. Of course, olives of all shapes, sizes and colours, tahina and big, fat juicy pickled cucumbers were also available. On Fridays, when the nation starts preparing for the beginning of the Sabbath, this place is jammed. Lucy would be there, basket in one hand, Ziggy the dog in the other, finding the best deals for the finest foods.

Come sundown, the tide subsides, and the bustling alleyways become eerily empty. All that remains are echoes of the vendors trying to undercut one another's prices just before the last shoppers disperse. And the smell of decomposing fruit. Huge, multicoloured pyramidal piles of discarded fruit and vegetables await the garbage collectors. They stand there like gigantic fruit salads awaiting someone to come along with a dab of fresh cream and a spoon.

For eight months, we lived on the roof, a view with a room. As September arrived, so, too, did the soft, white, feathery clouds that announce the impending winter rains. First they glided fleetingly across the skyline. But when they began to dock there day after day, we knew it was time to move. Soon our outdoor lounge extension would be flooded with water.

The more we looked, the more we realised that we couldn't move to a flat with no outdoor space. And most flats that advertise balconies are actually just a narrow strip large enough for one person to sit with their knees under their chin. That's when we realised we could only move from roof to roof.

Eventually, we found a new flat. A new roof two streets away. Only this time the exterior was smaller and the interior larger. The fridge wasn't inside the bathroom and the bath wasn't in the kitchen. The lounge was indoors and the bedroom had space to move around. It did, however, have an ensuite – not a bathroom but a kitchen, a rather strange, but welcome, design flaw that enabled me to bring Lucy breakfast in bed without straying more than three steps.

We figured we'd save on removal merchants by walking everything over. Eighty-eight steps down; eighty-eight steps up.

Never again.

One thing remained, however: the view from the roof. It was almost identical to our previous view. If we were home around sunset, we'd sit on the roof, facing west and bask in the view, awaiting the colour change: first furnace-oven orange; then fire-engine red.

CHAPTER TWENTY-FOUR

IT WAS STILL dark in downtown Tel Aviv, though subtle swathes of early morning light had started seeping through. The streets were bleary-eyed, slowly shaking off their slumber. The distant rumble of buses cranking up their engines was a clarion call to the city: daybreak.

The sweet smell of freshly baked pita bread drenched the brisk air, tantalising the taste buds of those who ventured out into the dawn.

We were alone, just Yaniv and me, in a nondescript café on the corner of Bograshov and Pinsker Streets, near the beach. In the weeks to come, this café was to become our local meeting place for two reasons: first, because it was among the few places open at such unearthly hours; and second, because it was an old school Eastern European establishment – a conditoria, frill-free, but famed for its bakery.

It had history on its side too. In the pre-state years, it was frequented by some of Tel Aviv's – and Israel's – greatest poets and philosophers. It remained steeped in the past. That was its timeless appeal.

The décor was simple. It was the sort of unpretentious place that you don't even notice unless you know of its whereabouts. A place that locals guard like a secret, petrified that real estate magnates or highflying developers may buy it out and transform it into yet another chic coffee parlour for yuppies and their mobile phones.

It's 5.45 am. And at this hour, after a long night prowling the streets, a shot of caffeine is critical. Halinka, the proprietress, defies her age. A short, wiry woman, she looks as though she is at least seventy, but her movement, dexterity and agility suggest otherwise. Dressed like she has just walked out of Poland circa 1930, she sounds as much too, with a thick, heavy-set European accent that even her Hebrew cannot conceal.

'Hevrai – friends, what will it be this morning?' she says buoyantly, waltzing around our window table, adjacent to a rack of freshly baked goods: rogaleh (a local version of a chocolate croissant), cinnamon twists, blueberry pastries, baked cheesecake and assorted biscuits and breads.

'One botz please,' I moan, barely summoning the strength to smile. Yaniv can only manage a nod accompanied by a two-fingered gesture to indicate his participation.

Botz means mud in Hebrew – not your average breakfast request. It's how Israelis describe Turkish coffee brewed over a low flame, because the sediment that lies at the bottom of the glass looks like mud.

Yaniv lights up a smoke. He is an addict, a no-holds-barred-thirty-a-day man. And he's not ashamed of it. Many Israelis have no smoking shame. Living on the edge of war, under the spectre of a seemingly eternal question mark, it's pointless trying to sell them the health card. They live for today, because they can't take tomorrow for granted. That much they have learned.

Even the slain Prime Minister, Yitzhak Rabin, was a compulsive smoker. If you already smoke, you may end up smoking more; if you don't smoke, chances are, after a while in town, you will. It may sound unorthodox for an ultra-Orthodox Jew – garbed in black hat, beard and side locks – to fire up a cigarette, but here in Israel it's nothing out of the ordinary.

I join Yaniv, and soon a cloud of smoke hovers above the table. Two glasses of 'mud' arrive.

Halinka bears a tray of freshly baked borekas, small triangular flaky pastries, with assorted fillings: spinach, sweet cheese, mushroom. They are fresh, warm and soft as a feather pillow.

There's no menu here. Regulars know exactly what they want.

'Min achla,' I say, borrowing the Arabic for 'tasty'. Many Arabic words have found their way into Hebrew dialect. Most are colloquial or informal words that have, as a result of the years of war and peace between the Arabs and the Jews, become adopted into the Hebrew vernacular. Ahalan is commonly used among the younger generation as a casual greeting instead of shalom (which can mean hello, goodbye or peace, depending on the context). Words like 'wallah' are as ubiquitous as they are indefinable. Inevitably, numerous expletives have harnessed themselves to Hebrew diction. Most of them are unpublishable and those that aren't lose their potency in the translation from Arabic to Hebrew and then to English.

Yaniv is the boss of the Tel Aviv branch of Meretz – the Civil Rights Party, the third largest party in the Knesset at the time, with twelve seats out of the 120-seat legislature. He is not old, and his tender olive skin and boyish good looks probably take some years off his real age. His head is completely shaved and his smile gives way to a mouthful of oversized, tobacco-stained teeth.

I was Yaniv's assistant – by default.

Ever since the spate of suicide bombs in February and March, my conscience had been plaguing me with guilt. As the election loomed, I worried about how I would live with myself if Labour were ousted from power and I had just been a spectator from the sidelines.

I had first arrived here in September 1994 at a time when the word 'peace' had taken on mantra status, when the Oslo Accords were but a year old, when Israel and Jordan were preparing to ini-tial an historic peace agreement. Within eighteen months, Yigal Amir had assassinated Prime Minister Yitzhak Rabin and Islamic terrorists had wreaked havoc on the country. Pachad, fear in Hebrew, was palpable on street corners, buses and markets. It was being used as fuel to rekindle the fire of the Likud Party and the Right wing as it attempted to wrest power from the Labour-led coalition.

All Israelis dream of peace, of the day when they can wake up in the morning and no longer have to listen to the news because there is no news. But the House of Israel is absolutely divided on the means to attain that end. Those on the Left, supporters of Labour and other satellite parties like Meretz, believe that peace with the Palestinians will only come about by separation – by withdrawing from most of the West Bank and Gaza Strip.

Those on the Right, supporters of Likud, smaller parties like Tsomet and some religious and ultra-Orthodox parties, think differently. They are unwilling to enter into an agreement with terrorists whose suicide bombs had claimed sixty-five innocent Jewish lives and injured 161 in the last two months alone, and who wish to reclaim the Chosen People's biblical birthright. Many members of the Likud camp will only begin to entertain peace negotiations when the security of Israel is guaranteed, when the bombs stop, the rhetoric dissipates and when Arafat lays down his gun. Security first, then peace is their mantra.

Perhaps it was fate. After living in Israel for a while, the general belief in fatalism begins to rub off on you. I entered the offices of the Meretz Tel Aviv branch thinking to myself that volunteering two nights a week for a month would be adequate.

'Do you have a driving licence and a month to spare?' asked Yaniv after a half-hour conversation.

'What? Why?'

He explained to me that his former assistant had just suffered a stroke and was bedridden.

'Did it have anything to do with the stress of the job?' I asked Yaniv cautiously.

'No.' His economy with the truth was transparent. But he had nothing to lose.

'Look, the election is less than one month away. We have a campaign to mount. Tel Aviv is the largest metropolitan area. I don't have the time to advertise for an assistant. I need someone who subscribes to Meretz's philosophy and can cope with long days and longer nights.

'Are you game?'

I tried to buy time. 'Are you putting me on the spot?'

'Yeah. I don't have a choice. Think about it and let me know in three hours. Call my mobile. I've got to run. Bye.'

I had entered the offices to volunteer my services for two nights a week ahead of the election. And here I was, less than an hour later, being offered a full-time, paid job as his assistant. If two nights was tantamount to dipping my toes in the paddling pool, this job was the equivalent of taking the political plunge. I discussed it with Lucy, though I spared her the details of my predecessor's cardiac arrest. She was adamant that I take it on. I called my father, who is a pillar of rationale and reason. He would give me the pros and cons of the job.

'Go for it,' he said. 'You'll never get another chance like it.'

I thought about the Hebron University job, when I had been on the verge of involving myself in an ethically questionable project that was well outside the bounds of legitimacy. This, I was convinced, was all above par. Meretz, though it was left of centre and advocated a Palestinian state, was well within the political spectrum. It was an offer I couldn't refuse.

I spent the next hour writing my resignation letter for my job at Hannah's CD-ROM company, cancelling all my diary appointments for the next month and tying up loose ends. I called Yaniv.

'Ahalan, Yaniv. It's me. Count me in.'

'Great. I'll pick you up in half an hour. We have to talk. It'll be a late night. Get some rest. Bye.' Click.

And with that he was gone. He was a man on a mission with no time for idle chitchat.

As I stood there holding the receiver, it occurred to me that I had just committed myself to a job without even asking what the job description was. All I actually knew was that my title was his deputy. By deduction, I figured I'd be helping him do his job. But then I realised I had no idea what he did. Regret began to creep into my mind while I tried to get some rest.

It was short-lived. Yaniv arrived bang on time, honking his horn with an impatience that I would soon learn was his trademark. We drove to Ben-Gurion airport to register my name as a driver of the campaign van. By midnight we were talking strategy over several cold Goldstar beers. My brief, he explained, would be to enable him to be free to do his job. In other words,

I would have to do the bulk of the street work while he took care of the office work. In practical terms, he explained, I'd spend a lot of time driving across town, putting up banners, posters and billboards, mobilising volunteers, ferrying youth to stand at junctions during rush hour, organising door-to-door mail-drops, demonstrations and a million and one other missions in between.

'Ben, it'll be non-stop,' concluded Yaniv. 'You'll need a holiday when it's over. And one more thing . . .' He closed in to such a degree that our noses almost touched. 'At night, under the cover of darkness, we will wage a propaganda war on this city.'

'Meaning?' I was not in tune with his vision.

'We will stage operations, a bit like we used to do in the army. Have you served in the army yet?'

I shook my head.

'Oh. Well, anyway, as the election draws closer they will intensify in quality and quantity. We will start off on a small scale, targeting certain areas of town and go out and plaster them with our propaganda.

'Then, on the election eve, we will turn Tel Aviv green with the colours of Meretz.'

I slurped my beer, and smoked another cigarette. Night missions sounded vaguely exciting, though the appeal waned on second thoughts, given that it compromised sleep.

At around 6 am on day one of my new job, all I could think about was resigning and going back to my cosy life devoid of politics.

Inside the café, the steam from my 'mud' coffee and the smoke from my cigarette were rising in unison; outside on the street, the curtain was rising on a new day.

'It was a successful mission,' conceded Yaniv. He was not big on acclaim; he was an intense character, wholly committed to the cause. 'The north of the city will awake to Meretz. We have started the ball rolling. Now we must prepare for round two. Get some rest. Meet me at the office at 10.30.'

I gawked. That left me precious little time to sleep. He had warned me about long days and longer nights, but I thought this was a touch excessive on the first day.

He took the van. I got on my scooter and made my way through the backstreets of the city. It was light by now and the city was beginning to stir. Market traders were already setting up shop at the Carmel Market. Fresh breads were being ferried across town to various outlets. Coffee machines were purring. The first chickpea balls were being dropped into sizzling oil and would be golden brown felafel within minutes. Traffic was beginning to clog the roads.

I rolled up to the flat, parked and climbed the eighty-eight steps to the roof. Ziggy heard me arrive. As I ascended the last flight of stairs, I could hear her sniffing the bottom of the door for a trace of my scent. She smothered me in sloppy kisses.

I lay down next to Lucy, who was sleeping curled up, and we locked together like pieces of a jigsaw puzzle. Piercing shafts of morning light filtered through the gaps in the blind, making it impossible for me to sleep. My eyelids just couldn't combat the glare. I grabbed my shades and put them on in bed. There were twenty-five days still to go. The clock had read 8.47 am the last time I looked, which left me less than an hour to sleep.

CHAPTER TWENTY-FIVE

ONE WEEK. That's what separates Israel from its fate. Seven days and nights before 29 May 1996, when the people will decide whose name will be inscribed in the history books when the next fateful chapter is written: Labour's Shimon Peres or Likud's Bibi Netanyahu?

Both, unsurprisingly, claim the pursuit of peace. Peres wants to continue down Rabin's peace path, if anything with more speed and less doubt. Netanyahu claims he wants to end the conflict too, but with less speed and more doubt.

When I began this job several weeks ago, there seemed no doubt about Peres' victory, just a question mark over the margin of his triumph. Now, polls show Bibi with a slim Jewish majority. But some 20 per cent of the population is non-Jewish (mainly Arabs and Christians), and Peres has a razor-thin majority overall.

The countdown has begun in earnest. I can tell that Yaniv has upgraded our mission to high intensity because the nondescript café at the corner of Bograshov and Pinsker Streets has become our unofficial HQ. Pre-operation plans and post-operation recovery sessions take place inside its smoke-filled interior.

WEDNESDAY

'I want you to go to Jaffa tomorrow,' says Yaniv, holding court in the café. 'The battle lines have shifted. Bibi now has a Jewish majority according to the polls. So the Israeli Arabs hold the key to our victory. We've got to rally their support to ensure an overall victory. They're still disgruntled after the Qana massacre.* We have to bring them back.'

'Will I be welcome, promoting a Jewish party in Arab Jaffa? I mean, I realise that we promote equal rights for Jews and Arabs, but won't most of the locals be supporting the Arab parties?' I ask, in between sipping sweet tea with fresh mint leaves, known locally as teh nana.

'Look you have nothing to worry about. First of all I would never endanger your life. Second, we have plenty of Arab members in our party; we even have Arab members of Knesset; and third we have a contact there, Ibrahim, who will help you. So, don't worry.'

'Oh,' he added crunching into a fresh cinnamon twist, 'we have a meeting at the Arab community centre tomorrow tonight. Yossi Sarid [Meretz party leader] and a few of the others will be hosting. So, apart from anything else, we need the place plastered with posters for their arrival.'

'OK. Give me Ibrahim's digits and I'll go down there tomorrow.'

THURSDAY

I spend Thursday morning at the National Driving Centre in Holon, a largely Sephardi-populated satellite town just to the south of Tel Aviv. I had been putting off converting my British driving licence to an Israeli one for some time, and my amnesty has run its course.

I simply cannot afford to lose my licence. Not now. Not six days before the election. Yaniv was irate but conceded that it was better to sort it out now – rather than have my licence revoked just when I needed it most.

Driving in Israel is one of life's least pleasurable experiences. With almost a million and a half cars on the roads, this country stakes a claim for most vehicles per square kilometre anywhere in the world. And everyone is in a rush. Everyone seems to think

---

* After Hezbollah rockets injured forty Israelis during the festival of Passover in April 1996, the IDF retaliated by hitting Beirut and Tyre. But they mistakenly fired on a UN camp in Qana, Lebanon, killing over 100 refugees.

they can drive better than the person in front. Horns blare at a moment's indecision. Overtaking on the inside lane appears to be an accepted practice. Hand gesticulations are par for the course. Expletives fly with next to no encouragement. Bus and taxi drivers are notoriously aggressive. Road rage is not uncommon; Israel has suffered over 20,000 road fatalities since 1948 – more than it has suffered in all its wars. Sad. Pathetic. But true. In short, driving in Israel is about as calming as a bungee jump.

My instructor, a middle-aged man named Ya'acov, sports Jesus sandals and greying curls. His fingers are stained from decades of nicotine abuse, and his grey moustache, which sags either side of his mouth, is discoloured from his addiction. I quickly check my fingers for evidence that I may be heading down that slippery slope. Fortunately, there is none.

I guess by his complexion that he is of Middle-Eastern descent, perhaps Iraqi. He explains the examination procedure to me in between clouds of smoke. We roll into action. After a few minutes of negotiating junctions, pedestrians, traffic and unexpected incidents, he falls silent. Then, 'The Arabs have twenty-two states to live in,' he says in Hebrew, after a long pause. 'We Jews have one.'

'Nachon – true,' I reply, trying to remain poker-faced. Despite my bewilderment and curiosity, my eyes never once leave the road. This is supposed to be a driving test, not a party political broadcast, I think to myself. What the hell is he banging on about politics for? I put it down to pre-election tension and train my eyes on the road ahead.

'So why do you support a Palestinian state in Eretz Yisrael, in the sliver of territory that is our God-given birthright?'*

I almost slam on the anchors in shock. Jolted by surprise, I am perplexed at how he could know my political persuasion since I had removed all evidence of it before I arrived.

'How . . . ?' I begin asking.

* Eretz Yisrael translates as the Land of Israel, but is used to refer to the biblical land between the Mediterranean Sea and the Jordan River (which includes the disputed West Bank).

Ya'acov interrupts. 'Habibi,' he says, 'what other business would you have with an Ibrahim in Jaffa?'

Now I am spooked. How does he know about Ibrahim? Who could've leaked such information? Was there a mole inside the party HQ? If he knew such privy information, imagine what else he may know.

Ya'acov was milking the moment. He blew a thin funnel of smoke in my direction, followed by a trail of teasing smoke rings. Then he pointed to my wrist where I had written Ibrahim's name and phone number in red ink. He would have known by the first three numbers that it was an address in Jaffa. Even if he didn't, Ibrahim is to Islam what Ya'acov is to Judaism – a name that reeks of religion.

Now I'm really pissed off, though my fears of a mole have been allayed. I need to pass my driving test, first and foremost. And I also need to get back to my beat but I've been driving straight now for some time and we are some way south of Holon. If I turn my head and engage him, he could fail me there and then. My head tells me to ignore him and focus on the test. But my heart overrides my brain, forcing it to concede defeat. Unable to contain myself, I bite the bait: 'Would you care to join me at Ibrahim's house tomorrow afternoon?' I ask. 'He's my cousin, you know. Actually he's your cousin, too. You can call him Abraham if you prefer.'

I've been lured into his corner. Now he has me by the horns – and I see my new licence evaporate into thin air right in front of my nose. Yaniv will go ballistic.

'No thank you. But, tell me, can he trace his ancestors back 3000 years? Am I mistaken or did the Arabs only arrive here in the seventh century?'

'When the bulk of our people arrived here at the turn of the twentieth century, this was not a land without a people for a people without a land,' I retort, debunking the old Zionist myth that Palestine (as it was called then) was *terra nullius*.

'We were here first. There was always a Jewish population here throughout the 2000-year exile. This is our birthright. Just because we were expelled into exile does not give them any right to take our homeland. Jerusalem is not even mentioned in the Koran. Muslims cite Sura 17, the passage about Mohammed's "Night Journey" as a reference to Jerusalem. Mecca is mentioned hundreds of times and Medina countless times, but the word "Jerusalem" is nowhere to be found. And yet Jerusalem is mentioned in the Torah over 700 times. We pray facing Jerusalem; they pray towards Mecca, with their backs to Jerusalem. So, where exactly is the evidence of their claim?'

'Does that "evidence" justify uprooting people from their homes and villages? Does it justify what happened at Deir Yassin?' I am referring to one of the 417 Arab villages and towns razed in the 1948 War. The most notable, Deir Yassin, was the site of what the Israelis claim was a battle and the Arabs insist was a massacre. Regardless, between 115 and 250 Arab villagers were killed by the Irgun and the Stern Gang (radical Jewish underground fighters). The news of Deir Yassin sparked a massive Palestinian exodus from other villages fearing that they would become the next victims.

'They have homes elsewhere.'

'Where? In Jordan? The PLO was expelled from there in 1970. In Lebanon? It was forcefully removed from there in 1982. The pages of the Palestinian history book are almost as black as ours. If any people should be compassionate towards a dispossessed people, surely it should be us Jews.'

'But we have been persecuted for 2000 years, suffered pogroms and anti-Semitism, let alone the Holocaust, a genocide which annihilated six million Jews – one third of our entire people.'

'That's exactly my point. Does that give us the right to a monopoly on persecution? Does the past injustice against us warrant our present injustice against the Palestinians?'

'You are young and naive. Trust me. I know my enemy. I grew up in his land. I have fought against him. I have witnessed war first hand . . . ' His voice trailed off. 'There is no other option. The only solution is to expel the Arabs to whichever Arab country they wish.'

'Sounds like you'd vote for Kahane.'

'Absolutely.'

I am gob-smacked. Kahane represented the most extreme Right-wing party in the history of Israel. He gained a seat in the 1984 elections with 25,000 votes, but was banned from running for parliament in 1988 for his blatantly racist platform, and was assassinated by an Egyptian in New York in 1990. His supporters are a dwindling minority on the political fringe of society.

And one of his diehard faithful was sitting next to me – examining my driving ability.

'But, now that the party is banned, I can't.'

'So, who will you vote for?' I am no longer focusing on the road. As far as I am concerned my test is over.

'No one. There's no party any longer which represents my position.'

'Thank God,' I whisper under my breath.

We return to the driving centre in silence. I am still reeling from the absurdity of the scenario. Only in Israel, I think to myself. Only in Israel.

I convince myself that it would be futile to ask whether our disparate views will affect my result. I also convince myself that he will fail me, but figure that I'll get no change out of stirring the political pot even more.

'I'll call you tomorrow with the result,' says Ya'acov, stiff as a starched shirt.

The distance between the centre of Tel Aviv and Old Jaffa is no longer than the time it takes to smoke one cigarette. The two places may exist cheek by jowl geographically, but they are far apart in most other ways.

Jaffa is 3000 years old; Tel Aviv is but 100 years young. Jaffa is largely Arab in character; Tel Aviv is largely Jewish. Jaffa is shrouded in history; Tel Aviv is crowded with secular hedonists. Jaffa's narrow pot-holed alleyways still cling to the past; Tel Aviv's hi-tech hub is lurching into the future at the speed of the megabyte.

Ibrahim's shop is on Yefet Street, the main artery that runs through the heart of Old Jaffa. He is a diminutive character, a Muslim Arab dressed in non-traditional clothes. His shop has a low entrance door with two steps down under the decorated lintel. His antiques are displayed on shelves inside the elegant, domed room.

I am wearing a Meretz T-shirt and am conscious that I am identifiable as an ally.

'Ahalan wa sahalan,' I greet him in Arabic, hoping to start on the right foot.

'Ahalan biq,' he greets me in reply.

'Kif halaq – How are you?'

'Al hamdu lillah – Praise be to God.'

He offers me gahawe, Turkish coffee.

'Aiwa. Shukran – yes. Thank you.' I accept his hospitality despite the fact that I have a busy schedule. It is considered impolite to refuse such an invitation.

I switch to Hebrew as my routine Arabic comes to a formidable end.

He opens out a map and marks the spots where there are billboards, which, he assures me, belong to him. He cannot come with me because he has to look after his shop but he invites me back for more coffee once I am finished.

He admits that he is concerned. 'Many of the Arabs don't want to vote at all. Those that do are split, too. There's Hadash, the United Arab Party and the Arab Alliance for Progress and Renaissance that are run by Arabs. Meretz is a predominantly Jewish-run party that supports equal rights for Arabs. They still feel aggrieved about the Qana massacre. And many Arabs just feel safer voting for Arabs. I can understand that.'

'Me too,' I reply.

'They cannot see the bigger picture,' continues Ibrahim. 'We will get the most mileage out of a party that has political power inside the government. What will we get from a party that has two seats against Meretz, which will get at least ten? We have to convince them that, in the long run, they will get more from Meretz than from the Arab parties.'

The first billboard I arrive at is plastered with red posters displaying Arabic writing. I cannot read or write Arabic – speaking it is difficult enough – but I recognise the logo from the television campaign advertisements as Hadash – the Communist Party. Alongside is another set of posters which, I think, belongs to the United Arab Party.

I back up the van alongside the billboard so that I can clamber on top of it to reach the billboard. My water and glue buckets and brushes at the ready, I begin plastering green Meretz posters on top of red Arab posters.

I am deep inside Jaffa, and although Meretz is tolerated here, it is not home turf. More worrying is the fact that I am concealing local Arab propaganda.

Horns begin to hoot. Shouts of abuse are hurled in my direction. Passersby stop and stare at me, perplexed. A group of six teenage Arab youths approach, muttering to each other in Arabic, pointing at the van. I sense they're looking for trouble and figure that standing here on a van roof in downtown Jaffa is hardly the most inconspicuous way to spend an afternoon.

Before I know it, they are raiding the back of the van. Helpless, and unwilling to chase kids through the streets of Jaffa, I resign myself to defeat. I drive to pick up a huge Meretz banner for the meeting tonight and receive similar abuse on the road. Ibrahim was not there by the time I returned.

The day ended with a woeful sixty Arabs attending the meeting at Jaffa's Arab Community Centre. Yaniv couldn't hide his worry. He was either on the mobile or smoking a cigarette – or both.

'They want to punish us,' he said, relieving his ear for a second. 'But they'll shoot themselves in the foot if they vote with their feet and stay at home. A victory for Bibi will be another blow for the Arabs.'

He was right. But he was preaching to the converted. And it seemed pointless trying to convince the local Arabs otherwise. The polls swung towards Bibi on the late-night news. Time was beginning to work against us. You could just about see the flames of rage inside Yaniv's belly.

FRIDAY

Today is the last Friday before the elections. Everyone is on the streets. Crowds swarm the city. Volunteers from opposing ends of the political spectrum brush past each other and exchange abuse at the city's main junctions. I ferry vanloads of volunteers north, south and east. I deliver more posters, more pamphlets and more propaganda for the peddlers to peddle. The traffic begins to clog the city centre. I ditch the van and grab my scooter in order to crisscross town.

Arriving at Shalom Junction, one of the main gateways to the city from the Jerusalem highway, I can see a couple of youths dismantling our banners.

'Hey! You can't do that,' I protest. 'We have an agreement. You have that corner; we have this one.'

They are clearly Likud supporters.

'The agreement is null and void. Just like your Arab-loving party,' said one, cutting the strings right in front of my face.

Next thing I know he's pushed me. Now we're fighting, fists are flying – and I am the minority receiving the majority of blows. The police intervene and save my ass from being minced to a pulp. The officer demands our ID cards. We are escorted to a police car. Fifteen minutes later we are both issued with a caution. There was no red blood spilled, just bad blood. Here in the heat of day, two guys want to beat each other up over a banner at a junction. Essentially we are brothers, but today, like Kane and Abel, we are bitterly divided.

I am seething with rage. It is a new phenomenon for me. I have only ever been involved in one fight before now – and that was fifteen years ago. My mobile phone rings.

It's Ya'acov. His timing is perfect. At that moment there wasn't a person I'd like to speak to less in the whole world. I answer, irate. 'Yes. What do you want? It's not a good time.'

'You passed,' he says, without emotion.

'Really? Are you winding me up?'

'No.'

'Wow. Thanks.'

'That's OK,' he says. 'Just so long as you fail in your job.'

I hang up on him, smiling. I burn down to the beach and launch myself into the Mediterranean. I dip my head underwater, washing off the anger and stress. There are no politics in these neutral waters – just the odd cigarette butt and plastic bag.

My cuts sting in the salt water. Souvenirs, I think to myself.

SATURDAY EVENING

We're driving back from north Tel Aviv in the transit van after a door-to-door blitz. It's around 11 pm. Across the street, we see three boys uprooting one of our billboards. I swerve over, stop and hold the horn down for five seconds. They see me. Instinctively, I jump from the van and race toward them as they make for their GMC van. I grab hold of their windscreen wipers to prevent them from driving off.

Only they drive off anyway. Now I'm hanging on to their bull bar. Lucy shrieks. The driver slams on the brakes. I hang on for dear life. We are staring at each other through the windscreen: one of his friends is egging him on to drive; the other is gesturing to me that he'd like to chop my testicles off and insert them in my throat. Lucy is begging me to get down. I am unable to decide whether to run like hell or pounce on them like a panther.

So I do neither. If I were a mental case, I think to myself, and I really wanted to antagonise them, I would spin around and drop my pants. But I'm scared shitless, so I just hang on tight. He revs the engine. All of a sudden I become aware that I have acquired extremely brown underwear. As the car screeches forward, I leap off the fender and land awkwardly on the ground. Lucy races to my rescue. She really wants to yell at me and tell me how goddamned stupid I am, but instead she nurses my wounds.

I spend the next hour on the phone trying to explain to the police what happened. They tell me they'll do everything to catch them, but make no guarantees. I have to make a statement and file a complaint at the station first thing in the morning.

SUNDAY

The day starts badly. Yaniv calls at 6 am to wake up with the news that my 'friends' in the GMC spent the night dismantling most of our billboards. He says he'll meet me at the police station.

I am refused entry to the police station before I have even set foot in it. This does not bode well. Fortunately, it's a simple case of removing my Meretz T-shirt since political affiliations are not tolerated inside the HQ. I spend the next hour waiting to see the right person. And the following hour being quizzed as if I were the guilty party. I leave at midday feeling like I've wasted my time – time we don't have.

That night we drive up the main highway, the coastal road linking Tel Aviv to Haifa and the north. Not far beyond the northern suburbs of Tel Aviv lies Kibbutz Ga'ash. We have arranged for a giant, fifteen-metre-high dove emblazoned with the Meretz slogan to be inflated in a field alongside the highway. Lucy and I are on guard duty from 2 am until 6 am. The local guard at the kibbutz gate warns us that there will be attempts to sabotage it. I am not at all amused at our defence ammunition: a mobile telephone.

'OK, so we get ambushed. I call the police. Then what?' I demand of Yaniv. 'They take twenty minutes to get out here by which time we have been gagged and bound to a mammoth inflatable that has just been unharnessed from the ground and released into the atmosphere. If we don't land in Nablus or Jenin, we'll land in Lebanon for all my luck.'

'Don't worry. The opposition won't know it's up until it hits the papers tomorrow morning. We leaked it to the press and they sent photographers to watch us inflate it.'

'Yeah, yeah. If I see anything suspect, I'm doing a runner. I'm not hanging around to be beaten up again.'

Yaniv is stoking the fire we lit to keep us warm. He ignores me, jumps in the transit and turns the ignition. 'I'll be back around 5 am. Don't fall asleep.'

'Bastard!' I spit as his wheels spin on the wet grass. Then he is gone, shrouded in a cloud of dust, exhaust fumes and smoke.

The night passes without ambush – and without sleep.

TUESDAY

Today is the penultimate day, 28 May 1996. It's 33 degrees and the heat is beginning to take its toll. My brain fries under my motorbike helmet in the midday sun as I bolt from junction to junction. I meander through the gridlock, noticing that there's barely a vehicle in the country that is not plastered with political stickers. There seem to be few, if any, drivers left who are neutral in this game.

But today something is different. On the eve of the election it feels like, all of a sudden, an army of religious youth has flooded the streets. They must have been bussed in from the West Bank settlements. They wear kippot srugot, knitted skull caps – the trademark of the religious Zionist youth (as opposed to black velvet ones, which are worn by the ultra-Orthodox).

But, worst of all, they are peddling a totally new message – 'Bibi is good for the Jews'. This is not only a new slogan, but a radical departure from the old philosophy. Here, they are making it patently clear, by deduction, that voting for Bibi is bad for the Arabs. It churns my stomach to see such division among our people. Such is the scale of their sheer numbers, we are simply overrun.

The final party political broadcasts are shown. Likud goes for the harrowing images of suicide bombs. The message: this is what Shimon Peres has brought us. They know how to shock the public. The footage is of charred buses, rabbis picking up pieces of flesh, mourning relatives. They are pressing the panic buttons with a vengeance. Elect this man at your country's peril. By contrast, the Peres adverts recall his diplomatic successes, all achieved together with his predecessor, Yitzhak Rabin: the Oslo Accords, the White House signing with Arafat, the Nobel Peace Prize, peace with Jordan. The polls carry percentage points too close to call. They all emphasise that the margin of error is greater than the margin between the two candidates. The nation is split on a knife-edge.

Israelis in the diplomatic missions around the world have already cast their ballots. They are in transit at this very moment.

Soldiers in Lebanon, the West Bank and the Gaza Strip cast their ballots today.

The waiting is over. The Day of Reckoning has arrived.

As I go to sleep it feels like Israel is holding its collective breath. No one knows. No one can be sure. I imagine that across Israel we are all laying our heads down tonight in a collective bed of doubt, our pillows cushioning our fears and reservations.

Tomorrow night they will either nurse painful headaches or celebratory hangovers.

CHAPTER TWENTY-SIX

TODAY IS Election Day. I rise at 3.45 am on Wednesday, 29 May 1996 and am greeted in the darkness by my dog's tongue. Her soggy kisses are enough to drown a swarm of mosquitoes. By 4 am I'm carrying placards from the office to the van. Yaniv struggles through the doorway wearing a fake smile that suggests he may be capable of extracting the teeth of anyone who annoys him. He has become the bane of my life. I yearn for tomorrow when it will all be over and I can return to normality. His blood pressure is running high, he tells me. I am suddenly reminded of my predecessor's fate. But I refrain from sharing my concern. We head off on our final mission.

By 7 am we are nursing bad moods and glasses of botz at the café. I beg Halinka for a shot of strong coffee. We have grown close over the last month and she pulls my cheek, hard enough to make me wince, and then shakes it like a rattle. 'Shalom, habibi. Would I deprive you?' If I had had the energy, I would have explained to her that grown men do not like having their cheeks pulled like infants – especially in public.

It's a public holiday across the country. Our sole focus is on the floating voters. And there appears to be a fair number of people in this category.

Yaniv heads off to the office and I sit staring into the bottom of my coffee cup at the murky centimetre of sediment. I realise that, for the first time in my life, I have scratched past the surface and have penetrated the heart and soul of the Israeli psyche.

Never have I known a people so politicised. Never have I witnessed such passion on the streets. Never had I dreamed that we could instil such hatred toward our own brothers and sisters. The chasm that divides us seems ominously unbridgeable. Politics is a potent force here. It can drive people crazy.

The morning newspaper corroborates this claim. It reports that an elderly couple have filed for divorce because he decided to vote Labour and she committed to Likud. They realised that their private and political lives were intertwined, so they decided to split once and for all. Both parties, it was reported, claimed to be quite content with the outcome. An amicable separation.

Amos Oz, one of Israel's greatest novelists, suggests a similar prescription between the Jews and the Palestinians. There will never be a happy marriage between our peoples, he says. So, we should work towards a painless divorce: 'We are talking about peacemaking, not a honeymoon: make peace, not love.'

The result of today's vote will go a long way towards determining the speed of our divorce from the Palestinians. There was no marriage ceremony; and our divorce proceedings have already been painful. Our prime minister has been assassinated, suicide bombers have wreaked havoc on civil society and our people have been torn apart at the seams over the means to achieve this divorce.

Over the past few weeks I have been pushed and shoved, spat on and cursed, arrested and cautioned, overworked and under-rested. I have been thrown into the deep end of Israeli politics to sink or swim. It has been brutal and ugly, nasty and vicious – but it has been real. It has opened my eyes to the vitality of the people; the fight for the country's soul is everyone's fight – and everyone does literally fight. That, in itself, is a testament to the democratic spirit of the people.

I have to cast my vote for the first time as an Israeli citizen. The polling station is in a school on Ahad Ha'am Street, named after one of the great Zionist thinkers. Most Israeli streets are named after famous people or historic events, making a wander to the local shops a journey down the annals of Jewish history.

I hand in my ID card and my voter's registration card. I receive a ballot paper in return and head to a booth. I have two votes for the first time in Israeli history: one for prime minister and one for the party. There are only two choices for the former. I vote Shimon Peres for prime minister.

But there are some twenty different parties listed, indicative of the ultra-democracy of Israeli politics.

Though I know which party I'm voting for, I flirt with the alternative choices in any case. Outside of the main parties, there's a host of single-issue parties that tease me. The casino party is dedicated to legalising casinos in Israel. At present, you either have to go to the West Bank town of Jericho or travel down to Eilat and get on a boat to play roulette. The Green Leaf Party intrigues me because the legalisation of cannabis may chill the cauldron of politics and increase the peace – if only until the buzz wears off. Elsewhere on the list are ultra-Orthodox parties, ultra-secular parties, Left-wing and Right-wing parties, Sephardi and Ashkenazi parties, Arab parties, immigrants' parties, you name it. There's even a Men's Family Rights Party, which wants women to pay family support to their divorced husbands.

Small wonder that the Knesset is so fractured and all Israeli prime ministers have to cobble together a coalition of at least 61 seats in the 120-seat legislature. I cast my ballot and know that here, if anywhere in the world, is the one place where the power of one has real meaning.

Exit polls start flooding in by early evening. Unsurprisingly, it's neck and neck. Yaniv is uncontrollable. At the party HQ, there is a crowd huddling around the television. It's impossible to hear anything above the commotion. Lucy arrives with Henry 'the mild-mannered janitor', an old friend from England who has set up base camp in a tent on our roof. He works as a janitor/cleaner in downtown Tel Aviv and so his residency in our flat, formerly a janitor's cupboard, is appropriate.

Head shaved and rarely without a rolled cigarette in his mouth, he is one of those larger-than-life characters with enough buoyancy to ignite a funeral parade. With a wardrobe that relies heavily on recycled camouflage gear from army surplus stores, he looks like Che Guevara meets the Isley Brothers. Henry has been helping distribute Meretz fliers around town.

Yaniv cannot bear it and lets loose on the crowd, screaming at the top of his voice. Veins start bulging from his forehead. I worry about his blood pressure and urge an end to the suspense. By midnight it's still a cliffhanger. The nation is equally divided. I just want to go home.

By around 2.30 am we're in bed. Peres holds a razor-thin lead over Bibi. Most of the votes are in and counted. Surely he can't be beaten. He must have won, but will struggle to cobble together a coalition with any real teeth. By 3 am I figure it's over. We have won, by the slenderest of margins. But we have won! After days, weeks of doubt, worry, fear, there is no longer any need for concern. The future is secure. Just.

So, we, like most of the country, shut our eyes thinking that Peres has scraped across the line. The vote counters will continue slowly ploughing through the final few thousand votes throughout the night, tallying the scores to confirm what we already know.

We wake around ten the following morning. I am exhausted but relieved I don't have to get up and face Yaniv. I have earned my rest. Lucy turns on the television.

'What?'

'No!'

'Bullshit!'

'How?'

'It can't be!'

The presenter was still trying to grapple with the extraordinary circumstances. Some time during the night Bibi had erased the narrow deficit and, by the slimmest margin in the history of Israel, had won the election. His margin was all of 0.9 per cent, some 29,000 votes. Shimon Peres had managed, in miraculous fashion, to snatch defeat from the jaws of victory at the eleventh hour.

I am totally deflated, defeated and dejected – shocked and stunned into silence. I bury my head in the pillows. It must be a nightmare. It can't be true.

The phone rings. The answer machine picks up.

'Yo! Coos achto [unpublishable Arabic expletive].
This country is crazy. First we kill Rabin, then we defeat Peres.
Unbelievable! Call me. We gotta get out of town.
[Loud yell, nervous laughter.]
Sinai? Chill out and get away from this madhouse.
This shit is way, way too intense.
[Frantic coughing, choking, wheezing.]
Bibi is prime minister.
[Long, indecipherable Arabic expletive.]
Later.'

It was Hannah's boyfriend, Rami, one of the nicest blokes around. He'd just about walk on glass if you asked him to. He was also an ardent Labour supporter and despised the new Likud prime minister. Which explains why he wanted to leave town and go to the Sinai for what Israelis call 'nikui rosh'. It loses a little in the translation, but it basically means a cleansing of the mind. But, by the sounds of things, Rami was not planning to cleanse his mind, but to really mess with it.

Lucy and I were extremely tempted by the offer. We needed to breathe. It felt like we were suffocating under the weight of defeat. But Rami and Hannah left straight away, promising that we'd meet up somewhere between Tarrabin and Nuweiba. I knew they'd be half-way to the moon by the time we got down to Sinai and so the chances of us meeting them were slim.

I had learned, over the past month, that to live life in Israel is to live history in the present tense. I took an active part in what future historians will chronicle as the closest race in Israeli history. All I was left with was that sinking feeling – not dissimilar to Scotland being knocked out of the World Cup on goal difference. And having to wait four years for another chance.

CHAPTER TWENTY-SEVEN

IMAGINE LIVING inside a pressure cooker. That's what the last few months, with the suicide bombings followed by the elections, had felt like. Sinai was the only place where we could go to let off steam.

Many Israelis head to the resort town of Eilat – Israel's Red Sea playground. Separated from Be'er Sheva and the rest of the country by the triangular-shaped Negev Desert, Eilat was originally established as a border outpost to safeguard Israel's Red Sea access that connected it to the Gulf of Suez and international trade routes.

Today, in the wake of a colossal building boom, Eilat is a five-star destination attracting the rich and the nouveau riche – a kind of French Riviera meets Las Vegas. Its attractions are manifold: crystal clear waters, coral reef teeming with fish, sandy beaches, year-round sunshine and a laid-back atmosphere that reflects the geographical gap between Eilat and the urban centres to the north.

The glam and the glitz, however, have come at a cost: the beach has been reduced to narrow banks of sand backed by ritzy hotels and tacky hostels. Schmaltzy touristy attractions dot the marina alongside casinos, which have sprouted on boats to circumvent the outlawing of gambling. And sunbathers, stripped to naked torsos, line up on the beach side by side, basting in oil like banana fritters.

There's little appeal left in Eilat for young Israelis and backpackers alike. The midnight run from Tel Aviv – six dark hours on a bumpy bus across the Negev Desert – ends on arrival in Eilat at 6 am. We'd usually bypass Eilat and make straight for the Sinai border crossing just beyond Eilat at Taba.

Rose had recently returned again from the Sinai. She said she had finally found her own piece of paradise. Ever since she had first set eyes on it in the mid 1980s, she has been serenaded by her own love affair with the Sinai. She said it was the overwhelming silence of the place that romanced her; the soothing sound of waves breaking upon the sandy shores purified her mind. She also felt embraced by the timeless appeal of the Bedouin, the desert nomads whose aim, it seemed to her, was to welcome in strangers. She was seduced by a humbleness she had never known existed.

I first went to Sinai in 1987 – five years after Israel withdrew from the peninsula – on my summer trip with Frankie and Freddy. During the occupation, Israel used the Sinai largely for military purposes: air fields, firing ranges and training grounds for military manoeuvres. To this end, a road was built along the coastline that enabled access to the Sinai's hidden secrets.

Sinai was still relatively untapped by 1987, and Dahab was little more than a cluster of straw huts straggled haphazardly around a sweeping cove. During the Israeli occupation, legend has it that IDF soldiers used to come here in search of some R and R. They were not looking for rest and recreation. Nor rock 'n' roll. But reefers and reefers of cheap marijuana.

It wasn't hard to understand why they named this place Dahab – gold in Arabic. When we arrived, we felt as though we'd stumbled upon a hidden treasure trove, and we revelled in its mind-altering jewels. We got high. Then we dived into the depths of the Red Sea in search of the kaleidoscopic coral reef.

But we avoided the Blue Hole. It is among the most famous and infamous dive sites on the planet, and seasoned scuba divers flock here to attempt to enter the subterranean Garden of Eden through the Blue Hole. Many never make it back from the narrow shaft that sinks down deep into the coral. Tributes to those who have lost their lives trying to master it are etched into the rocks alongside the site.

We rented a straw hut and engaged in the hedonistic pleasures of eating tahina, drinking sahlab (the bulb of an orchid mixed with hot milk, oats, raisins and coconut), swimming, snorkelling and playing shesh besh. The Bedouin we rented our hut from barely spoke any Hebrew or English. He came in each morning, stuck his index finger in the air and, pointing at each of us, hollered: 'One, one, one . . . one pound'. That was the cost of a night's accommodation back then, and an Egyptian pound was less than half of a US dollar. So we called him 'One-pound Wesley'.

Since then, Dahab's treasures have been discovered – and its coffers have been slowly drained. In backpacker circles it is now discussed with the same reverence – or irreverence, depending on whom you ask – as Thailand's Ko Pha-Ngan or India's Goa. Nowadays, Dahab resembles a blend between a post-hippie time warp and the yuppie creature comforts – air-conditioning, nightclubs and Western food – of the new millennium. Lucy called this phenomenon 'yippie' – a hybrid of hippie and yuppie that seemed a perfectly apt description of a place where yuppies acted like wannabe hippies and hippies wished they could afford the luxuries of yuppies.

The serenity of the place has been replaced by sound systems pumping trance and techno music, the straw huts now resemble concrete prison-like cinder blocks and although the sun-soaked beaches are still sun-soaked, they are no longer pristine. Traffic jams the main street: jeeps, seven-seater Peugeots, camels and the odd donkey seem to be either picking up or dropping off the next load of young Israelis, travellers or tourists. Savvy Bedouins, some of them now draped in expensive jewellery, sit behind the wheels of four-wheel-drive jeeps, their jelabiyeh breast pockets clutching mobile phones. They need not worry about performing the fifth pillar of Islam, the pilgrimage to Mecca known as the haj. They have their own kind of mecca right on their doorstep. And they are cashing in on it.

We returned year after year in search of new shores of paradise from which to escape the imbroglio of urban life in Israel. We moved north up the coast towards Nuweiba and discovered silicon sand dunes, called Duna, which shelter an oasis of palm trees by the sea. A string of small Bedouin camps have been set up to attract those seeking alternative solace away from the commercialisation of Dahab.

Because it was just off the main road, it was only a matter of time before it, too, became overrun by backpackers. The same fate awaits Tarrabin and Ras al-Satan, Devil's Head, another headland we frequented just off the main road near Nuweiba.

'I've think I've finally found it,' Rose whispered to Lucy and me on her balcony one steaming night in Tel Aviv just after the election.

'Why are you whispering?' I asked.

She giggled nervously, desperately trying to prevent laughter. 'I don't know. It feels kind of like a sacred space.'

'How d'you mean?'

'There's next to nothing there. Just a few Bedouin families.'

'What makes you think it's not just the next Dahab or Duna waiting to happen?'

She arranged her cigarette packet on the table and pulled out a match. She pointed to the packet with a match in her hand. 'Look. This is Sinai. Here's Nuweiba, this is Dahab, here's Sharm el-Sheikh.' One side of the packet had become the coastline and she located the three main towns. I was with her so far.

'What's it called?'

'Ras al-Jizra. It's on the edge of a national park. It's illegal to build settlements there. Building permits are never issued. It's a conservation area.

'Plus – and this is the big difference – it's miles from Dahab *and* miles from the main road.'

She began drawing on the packet again with her match.

'You know how the road goes inland after Dahab all the way south until just before Sharm?'

Lucy and I nodded, vaguely aware, though we rarely went past Dahab because it was so far from the border – and the border was so far from Tel Aviv.

'This whole area of coastline is untouched. Incredibly beautiful bays and beaches. Only dirt tracks and camel footprints criss-cross this area.'

'Why did we never think of that before?'

'Because we had Dahab, Duna and Ras al-Satan. And they were a hell of a lot closer to Taba. Plus, Ras al-Jizra is damn difficult to reach. There's no road. And when you get there, there's nothing there. No running water, no electricity, nothing.'

'So how d'you get there then?'

'That's the tricky part. There are three routes. The first is the shortest in terms of off-road distance. But it's also the longest, door-to-door.

'From Dahab, you take a taxi ride to Sharm. Then you get a ride up to Umm Sid. The dirt track ends there. You can't go farther north. But it's only an hour by foot. Or by camel if you can convince a local Bedouin. It's the most beautiful walk. There are pools along the track that are deep enough to plunge in. But it's a drag to go all the way south to Sharm only to have to double back up north along the coast.'

'So what are the other two routes?'

'I've only done one. But the Bedouin told me of another. If you head south from Na'ama Bay and follow the coastline, eventually you'll reach Ras al-Jizra. There must be a track, though I've read somewhere that there's also a scientific reserve here and it's illegal to trespass.'

'Sounds risky,' I offered.

'Yeah, maybe. But I took the high road.'

'The high road?'

'Yeah. I went over the mountain pass via the oasis of Ein Durba.'

'Where?' asked Lucy.

'Ein Durba.' Rose leaned back, shut her eyes and a soothing smirk washed across her face, triggering her two cute dimples. 'It's not marked on the map. It's a small goat-farming hamlet of Bedouin that lies in an oasis high in the hills.' She touched a vague spot on the packet with her match.

'Here. There's no signpost on the road, but when you get down there, maybe fifty kilometres short of Sharm, you turn off onto a track and head toward the coast. After an hour or so, you'll reach the oasis of Ein Durba. From there, it's a few hours by camel. The track meanders down the mountain into a wadi and then onto the coastal plain. Then you just keep following the headland . . . '

'Until what?'

'Until you reach the end of the road. You'll know when you've arrived in Ras al-Jizra.'

'How?'

'Trust me. You'll know.'

CHAPTER TWENTY-EIGHT

AHMED, OUR TAXI DRIVER, was wearing traditional Bedouin attire: an ankle-length deep-blue jelabiyeh and a white keffiyeh wrapped around his head to protect his scalp from the sun and his eyes from flying sand particles.

'Ahalan wa sahalan,' he greeted Lucy and me, revealing a mouthful of rusty, nicotine-stained, crooked teeth that would not have looked misplaced inside a camel's mouth.

'Dahab?'

'No.' It was clear that there was no way that I could begin to explain how to get to Ras al-Jizra, let alone Ein Durba. I needed a map.

'Nuweiba?'

'No.'

'Sharm?'

We shook our heads again.

Ahmed moved his head from side to side. 'Wallah, mish faahim – I don't understand,' he said despondently.

Then he thought he'd cracked it. 'Santa Katherina, aiwa?'

Our facial expressions left him perplexed.

He repositioned his keffiyeh and threw his hands up in the air, admitting defeat. 'Wallah . . .'

Finally, in pidgin Arabic and with the help of a map drawn in the sand, I narrowed down that we wanted to go past Dahab but before Sharm. Ahmed reluctantly agreed, adding that it may require Allah's assistance to find our destination.

'Wallah . . . mush mimkin – no problem. Inshallah – God willing.'

We pass through the last checkpoint at the Taba border and motor down the ruler-straight tarmac road through the desert. In the distance, the road seems to bake, evaporating on the horizon like a mirage.

Since the return of the Sinai to Egypt in 1982, much of the coastline between Taba and Nuweiba has been developed with flamboyant Egyptian castle-hotels adjacent to nondescript Bedouin shacks. The architectural contrast is conspicuous for its lack of planning.

Farther down the road, the desert begins to reveal itself – Bedouin shepherds, goats and camels start to appear in the wadis. They are the consummate nomads, eking out a living from the parched land, moving on when time and tide call it a day.

Ahmed chain-smokes Cleopatra cigarettes. He is a man of few words, though he is not short of speed and he attacks the few hairpin bends with alacrity. His Hebrew is as limited as our Arabic.

We pass the port of Nuweiba, from which Rose and I departed on our voyage to Petra two years previously, and approach one of several checkpoints, manned by Egyptian soldiers. A road runs off into the mountains towards Santa Katherina, home to Jebel Musa, believed to be Mount Sinai, the site where Moses received the Ten Commandments.

Nowadays, you can reach the summit of the holiest mountain on earth via a camel path that zigzags up to the peak, where you'll find a small mosque and a chapel – as well as a Bedouin selling Coca-Cola at grossly inflated prices. Nestled spectacularly below Mount Sinai is the monastery of Saint Katherine, a walled compound believed to be where the Burning Bush is located. 'Santa,' grunts Ahmed, pointing a long strip of ash on the end of his cigarette in the direction of the inland road.

We continue south past Dahab and, with the aid of a map we had bought in Nuweiba, we follow the road inland, searching for the unmarked turnoff that would lead us over the mountain pass to the oasis of Ein Durba and down to Ras al-Jizra. Ahmed slows down to 100 kilometres, trawling the empty wilderness for a clue.

He finally points to a solitary Bedouin goatskin tent, about fifty metres off road, before stopping.

Here we meet Hamad and wait in the shade of his tent until a ride to the oasis of Ein Durba arrives. We are gambling on supplies being ferried in: water, goats, camels, anything. It could be hours, days, even weeks.

Hamad looks like an elderly man, though I suspect the weather has taken its toll on his skin. He speaks no English but manages to converse a little in Hebrew – testament to the fifteen years the Israelis were here. Hamad's wife, cloaked in a black embroidered burqa (a veil worn to cover women's faces), with only a razor-thin slit for her eyes to reveal her identity, offers us sweet tea.

Hamad, meanwhile, is attaching bags of grains and jerry cans of water to his camel, negotiating the art of fine balance. His three semi-naked children are enthralled by our presence, and Lucy entertains them with a bottle of bubbles, which they chase under the piercing desert sun.

It's not too long before a battered old pick-up truck pulls in. Word seems to spread with the wind in this vast wilderness. We climb on the back, among sacks of root vegetables and decidedly dangerous cans of petrol, and brace ourselves for a bumpy ride. As we head off, the kids chase us through clouds of dust, laughing and yelling until one trips over and cries.

The dirt track twists across a flat wadi for the best part of an hour and then rises gently up a mountain pass. 'Ein Durba,' yells the driver from inside the cabin, pointing in the direction of the honey-coloured horizon where the green tips of palm trees rock gently in the breeze.

Over the ridge, the panorama opens out to disclose a hamlet of houses surrounded by barbed-wire fences nestled among the palm trees. A few goats skip across the ridge, their bleats drowned out by the truck's engine. Several hundred Bedouin seem to live here; the only remotely modern-looking building is a school. The rest of the homes are a hodgepodge of mud-brick dwellings, tin corrugated shacks, cinder-block and palm-frond shelters annexed to makeshift hardboard extensions.

We meet some of Hamad's family and are welcomed in traditional Bedouin style. Mahmoud, Hamad's nephew, is our host, a tall, lean man whose white jelabiyeh remains remarkably spotless despite the dusty surroundings. He only speaks broken Hebrew, but understands most of what we say. The embers on the fire murmur as he throws more wood on. His two daughters are busy kneading bread.

'Ras al-Jizra,' I say, pointing to the east.

'Aiwa,' he mutters as he uses the bottom of his jelabiyeh to fan the flames of the fire. 'Bukra el Ras al-Jizra – tomorrow to Ras al-Jizra. Inshallah – God willing.'

'Stage one,' I say to Lucy, forefinger in the air.

'One more leg to go. Tomorrow we'll reach the end of Rose's road,' she replies.

Mahmoud invites us to eat at sundown. Judging by the animal lying destitute near the fire, we will be eating chicken. He begins to spread the embers and digs a deep, half-metre trench in the sand. Then he lines the bed of the trench with embers, followed by the chicken, which has been doused in herbs and wrapped in foil. He places more embers over the chicken and fills the remainder of the trench with sand.

We are both vegetarian, though there is as much chance of an alternative vegetarian menu here in Ein Durba as there is of a spa suite and cable television.

'Kwayes – OK,' says Mahmoud, clapping his hands clean. He points to the sand, under which lies our dinner. 'Madfouneh.' I speculate that madfouneh is either the Arabic name for the dish he just made – or the type of sub-sand oven he has just constructed.

Two hours later we taste the sand-oven-baked chicken.

'Sachteen – bon appetite,' says Mahmoud.

'Shukran – thank you,' we reply.

'Al hamdu lillah – praise be to God.'

I avoid the embarrassment of rejecting the food by eating Lucy's portion and mine. And, I admit, it is truly delicious. Lucy eats pita bread, tahina and salad. We spend the rest of the night drinking sweet tea and more sweet tea, before reclining inside our sleeping bags adjacent to the smouldering fire.

Immediately, we are star-struck by the view: it's raining stars. They seem to be falling out of the sky in pairs. Lucy snuggles into a comfortable position, eyes glued to the sky. She is beaming. Sinai is where we first fell in love. It brings back magical memories.

The babble of goats and chickens wakes us early, and a Bedouin elder who speaks not a word of Hebrew, let alone English, greets us.

'Sabah al-kheir – good morning.'

'Sabah al-noor,' I reply, rubbing my eyes.

He sits himself down and tends to the ashes of the fire as the sun rises slowly, yawning the day into action. Mahmoud arrives and explains that he's found some locals with a pick-up truck who will drive us down to Ras al-Jizra for a small amount of money. Otherwise it's a long haul on his camels.

Lucy is keen for camels. Despite being short of padding on our posteriors, we decide that we have come this far and the final furlong merits the authentic approach. Mahmoud loads our bags on the gangly animals and we soon disappear into the distance, our shadows inching across the empty desert.

After a couple of bum-busting hours, Mahmoud begins collecting twigs – a signal, we soon learn, that he is going to prepare a small fire to boil some sweet tea. Two Bedouin kids, garbed in mini jelabiyehs and without shoes, sprint towards us out of nowhere, waving their hands and clearly rejoicing that strangers have arrived to break the monotony of an average day in the desert. They exchange words with Mahmoud and we approach a small cluster of palms, under which a small goatskin tent is perched. A Bedouin woman, wearing an elaborately designed colourful burqa, waves her hand, beckoning us in.

Somehow, there always seem to be embers of a fire smouldering inside a Bedouin tent. I've been invited to drink tea with many Bedouin and I can never recall having to watch them set and light a brand new fire. They seem to keep it going, a bit like the ner tamid (the eternal flame) that flickers above the Aron HaKodesh (the Holy Ark where the Torah scrolls are kept) in every synagogue. Her nose is pierced with the largest golden ring I have ever seen connected to a nostril.

We spend several hours there, shaded from the heat of the sun, drinking yet more sweet tea before we press on. Soon the sky begins to turn dusty pink. Our camels yank themselves up the final ridge, their lanky legs at times seem to be on the verge of collapse. The trail runs along the ridge edge before rising slightly.

'Ras al-Jizra,' announces Mahmoud, 'is around the next corner.'

There, below us, is a deserted headland, beyond which lies a deep blue lagoon in the most virginal, unspoilt surroundings. Only a short distance by foot or camel north of the modern Egyptian coastal resort of Sharm el-Sheikh, it was worlds apart in every other sense.

A straggle of goatskin tents and bamboo huts lines the lagoon – almost a carbon copy, I figure, of what Dahab would have looked like when it was first established. The moon is slowly beginning to rise and dapples soft light on the edge of the water, where small waves gently press against the shore, leaving a trace of their watermark before receding.

'Listen to the silence,' I say to Lucy.

Lucy is grinning. 'Mmmm . . . Now I know what Rose meant by the end of the road.'

CHAPTER TWENTY-NINE

WE SPENT several days revelling in the beauty of Ras al-Jizra, swimming in the cove, frolicking in the rock pools and filtering out the dirt that had tarnished our minds over the last few months.

Then we started the long haul home, leaving only a crisscross of our footprints in the sand, soon to be erased by the tide. It would be a twenty-four-hour trip door-to-door if all modes of transport – hitch to Ein Durba, taxi to Taba, minibus to Eilat, bus to Tel Aviv – ran back-to-back. In all likelihood, though, it would take much longer.

There is great commotion at Ein Durba when we arrive. All the camels are gathered together in the village centre and the locals are busy decorating some of them with frills, embroidered saddle covers and bells.

I seek out Mahmoud amid the crowd. 'What's happening?'

'The camel race is tomorrow. To celebrate Moulid an-Nabi . . . you know . . . the birthday of the Prophet.'

Perplexed by his enthusiasm, I think about asking for clarification. Camel race? It sounds like an oxymoron to me. His camels crawled across the desert to Ras al-Jizra, at times wheezing in fits that suggested they might keel over and die there and then. And every time we camel trekked anywhere in Sinai, our Bedouin shepherd walked barefoot in the sand . . . ahead of the camel.

But who am I to dispute Mahmoud? And why would we turn down the offer to attend a camel race?

Mahmoud explains that the camel race is an annual affair. Once a year, members of the fourteen Bedouin tribes, comprising around 50,000 Bedouin, gather from across the peninsula. Each clan selects its best camel to race against the others across twenty kilometres in a flat wadi. The venue alternates each year.

Mahmoud is clearly excited. 'You must come. You must.'

The race this year is to be run to the north and since we're headed in that direction, we figure we've got nothing to lose. In any case, the very notion of a camel race intrigues us.

'Count us in.'

'Kwayes. Al hamdu lillah.'

The gathering begins early, not long after daybreak. It is cold and small pockets of Bedouin, wrapped up in robes against the elements, are warming themselves around smouldering fires in an open wadi somewhere between Dahab and Nuweiba.

Camels appear out of the morning mist, led by their Bedouin jockeys. Some are decorated, like the ones from Ein Durba, with embroidered trimmings and decorative pompoms; others are naked, not even a saddle between their humps.

Hooting horns signal the arrival of tribes from elsewhere in the desert. The atmosphere is warming up. It's a festival.

It becomes increasingly evident to Lucy that she stands out in the crowd. 'There's not one other woman here,' she mutters under her breath. But she feels safe among these people. They are genuine, warm and hospitable. And it's not the first time that she's been in male Bedouin company.

They greet one another like long-lost brothers, their cheeks touching twice, maybe three times. 'Salaam aleikum – peace be with you.'

'Aleikum salaam,' comes the traditional response.

Bedouin time is a far cry from Western time. They generally don't wear watches, following the sun and the moon as their time clock. Punctuality is not sacred among these desert nomads.

Long after greetings have been exchanged and sweet tea and bitter coffee has been passed around, huddles of keffiyehs begin gesticulating, debating, laughing and squabbling.

Their body language suggests something other than the normal conversations held among brothers. Mahmoud confirms our suspicion.

'They're gambling, placing bets on the camels, arguing over odds and exchanging money.'

Here, mid-wadi, mid-desert, mid-morning, ancient nomads are engaging in this vice. It is both amusing and distressing.

Gradually, slowly, things get moving and the camels assemble behind a haphazard line drawn by a stick in the sand.

Hamad swings into action. 'Come, come now.'

The sound of a horn splits the desert air. Suddenly, these unwieldy, cumbersome, four-legged creatures hurl themselves into action. Their long necks stretch out ahead of them, their gangling legs desperately playing catch-up as they scamper awkwardly across the sand.

Squashed into the back of a Toyota pick-up truck, we are at least twenty keffiyeh-clad Bedouin strong, burning down the highway chasing camels that look like their legs are about to get tied in a knot. We are screaming, shouting, waving our hands at our jockey.

'Ya'allah! Ya'allah! – Come on! Come on!'

But he is impossible to identify. And all the camels blend into the camel-coloured desert, churning sand particles behind them as their feet scramble to lurch forward. And all the Bedouin are similarly dressed so that, in the prevailing sand storm, it's difficult to make out who is winning.

The jockeys whip their camels, urging them on even faster. Now they are flying at such speed that even the truck drivers have difficulty keeping up with them. There must be at least fifty vehicles in convoy all lurching at dangerously high speeds down the highway. One sharp bend and we'll all spill over the edge.

But that's not what troubles me most. Yes, we are driving at terrifying speeds. Our driver, like the others, has one eye on the road and the other on the camel race. An accident could turn the peaceful desert carnival into carnage. That doesn't trouble me too much either, though it does register some concern. What bothers me most is that our high-speed convoy is travelling not in one lane, but in both. Anyone attempting to approach from the opposite direction would meet a wall of pick-up trucks ferrying hundreds of Bedouin.

The locals do not appear remotely concerned for their lives – or for the lives of anyone approaching from the opposite direction. Perhaps someone has blocked the road at the end of the race. Or perhaps they have left it all in Allah's hands.

'Inshallah,' I say to Lucy, unable to assuage her fear.

She is desperate for a way off this joy ride, but, as the camels go faster, so too does the convoy. Mahmoud and his tribe are all screaming madly for their camel, waving their hands vigorously, whistling and shouting encouragement to their jockey. Finally, finally, we see the finishing line. The drivers reach for the anchors and brake sharply, sending scores of Bedouin clinging to the rails.

Our jockey does not win. But no one from Mahmoud's clan appears too disenchanted. It seems everyone is a winner today. Celebrations erupt. Food and drinks are being prepared around smouldering fires. Rababs (fiddles), ouds (lutes) and darboukas (drums) provide musical accompaniments.

It wasn't until we were back inside Israel the following day that we began to appreciate the uniqueness of what we had witnessed. There, on page two of the daily paper, was a colour photograph of camels charging across the desert. The jockeys looked like they were holding on for dear life. Their bodies were bucked rodeo-like in mid-air, their keffiyehs flapping in the wind.

The photograph told a story not often associated with these desert nomads – nor their camels. In the background, at closer inspection, a trail of pick-up trucks weighed down with scores of jelabiyeh-clad Bedouin could be made out. If it had been enlarged several hundred per cent it would have revealed the only two people without jelabiyehs.

CHAPTER THIRTY

WE RETURNED from Sinai sun kissed, batteries recharged, minds cleansed. The government had changed, but the country was still the same. Or so it seemed. Summer was beginning to kick in and, with the mercury rising in Tel Aviv, we decided a week or so later to head for the cooler climes of Jerusalem for the day.

We had run out of supplies of halva (sweet, chewy slabs of flaky sesame seed) and fresh Turkish coffee ground with hell (cardamom). The opportunity to restock our cupboards provided a good excuse for wandering aimlessly around the fragranced alleyways of the Old City's Arab souk.

If there's one window through which you can see Israelis, warts and all, it is the central bus station in Tel Aviv. Look closely at the queue for the bus – when it is not a push-and-shove affair – and you'll see a line-up of society: Ashkenazi and Sephardi, ultra-Orthodox and ultra-secular, Jew and Arab, Roman Catholic and Greek Orthodox, Ethiopian and Circassian, sabra and immigrant, soldier and draft dodger, Druze and Bedouin, kibbutznik and urban rat-racer.

Here at the bus station is one of the few occasions where you can take a snapshot photo of the real face of Israel in the harsh light of day.

In Tel Aviv, the relatively new structure, alleged to be the largest of its kind in the Middle East, is located in a seedy, impoverished neighbourhood south of the city centre. But it is more than just a commuter terminal: it is part shopping mall, part flea market, part food fiesta and part social venue. Its predecessor was an outdoor affair, surrounded by narrow market streets where moneychangers rubbed shoulders with pimps, pushers and prostitutes. No more.

The sixth floor, from where intercity buses depart, is perhaps the most animated part of the station. Bagels and borekas, shwarmas, pizzas and pretzels are all on sale in large quantities. Highly-strung salesmen flog bootleg CDs to passersby. Soldiers, wearing their olive fatigues, look constantly fatigued. They are either on their way to base or on their way home. They have an understandable and unrivalled capacity to sleep on buses from the moment they sit down, clutching their submachine guns like teddy bears because they can be court-martialled and jailed for leaving their guns unattended.

At street level, a shopping-mall atmosphere prevails. Security personnel – lurking behind RayBan sunglasses, earpiece in the ear, armed for action – scrutinise those who come and go. After the spate of suicide bombs, it felt like Fort Knox. At other times, you barely feel their presence. But, they are always there policing the shadows. And with over one and a half million national bus passengers per day, over 20 per cent of the population, security is on high alert, always.

Inevitably, with such a turnover of people, there's usually a commotion over a hafetz hashud, a suspicious object. The drill is fairly standard: security is alerted; the area is cordoned off; the bomb squad arrives; they survey the object, usually uncovering a bag of pretzels or dirty laundry. On the odd occasion where it is more serious, the object is detonated in a controlled fashion. Then life returns to normal and the voice over the loudspeaker reminds passengers never to leave their bags unattended.

A host of taxis lines up just outside the terminal. The drivers, a Mafioso of sorts, seemingly operating in a cartel, await passengers. They drink coffee while ploughing through kilos of sunflower seeds, delicately snapping the shell in between their front teeth, snaring the seed within and then discarding its case in one swift motion that takes a lifetime for a novice to master. The pavement beneath them is carpeted in empty shells and cigarette butts.

Across the road are berths where stretch taxis and minibuses are parked. This service is known locally as a sherut, a communal taxi that runs on the same route as the bus, carries seven passengers for a similar fare but only departs when full. It is a wonderful, low-risk way to travel the country.

Drivers try to lure the stream of passengers heading for the bus terminal.

'Alo! Alo!'

'Last seat to Jerusalem! Last seat!'

In light of the bus bombs, we almost always travelled intercity by sherut. We didn't even enter the bus station for a while. The time it took to wait for the sherut to fill up was a small price to pay for the security of knowing we'd arrive alive.

I didn't notice him at first. I was absorbed behind the newspaper, trawling the opinion pages for a hint of reason or rationale amid the political chaos and confusion under the new prime minister who was already foot-dragging with regards to the peace process. A couple sat in the back row. We were in the middle. I was penned in by the window on one side and Lucy on the other. A gaunt-looking ultra-Orthodox man approached, his wide-brimmed, black felt hat and the black-and-white pinstriped coat indicating that he may be a member of the Neturei Karta sect.

They are a curious breed, largely based in Mea She'arim, an ultra-Orthodox enclave of Jerusalem that clings religiously to the Old World. Virulently anti-Zionist, they do not believe in the modern state and therefore do not vote in elections, celebrate Independence Day, serve in the army or, in some extreme cases, pay taxes. Many religious and secular Zionists despise them as traitors (a mutual sentiment), and there are even elements that support the plight of the Palestinians in the hope that it will bring an end to the treasonous modern state. They believe that the coming of the Messiah will herald the dawn of Israel.

They do not stand in silence on Holocaust Memorial Day or Memorial Day to Israel's Fallen Soldiers, in part because they follow the two main fast days (known as Tisha b'Av and the Tenth of Tevet, the fourth month in the Hebrew calendar) to commemorate all disasters, especially the destruction of the First and Second Temples, and in part because standing silently at the sound of a siren is seen by them as a non-Jewish form of commemoration. Instead, they fast, recite lamentations and prayers, repent and study the Torah.

In addition, the date of Holocaust Remembrance Day was selected on the Hebrew anniversary of the Warsaw Ghetto uprising (19 April 1943). The government specifically chose the day that, in the face of indescribable adversity, the Jews took on the Nazis, when the triumph of the human spirit rose above the carnage of the camps. However, many haredim see this commemorative day as insensitive to those Jews who went 'like sheep to the slaughter' and did not fight back. According to the haredim, those who did not revolt, but maintained their faith in God, were as heroic as those who waged war against the Nazis.

Jewish, ultra-Orthodox, anti-Zionist and living in Israel, they almost defy definition and seem, at face value, to be a contradiction in terms.* In a sense, they are neither insiders nor outsiders, but outsiders on the inside praying feverishly for the Messiah to redeem Israel.

'Do you mind?' he asked in Yiddish, looking at me but pointing to Lucy. Speaking Hebrew would give tacit consent to the modern state that they so oppose, so they prefer speaking Yiddish, the language of their ancestors in Europe. He was stroking his beard, the elasticity of his hairs causing it to spring up and down. Although I didn't understand much of his language, I had been in such situations before. I started to swap places with Lucy.

He, like all ultra-Orthodox Jews, could not sit next to a woman he did not know. In fact, he is not supposed to look at a woman he does not know, let alone communicate with her. The laws of contact between these God-fearing Jewish men and women are

* Not all ultra-Orthodox Jews are anti-Zionist; many are simply non-Zionist. Many others participate in politics and use their people power to pursue their own goals.

strict. So much so that the signs at the entrances to the Mea She'arim compound in Jerusalem issue a strict warning: 'We do not tolerate people passing through our streets improperly dressed'. Violate this at your peril.

Lucy once told me about the time, many years ago, when she was going through a late-teens religious phase. She was studying at a rabbinic seminary in Safed (known as Tzfat in Hebrew), the home of Kabbalah (Jewish mysticism) in the Upper Galilee.* It is a hilltop town at 800 metres above sea level, and it can get bitterly cold in winter. Lucy was standing next to a heater trying to keep warm. All of a sudden, her skirt caught on fire.

In a mad panic she tore the flaming skirt off her body, threw it on the ground and began stamping on it. So there she was, standing in the middle of a room surrounded by rabbis and other ultra-Orthodox men, wearing nothing but stockings. Aghast, they immediately hid their faces from the sight of her semi-naked body. She was livid that none of them came to her rescue, and stormed out of the seminary in disgust. Unsurprisingly, she has never returned to Orthodoxy. Thankfully, she did return to Israel.

The laws of physical contact are even more rigid. When an ultra-Orthodox woman begins menstruating her husband cannot touch her, let alone sleep with her, because, according to Jewish law, she is considered 'impure' until seven days after the end of her period. In the Orthodox world, the man and the woman are only allowed to engage in sexual intimacy once they are married. And a woman must confirm the dates of her cycle to the rabbinate in order that she does not get married when she is menstruating.

Due to the hegemony the Orthodox wield over matters of personal status, specifically marriage and divorce, there is no civil marriage in Israel. Conservative or Liberal Jews can either get married by their own rabbis and then go through the Orthodox formality in order to be registered, or those who wish to avoid the rabbinate have to fly to Cyprus for the affair. And men must grant

* Kabbalists believe that each letter of the Torah has a numeric value, and that there are secret messages encoded within the script.

their wives a divorce; if he refuses, she cannot remarry and any children she may have in the future will be considered illegitimate. These are some of the rules and regulations that dictate the behaviour of these God-fearing Jews.

Live and let live, I say. I hold Lucy's hand and it suddenly dawns upon me that she is in fact menstruating. A smile breaks across my face, the irony of the situation almost forcing a giggle.

'What?' asks Lucy.

'Nothing,' I lie.

We fill up without delay and begin the fifty-minute journey to the Holy City of Jerusalem. With no prompt, money begins to exchange hands. I tap the shoulder of the man in the front passenger seat and pass him twenty shekels.

'Pa'amayim – twice.' Seconds later I get a tap on my shoulder and money is passed from back to front.

'Who gave me twenty?' asks the driver, as he hands back change that is then passed through the cab to the back seat. For five minutes, money is passed to and fro; change is returned along the line. It's a quaint affair, and there's a bond that is experienced on every journey. But, most of all, it feels safe. A bus carrying fifty people is a much bigger target than a car carrying seven.

We enter the Ayalon, the main highway out of Tel Aviv, and head inland past citrus orchards, the scent of blossom hanging in the breeze.

The sweet smell is short-lived, however. In the distance, behind the orchards, a mountain of garbage towers high into the sky. Flocks of birds circle ominously above, awaiting their moment to swoop into the lucky dip as trucks dump more waste on the landfill. Tel Aviv's unsightly dump came into existence long after the Land of Milk and Honey was described.

Allegedly, this area used to belong to an Arab village called Hir, meaning good. But local Israelis refer to it as the Hiriyah, derived in Hebrew from harah, meaning shit. Looking at this blight on the landscape, it is easy to understand why. Shit is an understatement. After 1948 the area was used as a transit camp for new Jewish immigrants until they were resettled. The area then lay empty and, since it was outside the city, which was growing by the day, it soon became its dumping ground. The dump then became a mound and is now a hill rising some 100 metres – an unfortunate landmark that, until recently, greeted every tourist arriving or departing from Tel Aviv.

A signpost announces that Ben-Gurion airport is approaching, as is Kfar Habad, a Hassidic enclave of 5000 or so Lubavitcher Jews that resembles an eighteenth-century Eastern European town transplanted to the Middle East. They follow their own leader, Rabbi Menachem Mendel Schneerson, who was, in the eyes of his flock, the Messiah. But he died in 1994, aged ninety-two. To this day, some still cling to the hope that he is the Messiah.

Eucalyptus trees line the roadside at Latrun, strategically located on a ridge between Jerusalem and Tel Aviv, enabling those in control of this area to blockade the road to Jerusalem. In the 1948 War of Independence it was a major battleground as the Arabs tried to seal off the city from the rest of the country.

The plain begins to give way to undulating terrain dotted with fig trees and olive groves, dates and carobs. It then rises and dips in crests and troughs as the approach to Jerusalem beckons.

Strewn along this part of the highway are the charred, rusted remains of armoured supply vehicles that tried to defeat the Arab siege of Jerusalem and keep this road, the only supply line into the city, open during the 1948 war. They remain as a chilling memorial to those who lost their lives in the battle for Israel's independence.

And so begins the final, snaking climb to the summit. As the road corkscrews its way up and around the pine-forested mountainside, it feels like the last steep incline before the Gates of Heaven.

Beyond the final right-hand bend is the first vista of Jerusalem, a city of golden stone atop the mountain. (Under the British Mandate, planning guidelines stipulated that facades of all buildings be built from Jerusalem stone.) 'Welcome to Jerusalem,' proclaims the flower arrangement set in a garden at the gateway to the city. National and municipal flags flank the boulevard entrance, fluttering in the breeze.

We have arrived. From the profanity of Sin City – where prostitutes work the night, crime and crack work the streets and scantily-clad women tan their already bronzed bodies on the beach – to the sanctity of the Holy City where the psalm 'If I forget thee, O Jerusalem, let my right hand forget her cunning', whispered throughout 2000 years of exile, still murmurs in the twilight wind.

It is, as Yehuda Amichai, the capital's unofficial 'poet laureate', once wrote, 'the only city in the world where the right to vote is granted even to the dead'.

CHAPTER THIRTY-ONE

GOD IS ONLINE. If you think that sounds absurd, think of the only place on the planet where an umbilical cord connects heaven and earth.

Jerusalem. Al-Quds – the Holy in Arabic; Yerushalayim – City of Peace in Hebrew. Impressive names in principle. But in practice, there is little these days that remains holy here, and peace, sadly, continues to elude this sacred spot. According to the Orthodox, peace will only prevail when the Messiah arrives on the Mount of Olives, the largest and oldest Jewish cemetery in the world, and enters the Old City through the Golden Gate to the sound of the shofar to redeem the Chosen People and rebuild the Temple.

For now though, this stunning old city, whose camel-coloured walls shelter some 30,000 Jewish, Christian and Muslim souls, is the most contested 2.6 square kilometres on earth. No other city has been held hostage to history like Jerusalem. No other place has witnessed the wars, battles, sieges and uprisings that this city has. Historians count twenty sieges and two exiles to date in over 3000 years. Jerusalem has been conquered by the Israelites, Persians, Greeks, Hasmoneans, Romans, Byzantines, Arabs, Crusaders, Mamelukes, Ottomans, British and Israelis. Peace is not on her side.

Lucy and I enter through the Jaffa Gate and amble down the Arab souk, dodging the barrage of vendors as we weave through the human traffic on our way to the Western Wall.

'God online?' quizzes Lucy.

'Yeah. You can visit the Gates of Heaven on the web,' I answer.

'Let me guess . . . www.holyone.blessed.be.he?'

'Not quite. Messages can be sent via www.kotelkam.com. They print them out and deliver them to the Western Wall. Then they scrunch them up and insert them in between the cracks.'

'What if you don't have email?'

'No problem. God's fax line has been up and running for years. Jerusalem 561 2222.'

Lucy's facial expression is somewhere between aghast and impressed. 'So you're telling me that people actually email and fax messages to God?'

'Yeah. I read about it in the paper the other day. Bezeq [Israel's national telephone company] says it receives around one hundred faxes a day. That's 600 a week or . . . around 30,000 messages a year. That's assuming they don't operate on Shabbat.'

'That's a hell of a lot of bits of paper.'

'It's a colossal wall.'

'True, but it's no Great Wall of China. One day there won't be any more room.'

We stop to poke around one of the stores down the main drag of the souk. It's full of bronze finjans (coffee pots), nargillehs (water pipes), worry beads, keffiyehs and oriental garments. And T-shirts, including one with the words 'I got stoned on the West Bank' scrawled across it.

Lucy is modelling a long, flowing embroidered skirt in the mirror. 'D'you reckon that the Prophet Mohammed has a fax line at the Ka'aba in Mecca?' she asks, trying to wind me up.

'I'm serious. God *is* online.'

'And Buddha has been spotted lurking around some Internet cafes in Bangkok and Kathmandu.'

'I'm not going to argue. We don't even need snail mail. We live here. But if you lived overseas, at least you'd have the option.'

She decides against the skirt (I never even flirted with the T-shirt) and we wander down towards the end of David Street, stopping to buy some pistachio baklawah from a vendor whose tiny store comprises huge round trays of sweets that look like they guarantee root canal treatment: dozens of varieties of baklawah,

Turkish delight, myriad types of halva, kanafeh (syrup-drenched vermicelli topped with nuts) and others I could not identify.

I'm still obsessed by the idea that God is online. 'The irony of it is that the rabbis recently issued an edict banning their flock from using the Internet in case it leads them astray.'

'So, you can fax a message but you can't email it?'

'Yep.'

'That's absurd.'

'This is Israel.'

We stop to buy some freshly ground Turkish coffee. At the end of David Street, we take a right and weave our way along the alley-way towards the security checkpoint on the steps above the Western Wall plaza.

In front of us is the Western Wall. Just above us, to our left, is a massive yeshivah with six everlasting lights on the roof along-side the word Yizkor – he shall remember, a solemn tribute to the six million Jews who perished in the Holocaust, who died still in exile, who never lived to see the Western Wall return to Jewish sovereignty after 2000 years. Yizkor is also the name for the memorial prayer for the dead. This is where history and memory converge. Just standing there, I feel saturated by them both.

Thirty or so metres above the Wall, the Dome of the Rock, the architectural *piece de resistance* of the Old City, glistens in the sunlight. Adjacent is the silver-domed Al-Aqsa mosque. And just behind us is the grey dome of the Church of the Holy Sepulchre.

Here, at the intersection of monotheism – the focal point of 1.8 billion Christians, 1.2 billion Muslims and some 13 million Jews – you can fill your soul three times over every weekend: Friday for Muslims, Saturday for Jews and Sunday for Christians.

It is within this square kilometre that the prayers led by muezzins, chazzans (cantors) and priests, and sermons delivered by rabbis, imams and ministers converge in a discordant Tower-of-Babel-like medley. Harmony eludes them, their notes merging tentatively on the fringes of the breeze, before gently fading with the light.

But, for some kindred spirits, the dream of Jerusalem becomes a nightmare and they find themselves consumed by the sanctity of the place. They soon become its casualties, believing they are Jesus, Mary or the Messiah himself.

In 1982, a medical syndrome was diagnosed for those overcome by this sacred spot. Yair Bar El, from Buenos Aires, named it the 'Jerusalem Syndrome' and casualties are treated in the Kfar Shaul Psychiatric Hospital on the outskirts of the city. Allegedly, some 200 people a year snap under the emotional weight of this city.

At the disputed Temple Mount/Al-Haram ash-Sharif, the crucible of the conflict, Jews and Muslims lay allegiance to one God. For Jews, HaKotel HaMa'aravi, the Western Wall, is the last remaining rampart belonging to the Second Temple built by Herod and destroyed by the Romans in AD 70, where the Holy of Holies, the most sacred spot on their earth, once stood; for Muslims it is where Mohammed ascended on his night flight to heaven. This spot is the epicentre of the earthquake that sends fault lines tremoring throughout Israel, the Palestinian Territories, the Middle East and beyond.

The last time I had been on the Temple Mount was back in 1987, when I was hitchhiking around the country with Freddy and Frankie, just before the messianists of Kiryat Arba duped us into a tour at Jerusalem bus station and then tried to brainwash us.

It was just before the Intifada broke out. I recall the sheer size of the place; the detail of the intricate mosaics and Koranic scriptures that surround the Dome of the Rock. Even the rock itself, like those gargantuan stones in the Western Wall, was dauntingly impressive.

Israel has maintained sovereignty over this area since it was recaptured in 1967, although the day-to-day administration of the area is supervised by the Muslim Waqf (Islamic religious authority). Secular Jews are allowed to visit the site, but they are not allowed to pray there. So we simply walk around the giant esplanade, gawking at the sheer beauty of the Islamic buildings.

We part ways. I take a cardboard yarmulke and enter the men's area; Lucy decides not to go to the women's section, separated from the men's section by a mechitzah (a partition that ensures that men and women do not come into contact during worship), and stays hovering around the back of the plaza.

Lucy has only ever touched the Western Wall once – in 1989. It freaked her out, the weight of her Jewish ancestry, genealogy, history and heritage proving too emotional to shoulder. Perhaps she suffers from a mild bout of Jerusalem Syndrome. If we Jews had to compress our territory into a 100-metre square, this would be it. Geographically, it is the hub of Jewish Jerusalem; symbolically it represents the heart of our nation's heritage.

I haven't written a message to scrunch in between the cracks of the titanic stones. I can do that by email from Tel Aviv if I really desire. In any case, I am not religious. I am not even Orthodox, let alone ultra-Orthodox. But I am still magnetised by this wall of stones and moss. It has nothing to do with religion, but with a connection to my ancestors, my family, my people, my heritage, my history.

Hundreds, perhaps thousands, of Jewish pilgrims from the four corners of the earth gaze up at the wall in awe and wonder. Some have glazed eyes, tears rolling down their cheeks. Theirs are tears of joy, tears of pain, tears of hope, tears of shame.

Their tears are my tears too: tears of joy at our return home from exile; pain that the wall is all that remains of the Temple; hope that one day peace will prevail; and shame because we know, in the basement of our souls, that war begets no winners, that our children are the ultimate losers and we, Jews and Palestinians, may be writing their epitaph before they are even born.

I return to where Lucy is waiting and we make our way back through the Jewish Quarter. 'Do you think we'll ever share Jerusalem with the Palestinians?' she asks me.

'Not today or tomorrow. But when both sides realise that neither can win the battle outright, then maybe. The question that remains is, what price are we willing to pay? How many more parents, Jewish and Palestinian, must bury their children before peace prevails? Their extremists will never give up their demands; ours will never relinquish our birthright.'

Whenever people talk about the competing rights of the two peoples, I always get reminded of a Hassidic tale my father used to tell us when my brother, sister and I fought:

Two men come to a rabbi with a dispute. He listens to one and says, 'You're right'. Then the second man presents his case. The rabbi nods, strokes his beard and says, 'You know, you're right'. At this point the rabbi's wife interjects, 'How's that possible? They can't both be right.' To which the rabbi replies, 'You know, you're right!'

Likewise the Palestinians and Israelis, I say to Lucy. 'It's a case of right versus right. Surely the only solution is to accept that both sides are right and must be accommodated within an agreement that allows each to honour their "right".'

Lucy is amused but not impressed. 'If only people could see it in those simplistic terms.'

Lucy's grandparents used to live in a suburb called Yemin Moshe, one of the first neighbourhoods built outside the Old City walls, and we enjoy wandering around, wondering what it must have been like here when almost everyone lived within the Old City walls. Until the mid-eighteenth century, the Old City was the full extent of Jerusalem, and its gates were closed each night from sundown to sunrise to keep out bandits. This is where Lucy's father was born and grew up before moving to Australia. Technically, he is a Palestinian, since he was born before the creation of the state of Israel in 1948, when the territory, then ruled by the British, was known as Palestine.

These days it is a quaint, tranquil neighbourhood nestled beneath a windmill alongside rose-scented gardens. We amble through the neighbouring Mishkenot Sha'ananim, aptly translated as 'Dwellings of Tranquillity'. It is a suburb of narrow alleyways and lanes inhabited by artisans and artists, where magenta bougainvillea cascades down ancient walls, a grape vine winds its way around a pergola and pomegranate trees infuse their blossom scent into the breeze. The Jaffa Gate and the Old City walls rise opposite.

Hours later, we dragged our weary legs back to Jaffa Street to catch a sherut home. As we waited for it to fill up, I thought of Mick and Charlie. So many of my memories of Jerusalem are coloured with their dodgy antics.

Last I heard of Mick, he was working as a second-hand car dealer in East London, though if he stayed true to form, he had probably promoted himself from a run-of-the-mill doctor to the Minister of Health, dealing cars above the counter and 'medicine' below it.

He told me that he'd received a postcard from Charlie in Peru. Only one sentence was written on it – in Spanish: '*Plata y amore con tiempo para los gastallros.*' Mick said that he'd had it translated by a 'reliable' source, and it meant something along the lines of 'love and money with plenty of time to enjoy it'. It seemed like Charlie's ship had finally arrived.

As we began rolling down the hill towards the beach, it occurred to me that travelling from Jerusalem to Tel Aviv is an expedition in extremes, from the sacred to the profane. Tel Aviv may be the pulse of the nation, but Jerusalem, and the Old City in particular, is its sacred soul.

CHAPTER THIRTY-TWO

IT WAS ABOUT six months later, in early 1997, that a small, non-descript envelope, wedged in a package of mail bound by an elastic band, altered the course of our lives in Israel. My name, Benjamin Black, and address were printed in Hebrew letters inside the transparent window. Recognising the insignia in the top left-hand corner, I almost missed a heartbeat.

Though I was hoping it would never arrive, there was a certain predictability about it – like the first rain after a long, hot Israeli summer. But, deep down I knew I'd wake up one morning and find this bombshell among my bills. Still, I held out hope. Maybe they would have lost my address since I had last moved flats. Or maybe I would become a one-in-a-million statistical error like my mate Mike, and my ID number would be erased from the government microchip.

I could throw it away, burn it or simply pretend it had never arrived. But I soon realised that all these options would be futile. They had my digits, my details and my ID number. They knew where to find me. I didn't need to open it. The three-letter acronym on the top of the insignia revealed everything I needed to know: *Tsahal* – Tsvah Hagannah L'Israel – the Israel Defence Forces (IDF).

If I thought I would be spared the harrowing experience of dressing up in olive fatigues and a flak jacket, with an M16 or Uzi sub-machine gun slung across my shoulder, I was wrong.

And if I thought that peace would have prevailed by 1997 and, as a result, the final curtain on war in the region would have been drawn, burying mandatory conscription with it, I was simply naive.

My bubble had been burst. I hauled myself up the eighty-eight steps to the roof flat. Before I had even opened my mouth Lucy sensed my anguish.

'What is it?'

I pointed to the insignia on the envelope.

Her usually smooth face contorted. Her normally radiant deep blue eyes dulled. Her smile, which could almost ignite fireworks with its sparkle, disappeared.

I slowly opened the envelope just enough so that I could squint inside, as I used to do with my school examination results. If only this piece of paper carried such innocuous news. If only it recorded such banal issues as Grade A, B or C – pass or fail.

Outside of my particulars, it said that the Chief of General Staff of the Israel Defence Forces had ordered my conscription, according to Israeli law. It was not an invitation. It was an order. There was no RSVP attached. No avenue for refusal. No box to tick for conscientious objection. Nothing to cushion the blow. Just the bare, brutal facts of life in Israel alongside my name and ID number.

I handed it to Lucy. She squinted briefly for confirmation. But she didn't need any. We embraced, squeezing each other tight. We had talked of this day for some time. We knew that it would arrive. But it still wrenched our hearts and sabotaged our dreams. I wasn't sure whether I was grieving for myself or for her. Imagine the feelings of isolation and desolation that a woman must suffer when she bids farewell to her partner as he goes off to the army.

We held on to each other long after our embrace was over.

In Israel, kids grow up knowing that when they reach the age of eighteen, they will spend the next two or three years serving in the army. They talk about it around the dinner table, discuss it among friends, think about which unit of the army they'd like to join and watch their older brothers and sisters head off before them. The army is part of their life, as fundamental as school. They have eighteen years to get used to the idea. I had had less than one year.

I pinned my draft order onto the cork noticeboard in the·
kitchen. It hung there, incongruous, alongside a wedding invitation, two tickets for the Ahziv annual reggae festival, a sticker
with the words 'Peace, Shalom, Salaam' written on it and a
ridiculous photograph of me in Jordan, dressed up in Abdullah's
elephant-grey jelabiyeh, a white keffiyeh wrapped around my
head and Lucy's aviator sunglasses.

The bottom line was as simple as it was complex: if I didn't
conscript as ordered, the military police would take me to a military court, where I would be sentenced for breaking the law. Draft
dodging in Israel is illegal and punishable by jail. I was staring
two unenviable choices in the face: conscript to the IDF or serve
time in a military prison.

It wasn't worth comparing which of the options was better.
The thought of either drove me to the edge of agony. The only
other alternative was to go AWOL and, given that I had only
recently moved my whole life here to live in the Jewish state, the
thought of leaving and returning to the Diaspora, where some
eight million Jews are scattered across the globe, was the farthest
thing on my mind.

Maybe, just maybe I prayed, the army would realise the futil-
ity of drafting a skinny, flat-footed, muscle-less, vegetarian, vita-
min-deficient, 27-year-old Scot to the ranks of one of the most
revered military machines of the modern era.

We retreated from life for a few days as we began to grapple with
the additional piece of paper stuck on the noticeboard.

Rose was heading down to the Sinai again and I wanted to tell
her before she left. She admitted, like Lucy, that she was grateful
she was a woman and did not have to deal with the issue of the
army. But, she said, Avi, a distant friend of a friend, had had similar moral reservations and had managed to avoid military duty.
She told me to contact him.

It was Avi who first told me about 'Profile 21'. He mentioned it to
me in the same breath as 'Profile 97'. They are two ends of the same

scale – the scale that the Israeli army uses to measure the physical and mental combat ability of draftees, which now included me.

Once conscripted, the army requires all draftees to go through a series of tests: medicals, psychometric examinations and the like. Those who score a profile of 97 have the unenviable luxury of a front-row seat as a combat soldier or as a paratrooper. Perhaps as a pilot, or even as a member of one of the IDF's crack commando units. The gradings then drop from 97 to 92, 87 . . . And then, finally, to 21, the lowest rung on the ladder.

In military parlance, 'Profile 21' refers to those people whom the army deems unsuitable for duty. This could be due to poor physical or mental health, an intellectual disability, suicidal tendencies, drug addiction, alcoholism or even homosexuality.* It is even possible to be discharged on the grounds of an immature personality. Whatever the disposition, the army realises it would be taking an unnecessary risk and therefore grants the draftee permanent exemption by issuing him or her with a profile of 21.

Among the small but growing draft-dodging fraternity, 'Profile 21' has recently become an unlikely euphemism. Since the Defence Service Law does not account for conscientious objectors, Israelis who are unwilling to serve on moral grounds know that the ability to prove you are stark, raving mad can guarantee permanent exemption from the army. An increasing number of pseudo-lunatics are attempting to foil the army psychiatrist.

Whispering through a cloud of cigarette smoke, late one night in a funky south Tel Aviv bar that doubles as a laundromat, Avi explained to me how to fast-track 'Profile 21'. He had served in the army as an 18-year-old but now, as a reservist soldier, he could no longer justify conscription. Serving one month a year in the reserves was not for him. He realised his morals and ethics could not be reconciled with military service, and he had managed to con a profile of 21. Now he was exempt.

* Homosexuals are now formally drafted and the army says that there are no restrictions – even for high-level posts, though the facts on the ground have yet to corroborate this claim.

'This is totally in confidence habibi,' he said, brushing his long, curly hair off his face.

'You have my word.'

'I have an acquaintance, a friend of a friend who is a psychiatrist.'

'Keep talking,' I said, fine tuning my hearing into his whisper.

'You can go to him and he can write you a report to help you get "Profile 21".'

'Meaning?'

'He'll issue you with his psychiatric assessment which will explain why you're fucked up,' he said, his eyes darting around the bar.

'What would I have to tell him?'

'That you consider suicide as an option.'

'Oh. Is that all? Anything else?'

'Yeah. That you could not guarantee what would happen if you were issued with a weapon.'

'What?'

'You know. That you might fire on your own troops or simply not be able to fire at all. Or, better still, you might blow your own head off rather than shoot the enemy.'

'OK, I see. Sounds pretty easy. But what if he asks me loads of questions?'

'Look. He's in on the scam. It's a way for him to make good money.'

'How much?' I asked, secretly hoping it would be thousands of shekels beyond my budget.

'I'm not sure. I think about 500 shekels [US$150]. Look, he has to pretend to take his microscope over your mental make-up, but it's just to ease his conscience. If you're interested, I can get his details and find out how much it costs.'

'Yeah. I'm interested.'

I could not discard the idea immediately. But nor could I embrace it. What about my conscience? How would I live with the fact that not only had I dodged the draft, I had also lied and solicited false testimony? And what about the repercussions?

What would happen when I went for a job interview? Could access to my military files be requested? In the old days, army service was a rite of passage, and draft dodgers found it difficult to gain employment, lost their driving licences and became social pariahs overnight. Nowadays, so it seemed, the taboo had been broken. But I suspected there were still traces of that resentment lurking around.

What worried me most was that this seemed the most attractive option so far. Serving in the military was not a serious option. Neither was sitting in jail. Nor was being diagnosed as suicidal, but it certainly was the most appealing of the three. For the following few days, the issue of paying a psychiatrist to help me get a profile of 21 buzzed, like a mosquito, in my mind. But I soon realised that it could easily backfire. If I decided to pursue it, could it not end up pursuing me for the rest of my days? Would I spend the rest of my life in the shadow of my mentally ill alias? Or, worse, would it haunt me so much that over time I would actually become a legitimate candidate for 'Profile 21'?

CHAPTER THIRTY-THREE

LUCY WAS ALSO sceptical about me fast-tracking 'Profile 21'. While it was intriguing, there were other legal avenues I could explore before deciding to visit a shrink to tell him I was thinking of jumping off the roof of the 36-storey Shalom Tower. I dealt with my depressing reality by keeping a low profile, staying at home, sitting on the roof and listening to my brain churn through every possible scenario.

Lucy, on the other hand, had her own way of dealing with crises: shopping therapy. Whenever there was a desperate situation, it could always be semi-remedied by an afternoon at the market. And Jaffa's Shuk Hapishpishim (flea market) was her favourite spot.

Jaffa gave birth to Tel Aviv. The squalor and overcrowding in Jaffa at the turn of the twentieth century led a group of sixty Jewish families to move out and settle in the sand dunes just to the north. They planted the seeds of Tel Aviv in 1909, pledging to keep the area strictly residential.

Less than a century later, their pledge seems somewhat hollow. Tel Aviv is the commercial capital of the country and Jaffa now languishes like an aging mother left to wither away in the shadows while her child, old enough to stand on its own two feet, takes the spotlight.

The Arabs used to call Jaffa Arous el-Falestin – the pride of Palestine. That was before 1948, when Jaffa, home to between 70,000 and 100,000 Arabs, was among the finest towns on the Mediterranean. Yasser Arafat, Abu Iyad and George Habash, among other leading Palestinians, claim Jaffa as their home. It was graced with fine beaches, the houses were built in classical

Ottoman style – hidden under domed roofs and archways, laced with balustrades and decorated balconies, courtyards and round windows – and its ancient port was still among the main gateways to the Holy Land.

During the 1948 war, most of the Arabs fled; only some 3000 remained. In their place, Jewish immigrants, largely from Bulgaria, Romania, Libya, Morocco and Tunisia, arrived. Now, almost fifty years on, some 20,000 Arabs comprise about one-third of the total population of Jaffa. And, except for the 1929 and 1936 riots, the Jews and Arabs of Jaffa have managed to cohabit in relative harmony.

But Jaffa today is no longer the pride of Palestine, or even Israel for that matter. From a distance, you can smell the decay. It reeks of rot. The gentle breeze no longer trails the sweet smell of orange blossom for which this place was once famous. Open sewers and narrow, potholed streets, polluted by a bumper-to-bumper chain of vehicles, are its contemporary trademarks. Except for Old Jaffa. Perched on the crest of a hillock just above the port, the area was renovated by the government in the 1960s and transformed into an enchanting maze of quaint alleyways, expensive cafés, workshops and art galleries where artisans, artists and craftsmen ply their trade. Now, it is inhabited by a trickle of tourists, affluent consumers, empty spaces and ghost-like atmospheres.

Even the port, where much of Jaffa's 3000-year history took place, is no longer the gateway it once was. The stories of Jonah and the whale, of Andromeda and Poseidon took place here. When legions of armies and their armadas arrived to conquer the Holy Land, they landed at Jaffa; when boatloads of Christian pilgrims arrived to begin their trek to the Holy City, they disembarked here; and when Jewish refugees from war-torn Europe escaped Hitler's grasp, they too arrived in Jaffa, among other places.

Nowadays, Jaffa has been superseded by the larger ports at Ashdod in the south and Haifa in the north. Apart from the Arab bakeries – such as Abu Elafiah, Jaffa's first and finest bakery, which has been serving breads since 1880 – and hummous parlours

– Ali Caravan, Hummous Asli and Abu Marouwan, among others – as well as remnants of old buildings dressed in Ottoman architecture, Jaffa's day has largely been and gone.

Except, that is, if you're a market addict like Lucy or Rose. They could happily spend hours trawling the aisles of the market, pouring through the second-hand junk in search of additions to their eclectic wardrobes. A riot of colours spills out of the area opposite Al-Mahmudiya Mosque and the Ottoman Clock Tower into the surrounding streets. Anyone who wants to sell something, anything, packs their junk into an old battered suitcase, comes to Jaffa and tips it on the pavement in the hope that passersby like Lucy and Rose may be interested in a rusting wok or a set of cutlery that looks like it may have been stewed in bacteria. But Lucy could differentiate between vintage junk and trash. She and Rose returned home that day with an old, large, round brass tray, which we used to serve hummous, pita, coffee and tea on the roof.

Lucy also spent much of her time working in Jaffa, aiding the rehabilitation of blind and vision-impaired people by teaching them orientation and mobility – no mean feat in a place where pavements are sometimes non-existent, zebra crossings aren't strictly observed by drivers and potholes aren't always clearly marked.

She was shocked at how primitive the local infrastructure was and amazed at how many disabilities of the people she worked with were caused by war.* But, what touched her most was the way in which the largely Sephardi locals, spotting her walking with people with their long canes, would stop and say, 'Tihiyeh baree' – a blessing for good health. While it inaccurately typecast them as sick, Lucy nonetheless appreciated the ancient tradition and goodwill it came from. When some of these same locals told her she was performing a mitzvah (commandment or good deed) by aiding the less fortunate, Lucy would remonstrate that this was just her job for which she was paid like anyone else in the labour force.

* There are over 80,000 disabled war veterans in Israel. Interestingly, the only sport that Israel succeeds at on a world stage is the Paralympic Games, where Israel has won 266 medals, as opposed to only four at the Olympic Games.

I stayed home and tried to call the army's personnel department to discuss my problems. I rang for hours on end – to no avail. So, I decided to write a letter.

> Manpower Division
> Israel Defence Forces
> Tel Hashomer
> Tel Aviv

> Dear Sir,

> I recently received my conscription order to serve in the IDF. Ever since, I have been trying to phone you at Tel Hashomer. Each time the phone is engaged.

> My foremost concern is my health. I have spent the last few months going through tests for my lungs, since I suffered a lung abscess from a viral strain of pneumonia and recently experienced a relapse.

> In addition, however, I have other concerns. I work as a freelance writer and if drafted will lose all of my clients and be crippled financially. Plus, I am about to start my master's degree at Tel Aviv University and will still be studying when conscripted.

> Lastly, I have no family here. I live with my Australian girlfriend and, if I am drafted, she will be on her own, with no family.

> I would appreciate it if you could consult my draft papers and consider my case. I am very concerned about my health (and wealth!).

> Please contact me as soon as possible.

> I look forward to hearing from you.

> Benjamin Black

Days, then weeks, passed. No telephone call, no mail, nothing, until, one morning, a letter bearing the army's insignia arrived. Next to it was another letter with an Egyptian stamp on it. I recognised Rose's writing on the front.

I figured I'd read the bad news first. Inside, it made no mention of my letter. Instead, it simply restated my draft date and informed me that I was to come to Tel Hashomer to undergo physical and mental health checks in one week. It listed the date and the time. Nothing else.

I hoped Rose's news would offer some light amusement if nothing else. It was short, scrawled on tissue paper with a smudged symbol that could have been an Egyptian mummy in the top right-hand corner. She had written barely two dozen words. But to Lucy and me, those few words were heart warming. They were enough to offset my anger at the army's letter. If only for a day or two.

CHAPTER THIRTY-FOUR

I OPEN THE THROTTLE of my 49 cc Piaggio scooter and crawl across Tel Aviv to Tel Hashomer, a massive military barracks on the easternmost edge of the city, where I will undergo my medical examinations. Several soldiers patrol the entrance to the base. Only authorised military personnel or armoured vehicles can enter. I ditch my scooter, padlock it to a post and make for the first checkpoint. There is another checkpoint at the gate to the conscription section where I have to register for my tests. My bag is checked. My ID card scrutinised.

It's 8 am. Inside the gate, the plaza is teeming with teenagers. Today is their day. Their number is up. They will spend the next three years defending the nation. Their families are there to bid them farewell. Several girlfriends have come too, some of them are dressed up as if they are going on to a nightclub. Perhaps they have just come from one. Over the loudspeaker names are being read out.

Stunned, I stand there, wondering what these boys are thinking. I suspect a cocktail of emotions: excitement, fear, nerves, apprehension, doubt. And pride that we are once again a free nation. For most, if not all of them, they have grown up knowing this day would arrive. Some will be relishing the prospect, the challenge, the novelty, the opportunity to serve their country – perhaps even to die for it. Others will be wallowing in fear, loneliness, isolation.

Tears are scarce. At the age of eighteen, surrounded by their peers, there is a pressure on these young boys to act like grown men. They are about to become soldiers – and soldiers don't cry.

Still, I'm sure I can detect fear in their souls. They are plucked from the prime of their youth because they were born into a country where the state of nature is, tragically, a state of war. Their adolescence has been cut short and they have been plunged prematurely into adulthood.

Parents hug their sons, showering them with love and affection, tears and kisses, before they go off to train for war. They know that this is a milestone moment, that their boys are crossing the threshold. When they return, they will no longer be boys. These are the last few breaths that belong to the innocence of their youth.

The buses rev their engines. Army bags are tossed into the hold. How will I feel when my time comes? I have no family here (Ruth had left for London). Lucy would come to bid me farewell. My parents would be far away. In any case, I'll be twenty-eight years old. Too old to cry.

Like hell. Hairs stand on end down my back.

I see a father take his son aside for a few words, father to son, man to boy. 'Don't be a hero, son. Do you hear me?' he says in Hebrew. 'Look after yourself. Be brave, but don't try to be a hero. We will be waiting for you. OK?'

The son seems more embarrassed than emotional. 'Don't worry Dad. I'll be fine. Tismoch alay – trust me.'

His father is choked, his eyes well up. He was once a soldier too. Maybe he is still a reservist. He knows all about the pressure of tears and he fights them off with all his strength.

And then his son is gone, clambering aboard the bus. It could have been a summer camp if I hadn't known better. But these boys are headed for three months basic training where they will be physically and mentally deconstructed as boys – and then reconstructed as soldiers.

I muscle through the throng in the direction of the boy's father.

'How do you feel?' I ask without reservation.

'Terrible.' He is holding his weeping wife tight to his breast. 'Awful. But we have no choice. Maybe one day . . . '

I sit and watch the departure of the buses from afar. Parents wave and blow kisses. A boy presses his outstretched hand on the window screen. Is it a wave goodbye? Or a plea for help? Either way, it is too late. This is the lot he was cast in life. How does a mother feel when she waves goodbye to her son? After the spate of suicide bombs and the kidnapping and murder of Nachshon Wachsman, a renewed fear has been instilled in every mother that their uniformed son may be next.

Will she be among the unfortunate few who receive that knock on the door that bears the bad news? How do you tell a mother that her boy has been killed in battle?

The buses rumble off toward base camp. Parents, families and girlfriends drift away. Only the echoes of their pain remain.

I head inside for my medical examination.

CHAPTER THIRTY-FIVE

THIS IS THE FIRST STEP in my induction, where the army begins to assess my profile. Given my lung abscess and viral pneumonia I am sure to be ruled out of a profile of 97. But whether I am a candidate for 'Profile 21' is another matter entirely.

I'm in a queue awaiting the doctor, wearing nothing but boxer shorts. I am exposed, my lean frame, bulging rib cage, minuscule muscles, bandy legs, flat feet. It's cold; my nipples are erect. The room smells of bad feet. And sweaty scrotums.

There is an eclectic mix of people in the queue, including Russians, Eastern Europeans, Latin Americans, Ethiopians and Anglo-Saxons.* The one truism about the Israeli army is that it is a great leveller, equalising people from all backgrounds, all classes, all ages and all walks of life. As soon as we step into the olive uniforms, we are one. Our differences dissolve. That, I think, is one of the only things that attracts me to the army.

We fill out medical forms, chronicling any illnesses. Suddenly I remember what I was told not to forget. Avi, the guy who told me how to fast-track 'Profile 21', had advised me to drink a mixture of cigarette ash and water just prior to my medical.

'It creates an immediate high fever,' he had said to me. 'They won't know what to do with you. I also met a guy who banged his shin with a metal spoon over and over. He hobbled in there with a bulge the size of a football.'

It was too late for tricks. In any case, I wanted to see how far I could go on the truth, before contemplating the use of deceitful tricks.

* Close to one million Jews from the former Soviet Union immigrated to Israel during the 1990s. Nowadays, many street signs are written in Hebrew, Arabic, English and Russian.

There's a row of desks, where doctors sit, stethoscopes clasped around their necks ready to test the heartbeats of draftees. Beyond them is a small screen, behind which I assume one is to drop one's briefs and expose to the doctor the parts where the sun don't shine. I wonder what he's looking for. Sexually transmitted diseases? Or perhaps transsexuals. And what happens when he does spot what he is looking for?

The doctor quizzes me on my illnesses. I highlight my pneumonia and lung abscess and emphasise that ever since I have not fully recovered and even recently suffered a mild relapse. I also stress to him that my fitness, as a result, is not what it once was and therefore my ability to perform in the army is likely to be impaired. He does some elementary tests, listens to my lungs and concludes by telling me he'll refer me to a specialist for X-rays. I feel good. I am telling the truth and it appears to be leading somewhere. My profile, I am convinced, will be significantly lowered.

Now I'm three people away from dropping my pants.

The doctor is a short, bespectacled man, wearing a white, three-quarter length surgical coat. He stands about four metres away from me. I stare at him blankly. There is no dialogue. Everything is assumed. He motions his hand downward. I am about to be denuded. I imagine that if he were to verbalise his hand movement, he'd say: 'C'mon son, drop your underpants please. I have a thousand penises to check today.'

I oblige and reveal my shining armour in his direction. He barely blinks. He motions his hand upward. Then it's over. Reclothed, I wonder what he says when people ask him what he does for a living.

'Oh, I'm a doctor.'

'Really? How fascinating. What do you specialise in?'

'I work for the army. I inspect soldiers' weapons.'

CHAPTER THIRTY-SIX

AFTER MY MEDICAL EXAMINATION, I was guided downstairs to a room where the psychometric examinations are conducted to enable the army to ascertain whether or not I could endure the mental pressure of life on the front line. I already knew I couldn't. The two tests, and any additional information, would determine my profile, which would establish what unit I would be conscripted into.

Moral reservations aside, I decided to lie my ass off to save my soul. I wanted to fail. I wanted to fall so far short of the mark that they would either automatically give me a 'Profile 21' and beg me not to return anywhere near an army establishment ever, or summon me to see the kaban, the army psychiatrist.

I opened the document. It was a multiple-choice exam, with space for elaboration where necessary.

Do you ever wet your bed at night?
The choice of answers was:

> Never
> Sometimes
> Often
> Very Often

The last time I had wet my bed was over twenty years ago, but, for the purposes of this examination, I recalled an embarrassing incident last week, and another several weeks before that. I selected 'sometimes', preferring to err on the side of caution. I'll start off slowly, I thought to myself, and gently slide into mental insanity.

Do you ever experience migraines?

My gentle slide was about to become a deep-sea dive. Yes. Very often, I answered. After all, who defines the line between headaches and migraines? What is a headache to you is a migraine to me. I'm sensitive. Even the sunshine gives me migraines.

Do you panic in pressurised circumstances?

Absolutely. All the time. I even panic in unpressurised circumstances. After all, how do you measure panic? I appear calm and collected on the outside, but inside I suffer mental torture under pressure. I question everything.

Do you suffer from insomnia?

Is the Chief Rabbi Jewish? Yes. I barely slept last night. How could I sleep with my conscription notice hanging over my head? I lie awake counting down the days as if it's a death penalty.

Do you ever use recreational drugs?

What's the difference between often and very often? As a worldly kind of person, I am open to experimenting with everything and anything in moderation. Marijuana is recreational and I happen to have a taste for it. And I'm not averse to a wee dabble here and there with the odd mind-bending, reality-altering hallucinogenic.

I was on a roll and felt like I was cruising to a glorious failure.

Have you ever contemplated suicide?

My roll came to a grinding halt. I paused. I had made a conscious effort to leave my conscience at home. But I knew, deep in the recesses of my mind, that it would make an appearance somewhere along the line. Just when I was sure that failure had been secured, along came my conscience to spoil the party. This was the question that would separate the men from the boys, the question marks from the candidates for 'Profile 21'. No doubt about it. I wanted to concede that there had been moments of suicidal tendencies. But I felt the weight of guilt on my conscience.

Bed-wetting, migraines, insomnia and panic all seemed innocuous enough. But contemplating suicide crossed the line.

Would I honestly take my own life rather than conscript? I couldn't focus on the rest of the questions. My will to fail was broken.

At the end of the questionnaire, there was a blank space to add any other information. I pondered for a while and thought about adding: 'Ever since I received my draft order, I have suffered from a kind of schizophrenia, feelings of paranoia, fear, worry, panic and insomnia. I cannot explain it all here. I request to see the army psychiatrist.' Then I realised it would have totally exposed my folly.

I tried to think of all the reasons to justify lying. I remembered how an immigrant friend from Scotland, Jason, recalled his first day in the army. He told me how they were shown a film about how good life in the army can be, and then they were all given a piece of paper and led down a long corridor with doors on either side.

He had to go into every room with the piece of paper. In one room he was measured for a gas mask, in another he had a photograph of his teeth taken just in case his unidentifiable, charred body had to be identified from his dental records. And in another room he got two injections in each arm and one in the ass. In the final room, a huge wardrobe of sorts, he was kitted out with a uniform, which he had to don there and then. Then he was bussed to a military camp near the Gaza Strip for three months of training.

In one letter he wrote to me, he said that he spent most of his time standing to attention and being screamed at for not carrying out tasks fast enough. 'You can't even piss without permission,' he wrote. Still, he was able to see the funny side of it. 'There were times when I was standing at the front and the officers were screaming and I just laughed out of control. It was so surreal there was just no other way to deal with it. I was like a naughty schoolboy laughing all the time.'

But he had little to laugh about after basic training. He was sent to guard a religious kibbutz in Gush Etzion, a bloc of Jewish settlements south of Bethlehem surrounded by Arab villages and towns. He tried to get out of it by saying that he couldn't take a gun because his lack of Hebrew would endanger himself and the others he was guarding. He was sent to see the head officer, who gave him the choice of guarding or going to jail. He ended up guarding.

My mate spent months guarding a population largely comprised of Right-wing settlers, many of them American immigrants opposed to the peace process and virulent in their belief that this land is their birthright, given by God to Abraham.

It sounded as bad – worse even – than I expected it to be. Not something I could ever imagine myself wilfully choosing to do. And yet I found myself unable to confirm that I had indeed contemplated suicide. I did not tick any of the options. Instead, I handed my paper to the soldier and went to the manpower desk to request to see someone in charge.

The clerk on duty told me I had to lodge a formal request. I explained to her that I'd already lodged a complaint when I sent a letter soon after my notice arrived. But she was just a pen-pusher and although I laid on all my arguments, she was fairly blasé about the whole thing. Then I added one new piece of information. 'By the way,' I mumbled softly in Hebrew, 'I'm also a conscientious objector'.

She stopped scribbling and looked at me, eyebrows raised. Then she paused briefly for confirmation before returning to her form. Filing my request in the appropriate place, she told me that I would hear from the army in due course.

I left feeling empty. For the first time in my life I had wilfully tried to fail an examination, even though I drew the line between mild and extreme dishonesty.

At best, I had been more than a touch economical with the truth; at worst, I had intentionally disowned myself. Even if I could somehow justify that I hadn't lied outright, I could never justify that I'd told the whole truth.

CHAPTER THIRTY-SEVEN

ANOTHER ARMY LETTER arrived in the post several weeks later. I had become so cynical that I felt like smoking the damn thing, so when I read that the army was willing to hear my case in front of an appeals committee I almost kissed the little old lady from next door who was also fetching her mail.

I didn't quite know how to tell Lucy the news. 'The army rejected my appeal.'

She barely flinched. I placed the letter on the table in front of her. She continued grooming the dog. I nudged her. Finally, she twigged, and then beamed.

'Wow! Amazing!'

After all, we were in this together. If I was going to go to jail, she said she'd insist on coming too. And if I was thinking of going AWOL, she would be leaving too.

I tried to keep some perspective. The last thing we needed was to get excited only to have our hopes dashed again.

'Can I come?' asked Lucy.

'No way.'

'Why not? I'll sit outside.'

'OK. Yeah. I guess so. Why not?'

'When is it?'

'Not for a month.'

I pinned it up next to my draft notice. The news headlines came on the radio and soon we were lost in the latest developments of the peace process.

If the Ten Commandments given by God to Moses on Mount Sinai are the guiding principles of Orthodox and ultra-Orthodox Jews, then the doctrine of secular Jews – the unofficial eleventh commandment – is: Thou shalt not miss the news headlines. On the hour, every hour.

Israelis have always been, and seem destined to remain, obsessive-compulsive news addicts. The news runs through their veins. It's the lifeblood of the nation. Not by choice, but by circumstance. Wherever you go in Israel, the news seems to hover in the background, just within earshot. As the leaders stake their gambits over the final-status issues, and as extremists on both sides try to torpedo the peace process, Israelis glue their ears to the radio to hear the latest move in the end game of this Middle Eastern chess match. What percentage of the West Bank will become Palestine? Where will the borders be drawn? What will happen to the 200,000 or so Jewish settlers in the West Bank and Gaza Strip? Likewise, what will happen to the roughly 3.7 million Palestinian refugees? Will they be allowed the right of return? And, perhaps most significantly of all, what will be the fate of Jerusalem?*

In this sense the news of peace is even graver than the news of war because of its perceived permanency. Once these final-status issues are signed and sealed there will be no turning back, unless, that is, there is a full-scale war.

The country's minute size exacerbates this addictive disorder towards news. Like influenza, it is a contagious infection that spreads in the air. With six million people crammed into a space smaller than Vermont or New Hampshire, Albania or Tasmania, even if you don't know many people, it feels like you do.

Parents whose children are in the army instinctively listen out for 'no news'. It's their survival instinct. But, when there is news, and the newscaster cannot cite names until the families have been informed, thousands of parents sit frozen, petrified that this public news item may be privately addressed to them.

Even good news is greeted by its doomsayers. The heroic victory, against all odds, in 1967 was a watershed. Had Israel lost

* Not all of the Jewish settlers in the West Bank and Gaza Strip are ideological settlers; some simply moved there because the government offered financial incentives so as to create 'facts on the ground'. Likewise, not all Palestinian refugees would want to exercise the right to return.

this war, or any war for that matter, the nation would have ceased to exist. But no sooner had the echo of the bullets and bombs subsided, there were calls of panic and despair that the blessing of this six-day miracle would turn out to be a curse.

Public transport is perhaps the place where the sanctity of news is best understood. The moment those three beeps sound at the top of the hour, passengers fall silent. The driver automatically turns up the volume as everyone awaits the next chapter of their fate. When the news bells chime, and it is nowhere near the top of the hour, there is no doubt that what is about to be reported is bad news.

In the ten days leading up to the Six-Day War, the nation's ears pricked up on the hour as the winds of war began howling across the Middle East. Sentiments of doom pervaded the atmosphere. Few doubted that the Arabs would invade. But the moment the newscaster reported that Egyptian leader Gamal Abdel Nasser had closed the Straits of Tiran to Israeli shipping, Israel braced for war.

'I was leaning on a newspaper stall at the time,' recalled Abba Kovner, the leader of the Vilna Ghetto uprising of 1943. 'The newspaper seller was in the very act of stretching out his hand towards the paper I wanted when suddenly the [radio] voice caught his attention . . .

'"Oh! They've called me up too." He rolled up his papers and went.

' . . . A group of men stood huddled round a transistor in the middle of a patch of lawn. Whenever one of them heard his codeword read out by the announcer, he detached himself from the group and left. Without a word, another left. Then a third. Silently the group broke up . . . '

Kovner, who had seen nations march off to war, could not believe the manner in which Israelis went to war in 1967.

' . . . never before have I seen a city rise so silently to answer the call of duty. This nation went to war filled with a sense of destiny, gravely and quietly prepared, in a way that cannot be surpassed.'

Then, on 7 June 1967, the newscaster reported one of the defining moments in the state's short history: the voice of Colonel Mordechai (Motta) Gur, Paratroop Division Commander, was recorded on radio, announcing that 'The Temple Mount is in our hands!' Rabbi Shlomo Goren blasted a triumphant sound from the shofar and the Star of David flag was hoisted on the Temple Mount.

The battle for Jerusalem had been won. Jews, having prayed towards Jerusalem for 2000 years in exile, could finally return to their holiest shrine, the Western Wall.

Incredible then, that only a decade later, Israelis would hear the announcement that Egyptian President Anwar Sadat would make an historic visit to Jerusalem in 1977. For the first time ever, an Arab head of state would address the Israeli parliament in what would be the first tentative step down the road to a peace treaty.

If the report of the liberation of Jerusalem on 7 June 1967 was among the most joyous moments in the nation's history, the assassination of Prime Minister Yitzhak Rabin, announced on the night of 4 November 1995, was among the most traumatic. News of his murder attacked the central nervous system of the people of Israel. The unthinkable had happened in the centre of the Jewish homeland: the torch of hope Rabin embodied had been extinguished – not by a Palestinian terrorist, but by a religious Jew.

CHAPTER THIRTY-EIGHT

I WAS A LATE CONVERT to the olive school of thought. It was not an easy concession for me to make. Until I began living in Jerusalem in 1994, olives held pariah status in my gastronomic encyclopaedia. I loathed them; my palate would not tolerate them. They existed on a par with Parmesan cheese, which, to me, smells worse than bad feet.

Now I'm a self-proclaimed olive junkie. Green, black, pitted, marinated, you name it. If it's olive-oriented, I'm into it. And I'm not alone. Israel is one of the largest bastions of olive addicts in the world.

While I was waiting for my appeal, I was commissioned by a features magazine to write an article on the olive industry. I contacted the former director and curator of the Olive Oil Industry Museum in Haifa, and one of Israel's leading olive aficionados, David 'Dudu' Eitam. He lives in Hararit, a tiny hilltop settlement above the olive-drenched Sakhnin Valley in the Galilee, and I asked him if he would be prepared to talk. He told me to meet him at the museum.

Haifa, Israel's third largest city with a population of around a quarter of a million people, is that thumb-shaped peninsula that juts awkwardly out into the Mediterranean Sea in the northwest of the country. From the sweeping slopes of the pine-coated Mount Carmel, the port area below looks like a sprawling industrial mess. But from the port, the city above looks like a tiered wedding cake, the terraced layers climbing up the hillside.

Its centrepiece, halfway up – and Haifa's architectural crown – is the golden dome of the Baha'i's Shrine of Bab, surrounded by manicured terraced gardens. At the top, the university towers above the city.*

The taxi driver, an olive-skinned chap wearing a crocheted yarmulke, raised his eyebrows when I asked him to take me from the hilltop down to the olive oil museum. His English was patchy. He flicked his wrist in a way that suggested I was mistaken. 'Where? No. No possible. I never hearing this place.'

'It's near the port,' I offered.

'Sure you no meaning de railway museum?'

'Yeah, I'm sure. It's past there – across the tracks.'

He was unconvinced and it took me a while to persuade him to gamble on my assurance. He scowled at me as though I had twisted his arm, and in the process forced him to give up his remaining half cigarette. I flashed him a warm smile. He was not amused.

'You no sabra [native Israeli] huh? Where you from?'

'Scotland. You?'

'Me? Morocco. But forty years I living here.'

The inside of the cab is decorated like a kitsch shrine. Fake fur lines the dashboard. Hanging from the top of the windscreen are small trinkets and amulets with bells. Attached to the panoramic mirror is a beautiful blue glass hamsa, an oriental charm designed in the shape of a hand, which is believed to ward off the evil eye. Stuck on top of the speedometer is Tefillat Derech, the Hebrew prayer for safe travel. And attached to the length of the dashboard in front of the passenger seat is a collage of photos. Some of them are of children; others are of strange-looking, bearded characters.

We descend the wooded slopes of Mount Carmel. Behind us, the university tower rises skywards, and beyond it the road winds across the mountaintop to the Druze villages of Daliat el-Carmel and Isfiya. Ahead of us the panorama view fans out effortlessly to the east across the Galilee towards Tiberias and Lake Kinneret; to

* The universalist Baha'i, named after its founder Baha'u'llah, is an extension of Islam and has some four million followers worldwide. They believe in the prophecies of Mirza Ali Mohammed, a Sh'ite Muslim, and pray for a single world government, believing that all religions are, in essence, the same.

the north the crescent-shaped coastline sweeps past the ancient walled city of Akko and up toward Kibbutz Rosh HaNikra and the Lebanese border.

Much of the terrain in this part of the country is clothed with olive groves, their gnarled, wrinkled trunks and silvery leaves giveaway trademarks. Some have been here for generations; others for millennia.

After the Great Flood, Noah sent a dove out to see if there was any life on land. The dove returned with an olive twig in its beak – the first sign of life. The Torah names the olive as one of the seven species that bless the land of Israel: 'A land of wheat and barley, of vines, figs and pomegranates, a land of olive trees and honey.' Scientific evidence suggests that domestic olives have graced these parts for at least 6000 years. The Koran, too, makes several references to olives. And two olive branches surround the menorah, the seven-branched candelabra that is the national emblem of Israel.

Lastly, the olive branch is also the symbol of peace. So when Yasser Arafat, concluding his maiden speech to the UN General Assembly in November 1974, held up an olive branch, he was invoking the power of this symbol: 'I have come bearing an olive branch and a freedom fighter's gun. Do not let the olive branch fall from my hand.' Arafat's gun holster was visible when he raised the olive branch, though he claimed it was empty.

'Zayit' in Hebrew and 'zaytunah' in Arabic, the olive – with all its religious and historical connotations – symbolises this land and its people. But native-born Israelis are commonly referred to as 'sabras', named after a native, pear-shaped fruit that grows on a cactus, because they are prickly on the outside but sweet on the inside.

The logic of this nickname becomes increasingly apparent the longer you stay in Israel. Israelis can be short-fused, impatient, abrupt and uncompromising at times. Their prickly exterior has perhaps been hardened over time because they have suffered and endured so many traumas and tragedies. But that is not the whole truth. The rest lurks deep inside. And those on the long haul will soon unearth the treasure that lies within – the sweet centre of the people. As a result, 'sabra' has become part of the Hebrew lexicon – a self-proclaimed acknowledgment of the contrasting characteristics of the native Israeli.

For me, the one fruit that accurately symbolises the land and the people – Jew and Arab – it is not the sabra. It is the olive, the hallmark of the Holy Land.

We make our way through the commercial precinct of Hadar and the narrow, winding alleyways of the Arab quarter of Wadi Nisnas and Wadi Salib, past the el-Istakal Mosque. Most Arabs fled Haifa in the 1948 war, but those that remained stayed in this area. In Haifa, as in Jaffa, Jews and Arabs manage to co-exist in relative harmony.

'Who are they?' I ask, pointing at the dashboard.

He launches into a Hebrew monologue. 'My children. Reuven, Aryeh, Chaya and Nechamah. May they be blessed. May Reuven recover from his accident. Aryeh will grow to be a scholar, God willing. Let Chaya be fruitful and multiply. And Nechamah . . . bless her sweet soul.'

'No. I mean them,' I stress, pointing to the beards.

His face breaks out into a smile. 'Ahhhh . . . the zaddikim – the saints.'

In a country laden with rabbis, almost all of whom have beards and wear black hats, the untrained eye cannot determine who's who.

'This is Rabbi Israel Abouhatzeria. He's the Baba Sali. His tomb is down south in Netivot.'

'Oh.'

'You see him,' he says, pointing to the far end of the dashboard. 'That's Rabbi Haim Chouri. He's buried in Be'er Sheva. Here, that's Rabbi Simeon Bar Yochai. He's buried near here in Meron. Him? Rabbi Meir Ba'al Haness. Him too, he's buried in Tzfat. They're all zaddikim, saints, miracle makers. It's a North African tradition. Back in Morocco, each community had a saint. Now I'm here, I ask them all for their blessings. For me and my whole family.'

All of a sudden, a lorry pulls out from a blind corner in front of us. My Moroccan taxi driver slams on the anchors and swerves to avoid a collision. His hands are flying in the air, anger sizzling from his eyes and ears. 'Coos achto ya maniac (Arabic/Hebrew unpublishable expletive relating to the female anatomy)!'

The lorry driver returns fire, hands gesticulating out of his window. 'Al hazayin sheli (more unpublishable expletives, this time relating to the male anatomy)!'

Now my driver is furious, road rage combusting with deep-seated anger. The lorry driver blocks us from overtaking. I try to calm my driver. He mutters some Hebrew, firms his yarmulke on his head and touches his safe travel prayer with two fingers, which he then places on his lips. He casts a glance across at me. The intonation is clear. Stay put, shut up, fasten your seatbelt and hold on.

Road rage is not uncommon here. I begin to beg, plead, howl. Though the speedometer is partially concealed behind the safe travel prayer, I see the dial arching around, passing 80 kilometres. I didn't know about, let alone believe in, the zaddikim previously. But if ever we need them to come to our rescue it is now. Baba Sali and his friends look like honourable men. I shut my eyes. Just as I begin to beg the saints to save us, the barriers of the railway line go up, the lorry lurches across and my driver brakes, skidding millimetres short of the track. The train shuttles by.

The smell of burning rubber and boiling oil envelops the cabin. I heave a sigh of relief. My driver looks like he is a time bomb whose countdown has expired. I sense he wants to beat me up, but he soon calms down.

I have never tipped a taxi driver even 50 per cent of the fare before. This time I offer him double. My life, I figure, is worth at least 35 shekels (US$12).

Dudu, an archaeologist who has been studying the ancient olive oil industry for the last quarter of a century, is inside.

'Ahalan Ben! Come, come,' he beckons.

Upstairs is the attic of the building – Dudu's old office. He pulls two label-less bottles from a cupboard containing what appears to be olive oil and pours a small measure of each into four glasses. I figure I'm about to undergo my olive oil induction.

'OK. Look at these,' he says, pointing to the two glasses.

He picks up a glass, swirls the oil around and then inhales the scent as if he were a wine connoisseur about to embark on a tasting. I follow his lead with the other glass.

Before I know it, he gulps half the oil.

Stunned, I point to my glass. 'You don't . . . '

He nods, motioning a gulp with his hands. 'Taste it,' he says.

I am not normally averse to new experiences, but I can already see the pimples erupting on my chin. Had he offered me olive oil mixed with labaneh (white sour cheese) and a pinch of fresh bread, I would have had no problem. But a glass of pure oil was beyond reason.

I hold my nose.

To my chagrin, he changes glasses. The first batch is still dribbling down my throat into my oesophagus. The aftertaste is sharp.

'I want you to tell me which oil is extra virgin. Look at it, smell it, then taste it. Don't look so worried. Olive oil is extremely healthy for you. It's a secret not enough people know. It's low in acids and high in mono-unsaturated fats. Contrary to popular belief, it actually reduces cholesterol.'

That may well be. But right now, I'm not impressed. He takes his glass and goes through the same vintage-wine-tasting ritual.

I follow him – against my better judgment.

'OK. So what do you think?'

I draw a blank. Olive oil test over, he pulls his stool up close to mine and examines the bottles side by side.

'Look at the colour: one is transparent, the other is cloudy. Smell them: one is fragrant, fruity and fresh, the other is not. Taste them: one has a sharp aftertaste, the other is bland.

'That's the difference between extra virgin olive oil and pure olive oil,' he concludes.

'So, really, pure olive oil is actually a euphemism for impure olive oil?' I ponder out loud.

'Spot on. The lack of acidity is what differentiates the grade of oils. Up to 1 per cent acidity qualifies for extra virgin olive oil; up to 1.5 per cent is virgin; and up to 3.3 per cent is "pure" olive oil. These are the standards of the International Olive Oil Council.'

'The tricks of the trade,' I suggest, raising my glass of extra virgin olive oil in a toast to his test. I refrain from drinking.

My induction over, I cruise around the museum and arrange to meet Dudu out the front, alongside the remnants of ancient olive presses. I soon discover that what crude oil is to the Gulf States today, olive oil was to ancient Israel: a major source of income. Excavations of ancient olive presses and pips indicate that olive oil was a massive industry in the region as far back as the Chalcolithic era, some 6000 years ago.

I also learn that Israeli Arabs consume seventeen litres of oil per capita per year whereas Israeli Jews only consume half a litre. I am an olive oil anomaly, consuming far more than half a litre a year.

I meet Dudu outside. 'Here,' he says, handing me a label-less bottle of extra virgin, cold-pressed olive oil made from the choicest hand-picked olives in the Holy Land.

'Thanks. That's very kind of you.'

'It's liquid gold. Use it sparingly.'

I leave him outside the museum, cigarette smoke trailing his afternoon shadow.

I took a taxi back up to Hadar and caught a bus home. Exhausted I soon fell asleep, awaking to a driver prodding my rib cage. Lucy was home when I arrived.

'Hi. I bought you a present.'

To be honest, I did not actually 'buy' the present. And, right there, I realised I did not have it either. Somewhere in Tel Aviv is a privileged Egged bus driver who is now the proud owner of Israel's finest liquid gold.

CHAPTER THIRTY-NINE

I HAD STARTED my master's degree at Tel Aviv University several months after the election debacle. I was able to study part-time, which allowed me to keep working part-time. In order to graduate I had to gain an exemption in Hebrew, which reminded me of those Jerusalem days when I had first met Mick and Charlie. Technically speaking, I was on the hunt for two exemptions.

There was more than a hint of irony in the fact that I was enrolled in a degree course entitled 'Security Studies and International Relations'. Almost everyone else on the course had served in the military, and most had served beyond the call of duty, completing an officers' course or higher. Many of them openly admitted that they wanted to enter the Ministry of Defence after graduation. And some of them were already full-time military personnel, being sponsored by the army to complete a post-graduate degree. At least 20 per cent of my mostly male class arrived at lectures and seminars clothed in military attire.

My interest was in International Relations, not Security Studies, which involved learning about the 'theatre of war', the 'operational art of war', IDF tank movements and other mildly uninteresting military issues that I failed to follow because the Hebrew jargon was so complicated.

One of my lecturers was a hulk of a man whose muscles strained against his shirt. Everything he wore was skin-tight. He was completely bald, and he wore tiny, round spectacles that exaggerated the size of his face even more. He was one of those guys who wore his trousers all the way up under his armpits, and even when he talked normally his deep voice boomed around the lecture theatre.

My interest was aroused during a class about the peace treaty with Egypt. The lecturer was trying to analyse why Egyptian President Anwar Sadat had finally agreed to come to Jerusalem in 1977, and then go to Camp David in 1978 to negotiate a peace treaty with Israel that would ostracise Egypt from the rest of the Arab world.

After all, the lecturer said, it was Sadat's predecessor, Gamal Abdul Nasser, who had initiated the Six-Day War with Israel in 1967. And in 1973, Egypt, together with Syria, had launched a two-pronged attack on Israel, almost defeating it on Yom Kippur, the holiest day in the Jewish calendar.

'So what made Sadat take this unprecedented U-turn and risk pariah status in the Arab world?' he hollered.

Nir was one of those guys who sat at the front of every class and answered all the questions. He even answered questions that weren't asked. When we were discussing tank manoeuvres and the like, his familiarity with the minutiae of tank accessories suggested that he was either an avid subscriber to *Tank Magazine* or, more likely, he served in a tank in the army. Still, he was annoyingly on the ball, always right (even when he seemed to be wrong) and always stayed around to ask the lecturer excruciatingly banal questions long after everyone else had dispersed. And he would sometimes even position himself strategically at the door to catch the lecturer on his way into the theatre.

His hand was up in a flash. He didn't even wait to be asked.

'Sadat realised he had no alternative. The IDF crushed the Egyptians in the 1956, 1967 and 1973 wars. Egypt in the 1970s was suffering from massive domestic poverty. Sadat knew that the alternative to peace was worse. That he would be defeated on the battlefield again and again. Likewise the Palestinians. Arafat realised that his people could never defeat us on the ground. So, he decided to forsake the battlefield for the negotiating table. King Hussein too. The Arabs – Syria aside – have all accepted that they will never defeat the IDF, backed by the US, on the battlefield.'

The lecturer interjected. 'And what about then Prime Minister Begin?* He called the leaders of all Arab states to come, unconditionally, to the negotiating table on the eve of his election in 1977. You have to account for both sides of the coin in any analysis.'

Nir looked momentarily meek.

I was particularly drawn to this lecture (ordinarily I'd tune out as soon as Nir tuned in) because it highlighted an issue I had been trying to verbalise about my impending army service. Though I hated to admit it, Nir was right. The IDF had forced the hand of the enemy. They realised that they could not defeat Israel in a war, so they slowly began to embrace the notion of peace.

The war for the survival of the state was over. The 1948, 1956, 1967 and 1973 wars were existential wars. But today the goalposts have shifted. The Cold War is over. Israel is a military powerhouse. The United States is its loyal ally. Israel's survival is no longer in doubt.

It's precisely because of the military power of the IDF that Israel is now in a position to pursue peace. The war, as we knew it then, is over. Had my draft date been 1967 or 1973 I have no doubt I would have conscripted and would have had no moral scruples about it. Israel was fighting for its life. But even though the army is still required to safeguard national security and to act as a deterrent, and while it is necessary until such time as peace is secured and there is a normalisation of relations, I don't feel morally bound to conscript.

We already have peace treaties with Egypt and Jordan and I believe we have reached the end game with the Palestinians. The only missing link is the Syrians and when they come to the party, they'll bring the Lebanese with them.

As I left the lecture theatre I overheard Nir making some convoluted excuse about why he had failed to mention Begin's role in Sadat's decision to embrace peace. I suspect he is, by now,

* Menachem Begin was the first ever Likud Prime Minister, elected in 1977. Between 1948 and 1977 Labour had always led the government until Begin won what is known as the 'earthquake' election that altered the political map of Israel.

knee-deep in papers at the Ministry of Defence in Tel Aviv. And still subscribing to *Tank Magazine*.

When he was Chief of Staff between 1964 and 1968, Yitzhak Rabin said that the IDF's aim was to 'ensure the existence of our people in our homeland and to affirm, even at the cost of their lives, the right of the Jewish people to live their lives in their own state, free, independent and in peace.'

I believe that most of this aim has been achieved. Israel's existence is no longer in doubt, thanks to the strength of the IDF. We live in our own independent state. And we Jews are free people on the cusp of peace – everyone except our soldiers, who are still fateful pawns in a deadly game of political chess.

CHAPTER FORTY

I HAD ONE WEEK before my appeal hearing. Though I was slightly encouraged by the fact that the army had agreed to hear my case, I was still dubious about whether it would lead to anything.

I decided not to even tell my parents about the appeal; it would get their hopes up only to be dashed again if it were rejected. My mother, needless to say, was not exactly ecstatic about the prospect of me conscripting. Neither was my father, though he looked at it through a philosophical, as opposed to an emotional, lens.

He was a staunch supporter of land for peace. He was already advocating talks with the PLO in the mid 1980s, breaking ranks with the mainstream Jewish community long before that taboo had been broken. He sympathised with my dilemma.

In the late 1950s and 1960s, my parents had both hitchhiked through France to Marseilles and had caught the five-day boat to Israel. They were there in 1967, and just before the outbreak of war, my father sent my mother home to Britain to look after my brother and sister. He stayed on Kibbutz Lahav on the fringes of the Negev Desert where he had previously volunteered. Since all the men had been called up to fight in the war, he had the somewhat suspicious job of looking after all the women.

He still had friends there. 'You should go visit Amos. He'd be a good guy to talk to. And he'd like you to visit. We used to be good mates in the 1960s. We keep in touch every so often. He's a dude. Ask him about his army experience.'

I was open to anything at this stage and it was a good opportunity for Lucy and me to escape the city for the day and head south to the desert.

Amos is an archetypal kibbutznik: slippers, flannel shirt, stubble, shades. We soon got onto army talk.

'I can still see it clearly,' he said. 'We were patrolling the western Negev. In those days, around the time of the Six-Day War, the order was to shoot to kill. I was covering my platoon as they advanced to the Egyptian border. Their lives could have been at risk.

'That moment is scorched in my brain. I can freeze every frame again and again.' His eyes began blurring; his nostrils flared. 'I saw him move towards us. I caught him on my radar crawling on his stomach, inching his way towards us. I remember staring at him, wanting to know him. But my training prevailed over my instincts. I fired three bullets.'

He paused for more than a moment. Do you understand what "Know Thine Enemy" means?'

'No. I have never been to war. I don't understand. I can't understand. But you should have no remorse,' I said. 'You fought for your country. You killed the enemy and thwarted him killing more of us.'

I was trying to be compassionate. I wanted him to know that I did not judge him. I wanted him to know that I would have had similar reservations. But I had made an assumption, and it was entirely false.

Tears began streaming from Amos' weathered eyes.

'Maybe he had children? Who told his wife? Would his body have been left there to decompose or did he get an honourable funeral? These questions have haunted me since I fired those bullets.'

I had no words of comfort worthy of the situation. If in the last thirty years Amos has been unable to shake his guilt, how could my naive comments help?

'I have to live with this man's face in my subconscious. Day and night. Some nights I wake up shivering because, in my dreams, I have been sentenced to death for murder. I have no defence. I killed a man.'

He said it felt like his arteries were slowly being wrung dry of blood. And that he was heaving his last few heavy breaths. He was a broken man.

'Amos. You killed a man in your defence. I have not killed a man. But nor have I defended the state.'

'I will never be able to shake that moment from my memory. That man will die with me. As I did with him. Barely a day goes by when I don't think of him or his family. I wonder who they are, how they are faring. I beg to be taken to them so that I can help them. I yearn to humanise them so that maybe I can perhaps make their suffering easier. But I can't. I will never know who he was.

'The only positive thing I have learned from all these years is that war begets no victors, only losers. OK, we won the wars of 1948, '67, '73, but I lost my soul. So did many others like me. We paid the price of the victor over the vanquished. What we call the 1948 War of Independence, the Palestinians call Al-Naqba – the Catastrophe. It was zero–sum. Our victory was their defeat. Our return home was their exile. In 1967, we occupied their land because we believed it promised us security. But we lost our freedom in exchange.'

'Amos,' I said not really knowing how to console a man whose heart and soul had been ripped to shreds, 'I agree that we have lost more than we have gained in our wars. But I also understand that if we had lost just one of those wars, we would have all been buried at sea. That, surely, is your primary defence. You carry your guilt because of your action. I carry my guilt because of my inaction.'

'Habibi,' he said, rubbing his eyes. 'The man I killed was just crawling back to an abandoned well to pour some water into his parched mouth. I thought he was an enemy soldier. So I shot him. He was no threat to our people. He had no weapon. He was caught beyond enemy lines and was dying of thirst in the desert.'

CHAPTER FORTY-ONE

THERE IS ONE moment of life in Israel I will never forget. A moment so far removed from conventional life that it still sends a shiver down my spine.

It wasn't katyushas flying overhead on the northern border near Kibbutz Rosh HaNikra. Neither was it watching human flesh being scraped from the pavement after the suicide bomb in downtown Tel Aviv. Nor was it standing in silence at the siren on Memorial Day for Israel's Fallen Soldiers alongside Hannah, mourning her brother Alex, who had been killed in action in Lebanon.

They were all horrific. But this was not a moment from war. It was a moment preparing for it. A moment when the thought that it could happen brought the notion of death to my doorstep.

Saddam Hussein, dubbed 'The Butcher of Baghdad', invaded Kuwait on 2 August 1990, prompting a US-led coalition based in Saudi Arabia. But, as Operation Desert Shield launched a bombing campaign on Iraq and Saddam's defeat by the allied armies seemed imminent, he played his joker card: he fired batteries of scud missiles at Israel in January 1991 in an attempt to lure it into a war against Iraq, thereby dividing the allied coalition and diverting the focus from the crisis in the Gulf to an Israeli–Arab war. Yasser Arafat supported Saddam Hussein during the Gulf crisis, hoping that Saddam would attack Israel, thereby triggering an Arab–Israeli war on behalf of the Palestinians.

Hussein's logic was simple. If he could snare Israel into the war, the Arab members of the allied forces, such as Egypt and Saudi Arabia, would surely join Iraq as the Kuwait crisis became an all-out Arab–Israeli war. But Israel, for the first time in its history, did not retaliate under attack, after the United States exerted immense pressure on the government to exercise self-restraint.

For six weeks, Israelis scuttled to their sealed rooms at the sound of the siren, donning gas masks, sticking masking tape across any gaps and lining their doorways with wet towels. Thirty-nine scud missiles hit Israel. Luckily the warheads on them were conventional, not nuclear or biological. Fortunately, no one was killed, although the damage was extensive.

In his war diary, renowned Israeli novelist David Grossman recorded his feelings from inside his sealed room.

'In the masks everyone looks alike . . . We speak only of missiles and methods of sealing our rooms, and mobile launchers. Our vocabulary has dwindled. Even our souls have shrunk.'

'In Europe and America,' continued Grossman, 'parents cringe when they have to tell their children the facts of life. In the land of the Jews, long before they learn the facts of life, we must tell them the facts of death.'

Saddam started his war games again in early 1998. This time I wasn't watching it on television from a safe distance, as I had when Operation Desert Storm was waged. Nearly a decade later, would it all happen again – with me and Lucy in the thick of it? While the threat of an attack was not physically perceptible on the ground – Jordan separates Israel from Iraq – it was tangible in the air.

We received a notice in the post instructing us to collect our gas masks from one of the various public depots; we were also told to allocate a 'sealed room' in the event that Saddam's threats would arrive by missile. The panic was probably less acute than in 1991 because most people had been through the drill once before. But, for us, it was uncharted territory.

The concept of a sealed room had been unimaginable to me back in 1991, although my sister and her family were cowering behind gas masks in their sealed room in Jerusalem. And while the first avalanche of scuds killed no civilians, they did land within range. This time, however, the threat was compounded by the possibility that Saddam could attach nuclear or biological warheads to his missiles.

On Sheinkin Street and in the Carmel Market, people seemed to go about their daily business as usual. There was little or no perceptible edge to the atmosphere. But at the checkout tills in the local supermarket, piles of masking tape and plastic sheets were being stacked high. Lucy immediately sensed the danger. We took our ID cards and decided to get a taxi to the bus station to collect our gas masks because my scooter couldn't handle two people and two gas masks.

She was in no mood for my taxi antics. 'Do me a favour. Don't start a fight with the driver.'

'I won't. I never do – unless they start with me.'

'Nonsense. You always have to open your mouth, talk politics, sport or anything controversial.'

'Not true. I just like communicating. They're interesting people who listen to the radio all day and smoke too many smokes.'

I barely opened my mouth the whole journey. And I even managed to refrain from biting the bait when the host of a talk-back radio show explained that the MonicaGate sex scandal rocking the White House had been described by Hamas spiritual leader Sheikh Ahmed Yassin as a Zionist plot because Lewinsky was Jewish.

We were directed down to the basement. A disorderly queue meandered back from the door, where a couple of IDF soldiers held the fort. As we waited, people exited from another door and strolled away bearing rectangular cardboard boxes under their arms. Had this not been Israel, it would have been possible to imagine that Santa Claus may have been in the room distributing Christmas gifts. There were mothers, holding children, perplexed but excited by the novelty of a new 'toy'.

We inched our way forward. The talk in the queue revolved around one subject.

'Mah pitom! No, I don't think he'll attack. But I'd rather have a mask just in case. You never know with him.'

'Hoo meshugah! – he's crazy! He fired last time. So why won't he do it again?'

'I haven't got any tape yet.'

'Nuuuu. What are you waiting for?'

'How can I be sure my room is sealed?'

'Last time we sealed the lounge. This time I think we'll do the kitchen. Who knows how long it will be for? We can't starve. Mah la'asot? — what can I do?'

I had been thinking similar things. How do you know that your room is sealed? Surely the acid test is under attack – by which time it would be too late to rectify.

Although we lived in a flat, it was on a roof. It opened out onto a huge exposed balcony and it would be difficult to seal a room.

'Which room can we seal?' asked Lucy.

Our bedroom had no door; our kitchen was in our bedroom; and our lounge was essentially the front hallway. In fact, the only room that had a door and that could be 'sealed' was the bathroom. Only it was tiny. In the event, one of us would have to sit on the toilet seat; the other in the bath. Otherwise it would be standing room only.

I couldn't help laughing at the absurdity of the scenario. The bathroom was in such a state of disrepair when we moved in that we had decided to renovate. The landlord was planning on tearing the roof flat down to rebuild a penthouse for his retirement, so he gave us the green light to trash the place if we felt inclined. The result was a bathroom straight out of a seedy nightclub, with deep purple walls and bright turquoise fur trimming that surrounded the mirror and shelves. I removed the faucet because the sink was too small and the water just ended up on the floor. Now it just bubbled out of the hole in the pipe.

The only part of the whole room of any note was the toilet seat. Lucy had replaced the ageing dyed plastic seat with a new wooden one. After all, it was the throne.

Within an hour, we were at the front of the queue displaying our ID cards to the guards. We could see inside. Cardboard boxes were piled floor to ceiling, wall to wall. Three or four female soldiers were talking people through the routine.

The soldier looked at us and guessed the size we would require. Then she grabbed two boxes from the stockpile. It all seemed extremely routine for her and, no doubt, she had no idea that we were not born sabras. It was her job to dispatch gas masks as quickly and efficiently as possible, not to worry about whether we were suffering an emotional crisis. She tightened the straps around Lucy's mask.

Then came that moment.

I looked at her, my love, and she was different. The mask was big, black, bulky and ugly. It had an enormous cylindrical breathing apparatus down near the mouth. Two huge oval-shaped eyepieces enabled her to see out – and me to see in.

We locked onto each other's eyes. She seemed remote, distant, scared. Her eyes began to well up. She was petrified, and I could not reassure her that everything would be OK. The soldier fastened me in and tightened my straps. Her tears sparked mine. Now we were separated twice. Two lovers behind two masks that would, ostensibly, protect us from whatever poison may emanate from Saddam's scuds. Perhaps these masks could save us from anthrax or cholera, but they could not mask our fear.

For the first time in my life, I felt like a prisoner of war in my own home. There we were dressed up like aliens – and all we could both think about was why we had chosen this life when it felt, at that moment, close to death.

We could have been riding the surf at Bondi or soaking up the vibes in Soho, but instead here we were petrified, staring at each other from inside gas masks.

It was a split second. But it will last a lifetime.

We shoved the two boxes under our bed, hoping that we'd never have to use them. My fear was compounded by the fact that my pending draft might mean that Lucy would be left alone. That was bad enough, but alone during a scud missile attack? I would never allow that to happen.

Fortunately, Saddam's scuds didn't eventuate and we never discovered what it would be like to seal our bathroom and don gas masks while missiles rained down on us from Baghdad.

CHAPTER FORTY-TWO

TIME HAD just about expired. I had one last hope left, but I had to think beyond my appeal; to work out what would happen if my appeal were denied. Every time I thought I was sure, something else inside me questioned my logic.

I arranged to meet Yonni. We had grown up together in the youth movement; he was a year younger than me. Then he had been Jonathan; now that he was in Israel, he was called by the Hebrew equivalent – Yonatan, shortened to Yonni. We came from the same stock. He had arrived in Israel a couple of years ahead of me – so he was called up before me. He had already completed his service by the time I received my draft papers, and I wanted to know what the army was like for an older person, someone who hadn't been born here and someone who had grown up with the same 'bleeding-heart' liberal ideology as me.

'Hell can't be anywhere near as bad as Lebanon,' he told me, as we strolled down the promenade alongside Tel Aviv beach. 'Everyone laughed at how my service wouldn't involve anything "real". But 1995 to 1996 was a bad year to be in the army.'

'Is there a good year to be in the army?'

'Dunno. Mine sure was bad. It was the year of Rabin's murder, the year of all the suicide bombings and the year that there was massive action in Lebanon, Operation Grapes of Wrath, and in the Territories, Operation . . . what was it called again . . . Fuck Hamas up the Shitter . . . '

He was the 'loader' in a tank. 'My job,' he continued, 'was loading the shells and playing with all the bang-bang things – machine guns, mortars, grenades and all that.'

'I was in a platoon of 18-year-olds. My officers were twenty-one. From the very beginning, there were things I hated about the army, and I'm not talking about the running up hills carrying sacks that felt like they were loaded with rocks. I hated that too, but I hated more the way that they always refer to the "enemy" as "the Arabs". I know that the enemy was the Arabs, but it struck a nasty note in me, right from the beginning. I always felt that when you get too used to calling the enemy Arabs, then you inevitably start thinking of all Arabs as enemies . . . '

His voice trailed off. 'And these are 18-year-old Israelis – in their most formative years. Do you know what I mean?'

I nodded in agreement but remained silent, not wanting to break his pace. It seemed like he'd turned the tap on and his memories were gushing out.

'We did basic training in the desert in the middle of summer and then my "one year of nothing real" turned surreal: the [Occupied] Territories and Lebanon.

'After the Dizengoff suicide bomb, we were sent into the Territories, south of Hebron. The aim of our mission was to try to force Hamas out of that area. The army had placed a curfew on the whole area and, as soon as we arrived, we went through a village to ensure that no one was defying the order.

'We walked through streets and alleyways, peering into people's windows, and looking mean. Literally. It was a show of military might. We were supposed to look mean – and I hated it.

'I didn't look through a single window – all I could think of was what it must be like to be an Arab kid watching Israeli soldiers staring through your front window. I understand why it had to be done – after all, over sixty innocent civilians had been killed by Hamas bombs that week – but it was horrible.'

'I also understand why it had to be done,' I said. 'I saw some of those civilians' dismembered limbs and torsos splattered across Dizengoff junction. I can still see those ultra-Orthodox guys, wearing rubber gloves and carrying plastic bags, scraping pieces of flesh off the pavement.'

'There was only one actual act of violence carried out by our platoon that day – and it was by me! A guy got out of his car when we were searching it and attacked me – he tried to punch me in the face, so I had to hit him in the face with my gun. Me! Can you picture it? The whole platoon thought it was hysterical – everyone called me "Lefty" and the fact that I was the only guy who hit anyone that day amused a lot of people. Not me. I was shaking like a leaf, and I swear I almost threw up.'

'Jesus! I would have. And Lebanon?' I prompted.

'Lebanon . . . '

Yonni sat down on a low wall alongside an ice-cream van, lit a cigarette and drew on it heavily. Kids were running riot on the sand just behind us laughing, screaming, crying. House music was pounding out of the speakers next to the café at Banana Beach.

Lebanon has been Israel's Achilles heel since 1978 when the first Israeli operation crossed the northern border.* And the closest I'd ever been to Lebanon was on the hill above Kibbutz Rosh HaNikra gazing down the slopes towards Tyre (Sour).

I had read a description of southern Lebanon as 'Hell's boot camp'. Robert Young Pelton, in his aptly named book *The World's Most Dangerous Places,* opens the chapter by writing: 'If God created a training ground for the Armageddon, southern Lebanon would be the stage.' So I had a vague idea of how miserable Lebanon was. And anyone I've met who has fought in Lebanon seems to pause before talking about it. It's as if the scars, aches and pains are stored in a separate memory bank, and a special code is required to access the data.

'I was there during operation "Grapes of Wrath".† It was just before the 1996 election so it was a sensitive time politically.

'We went into Lebanon early one morning and drove quite

* On 14 March 1978 the IDF launched Operation Litani in response to the massacre of thirty-seven civilians by Palestinian terrorists from Lebanon who hijacked two Egged buses. The IDF initially occupied southern Lebanon up to the Litani River in an attempt to drive the PLO from the area. That was the precursor to the 1982 invasion.

† Operation Grapes of Wrath was the name of the military campaign launched on 10 April 1996 after Hezbollah rockets injured forty Israelis during the festival of Passover.

deep into the security zone. At one point we went through this big fucking wadi that had a reputation for Hezbollah ambushes, so we went through at full speed with all guns blazing. You can't imagine . . . Surreal is an understatement.

'Anyway, we then came to a hill where we had to cover the tank with camouflage netting and wait. We were there over six hours.

'I shat out of the back of the tank three times in that six hours. No joke.'

I started laughing. Until I realised Yonni was not laughing at all.

'Then we saw Hezbollah guerillas setting up an ambush. We were ordered to open fire. All of us. This meant that three people all fired at once, so we all hit them.'

'What? You killed these guys?'

I was still naive. You don't go to south Lebanon to sunbathe. You go to fight a war against guerrillas who are waging jihad against 'Zionist infidels'. That's why so many soldiers I knew actually preferred being sent to Lebanon as opposed to the West Bank: after being trained to fight in war, they say, the last thing you want is to be ordered to chase kids down alleyways in Nablus or Hebron. In Lebanon, they argued, it's the real deal.

Yonni didn't reply to my infantile question. His eyes were unfocused and he seemed distant. At that moment, I figured, he was back in Lebanon, standing over three dead bodies.

'We had to wait around for the intelligence people to arrive,' he mumbled nervously, eyes glazed. 'When we stood over these three dead bodies, I was so scared I was going to throw up or pass out. Or crap in my underwear.'

This time I didn't laugh. But I couldn't look him in the eye either.

'But, actually, I felt nothing. Not a thing. The whole thing was so insane – it felt like I was in a film. But I couldn't begin to believe that this guy from Britain had just killed three terrorists.'

He paused, stubbed his cigarette out several times over, crushing the butt to a pulp, and looked at me. He giggled nervously, wiping his nose though there was nothing to wipe. 'What would the neighbours say?'

He didn't expect a reply. I didn't know whether to laugh or cry, so I did neither.

'That night my platoon commander pulled me aside. He wanted to know how I felt. When I told him I didn't really feel anything at all, he told me that was good. He said that we hadn't done a good thing or a bad thing, we'd just done something that had to be done.

'Looking back? I don't know. In a way, I still feel that's true. I've not had one single bad dream about it, but I have to admit that barely a day goes by that I don't think about it at some point. I don't feel bad about it – and I understand that we were at war with the Hezbollah but I just wish that someone else had done it instead of me.

'But, then again, I know that Israelis slept safely that night along the northern border. And I realise that the army is not fun and games and that's what has to be done in the name of self-defence.'

I had no idea what to say.

'When we were returning to base that evening, we drove up towards this village. Though my night vision glasses, all I could see was locals running away – they looked like ants running out of a hole in the ground.

'That night, I was doing a shit in this toilet. The area was considered "hot" so we had to wear flak jackets and helmets everywhere – even on the toilet. No one showered here – the risk was too great.

'I was sitting there on the altar just staring at all these holes in the door from a mortar attack a few days before . . . That's when I realised that after I got out of Lebanon, I was never, ever going to set foot here again.

'It has the smell of death everywhere – I swear it's true. In southern Lebanon, I felt I was in a different world, one where you always watched everything, always kept your gun on you with a magazine at the ready – and you just never slept.'

'Do you regret it?'

'Believe it or not, I have no regrets. The year was hellish in so many ways, but as corny as it sounds, I learnt so much about a whole other world I knew nothing about. I learnt to appreciate things more. I learnt that a quiet life is the greatest thing in the world, and that you don't know how amazing peace is until you've tasted war. I only had a few days of it, and I'm still appreciating the fact that it's over. I never want to go through that again, and when I eventually have kids, I hope they never have to either.

'All the films that portray war, they just don't get it. There's no coolness, no heroism, just this mind-numbing disbelief, and your stomach turns to water.

'So,' he said, standing up again to continue walking, 'you just end up shitting loads'.

CHAPTER FORTY-THREE

YONNI CONFIRMED my worst fears. Even though the chances of my being sent to Lebanon were negligible, the mere thought of it scared the hell out of me. And I could never survive the torment that Amos went through day and night. But, no sooner had I convinced myself that I would never, ever conscript, and was busy weighing up the options of prison or exile, assuming my appeal was rejected, I was suddenly faced by a moral argument to serve in the army.

Ayal was one of my friends from university. He was the only one from there whom I trusted enough to discuss my position. The rest of them were diehard soldiers on a fast track to the Ministry of Defence. He came over one afternoon to watch the sunset from the roof.

I didn't tell him about my appeal.

'What are you going to do?'

'I'm still thinking. But I simply can't justify serving. If I would never send my kid to the army, how can I send myself? And what about miluim (reserve duty)? I'd be committing myself to a month a year for the next fifteen years. But then if everyone else does it, why shouldn't I? I just wish I could do national service as opposed to military service.'

'If you do decide to dodge, it'll be the army that loses out.'

'Eh? Why? You don't think there's enough meatheads out there who are dying to serve?'

'That's exactly my point.'

'I don't follow.'

Ayal tussled with his lighter, which was refusing to ignite. He tried a couple of tricks, to no avail, so he just sat there with an unlit cigarette in his mouth.

'It was not long after the Intifada broke out. I was serving in the Shtachim [the Occupied Territories]. Rabin, who was defence minister at that time, instructed us to break the bones of the Palestinian inciters in order to quell the violence.

'We were near Deir Ibzi, close to Ramallah, in the West Bank. Some of the soldiers in my platoon took his order too far; others, myself included, were more cautious.'

He shook his lighter and finally producing a flame.

'You remember those harrowing images of an IDF soldier hitting a Palestinian protestor over the head with a giant rock during the Intifada?'

I nodded, recalling the footage that was beamed around the world, adding to Israel's already damaged image.

'Had you or I been close by, we would not have stood aside. We have our own "red lines" beyond which we are not prepared to go. At any cost.

'Do you understand my point? What I'm getting at is the army needs people like you. Not everyone carries his conscience in the army. I know a few more soldiers who would've done the same as those guys did.'

It was a valid argument. 'Then there's no way out of my dilemma,' I said. 'If I go, I'm an accomplice to war. If I don't go, I risk others in my place abusing their powers like those guys.'

'No. Think about it. That's the difference. That's what makes conscripting not only acceptable, but morally important.'

'Maybe,' I replied. 'But at the moment it feels like I'm damned if I do – and damned if I don't.'

That night, Lucy and I watched the Eurovision Song Contest. Israel's entry was a song called 'Diva' by Dana International. Incredibly, she won. But Israel's pop diva is a transsexual; she was once a he – a guy called Yaron Cohen before he changed sex in a 1993 operation.

Her unlikely victory was greeted by extreme reactions, touching off a bitter battle between the Orthodox and secular. From our bedroom in downtown Tel Aviv, we could hear the spontaneous celebrations rocking Rabin Square, less than a kilometre away, long into the night. The secular soul of the nation, and the burgeoning gay and lesbian community in particular, took to the streets to celebrate their icon's success.

Up the holy hill in Jerusalem, however, Israel's Orthodox rabbis, inflamed that such a 'deviant' could represent the nation on a European stage, were already preparing edicts to ban the next contest from being held in Jerusalem lest the sanctity of the Holy City be tarnished. One compromise solution touted was to host the contest in Eilat, some 300 kilometres away by land and light years away in every other manner.

The very tenacity of the conflict (over an Israeli victory no less) highlighted the ongoing struggle for Israel's soul. The Israeli–Palestinian conflict may steal the limelight in the world media. But, backstage, the Israeli–Israeli conflict constantly simmers. Jews – secular and Orthodox, Ashkenazi and Sephardi, Left-wing and Right-wing, sabra and immigrant . . . – battle one another for hegemony. Like the Star of David, we are stretched in dichotomous directions, struggling to define ourselves.

CHAPTER FORTY-FOUR

IT'S THE NIGHT before I am due to go to Tel Hashomer to talk to the top brass. I'm in the bath, submerged in bubbles. Dense steam rises from the tub. Candlelights flicker, valiantly fending off the pervading damp. A soft crackle signals the demise of one candle. A thin thread of smoke rises gently, twisting and twirling until it melts into the steam. The already faint light dims.

My bath is my retreat from the fast fury of this brave new cyberworld. Sinking beyond the bubbles and beneath the water line, I am in search of clarity before my final fling at military exemption. The yin and yang of my conscience begin to play ball with each other.

– Ayal's argument about my own 'red lines' is powerful. Serve and try to influence from the inside.
– Nonsense. Look what happened to Yonni in Lebanon. He's barely lived a day without recalling his time there.
– True, but without him, and without the army, we would not have reached this point in the peace process.
– But we are at this stage in the peace process. The question is, could you handle living with the mental torture that Amos has lived with since he killed a man who wanted nothing more than water?
– But Yonni helped kill three guys and doesn't live with that torture because war is war and that's what has to be done. Is conscripting really such a big deal? In any case, you'll end up as a B-grade soldier, an office clerk or something innocuous like that.
– Maybe. But maybe not. There's no guarantee. What if you were sent to guard a West Bank settlement like Jason? How could you protect Right-wing settlers whose presence on the disputed land is one of the greatest obstacles to a peace agreement?

– But if you refused to go, you would be serving a sentence of a different kind: in prison. And if you were unwilling to serve, and equally unwilling to pay the penalty, then you would be condemning yourself to seven years in exile.

– If that were the case, then what would be the fate of your children? Could you guarantee them a Jewish life in the Diaspora? Wasn't one of your reasons for living in Israel in the first place so that you could guarantee your children would grow up Jewish?

– But one of the reasons you wouldn't serve in the army was precisely because you would never send your son or daughter off to war. Unless, that is, the existence of the state was at risk. In which case you too would go and fight for your country.

– And if you ask yourself honestly, are you and Lucy really happy here? Do you both not crave your families and the cultural normality that comes with living in the West?

The longer my dilemma stewed in my mind, the more I realised I was locked in a classic case of Catch-22. By now the bathwater was lukewarm and my fingers and toes were waterlogged. I had no choice but to retreat to reality. And reality offered me a last-gasp chance to save my soul.

So this is what it has boiled down to. Three sergeants will decide my fate. All other avenues have now been closed. This is my last chance.

I arrive at Tel Hashomer for the umpteenth time. Lucy is with me. She wishes me luck, we embrace and she waits outside in the empty courtyard. It's 10 am, and the roll call of inductees has been and gone.

Upstairs, I am told to sit and wait outside an office. As usual there's a hum of activity in the building, fast-moving soldiers and slow-moving draftees. There's a queue for medicals. The penis doctor is conducting his usual inspections. Psychometric examinations are being handed out. New immigrants are trying to recall whether or not they have amnesia, insomnia or have ever contemplated suicide. The cycle is spinning.

I am called in. The room is not large. There is a table, behind which sit three sergeants, two men and one woman. They are older than me, but only one of them looks to be in his forties. He is tall, lean and sports his military spoils on the shoulders of his olive shirt. His face reads like a condolence card: sad and glum. Even if he were to smile it would be hard to reverse the dour shape of his mouth. He has all the verve and panache of a funeral director.

I don't fancy my chances.

The younger of the two sergeants, though, appears somewhat dandy. He appears to be trying to brown-nose his boss, and he gives me a warmish, empathetic smile. He has short, dusty brown hair and a mole just to the right of his upper lip.

The sole woman seems intimidating. I barely cross eyes with her. I reckon she thinks I'm a wimp and nothing I say will sway her opinion. I may be wrong. And, I admit, I'm probably paranoid.

They have a file on their desk, which I assume has my particulars inside. No doubt it will hold my psychometric score. I'm convinced I'm not 'Profile 97'. I can't be. Putting me in a combat unit would be tantamount to military suicide.

Equally, I'm fairly sure I'm not 'Profile 21', though if I play my hand correctly I may, just may, walk out of here with a 'Profile 21'.

The elder of the two men begins. It's all in Hebrew.

'Benjamin, we understand that you have a problem with your conscription.'

'Yes,' I reply, catching his eye for a nanosecond.

'You spoke with one of the clerks and she has referred your case to our committee. What exactly is the nature of your problem?'

This is my moment. Do or die time. I want to emphasise at the outset that I am not just looking for a way out because I'm lazy or don't care about the country. On the contrary.

'I came to live here to be a part of this country. This is the only place in the world I consider home. You are born sabras, right?

You have never had to grow up feeling like a "guest" in someone else's land. Here I feel at home. But I do not feel able to serve in the military for conscientious reasons.'

My Hebrew begins to dry up. 'You see,' I stammer, trying to buy time while I translate in my head, 'we have already made peace with Egypt and Jordan. And we are on the brink of an agreement with the Palestinians. The Soviet Union, which used to supply the arsenal of arms to the Arabs, has collapsed. And the world's only superpower is our loyal ally. Today, we are not defending the state like we had to in 1948, 1956, 1967 or 1973. It's different. It's not the same war.'

Three heads nod cautiously. I am inspired. They seem to be warming to me.

'Israel's existence is no longer in danger. There is no existential threat today. And so, as a Left-wing Zionist, I do not feel I can justify joining the army.'

Then, without thinking about it, I drop a bomb.

'And I couldn't justify going to Lebanon.'

It takes only a second to say those seven words. And it takes only another second to realise that my calm introduction has just been obliterated by a senseless comment that has probably buried my chances of redemption.

'Why is that?' asks the younger of the male sergeants.

I could go for broke and explain why I think it's an illegal and immoral occupation. But I notice the elder sergeant scribbling notes in my file. Immediately, I regret touching such a sensitive nerve. I backtrack sheepishly.

'Well, all I mean is that nations have borders and we should use our borders to defend our state. The invasion of Lebanon was Israel's first non-defensive war. OK, the PLO were launching attacks and we had every right to defend ourselves, but sixteen years on we are still there . . . '*

I have not managed to salvage my mistake. Blank faces stare at me awaiting my next outrageous statement that flies in the face of Israeli nationalism. My destiny has just been confirmed. These

*The IDF withdrew from Lebanon in May 2000.

three sergeants have as much respect for me as a spider for a fly trapped in its web. I try one last-ditch effort to redeem myself.

'All I am saying is this: as a conscientious objector, I am ready, eager and willing to do national service, but not military service. I am happy to work for the state in any area except the military.'*

'You are aware that there is no such thing as a conscientious objector in this country,' pouts the woman.

'I see. So what is the penalty?'

'If you do not arrive for conscription on your call-up date, you will receive a hearing in a military court and the judge will sentence you.'

She is not big on compassion. I can almost hear her mind ticking away thinking, 'You jack ass, moralist daisy. How I'd love to haul your ass through basic training . . . '

'Uh-huh.'

'This is the law of the land,' emphasises the younger of the two men, showing the only ounce of compassion. 'Section 46(a) [of the 1986 Defence Service Law] makes it an offence punishable by up to two years' imprisonment for failure to obey an order such as reporting for military service.

'However, if you are considered to have evaded the IDF without permission, you could be charged with desertion, which is, technically, punishable by up to fifteen years' imprisonment.'

I interpret his use of the word 'technically' as a way of implying that fifteen years would be harsh. Jesus, fifteen days would be harsh. But would it be worth it?

'I realise that this is the law. But times have changed . . . '

'We will consider your appeal and let you know in due course,' concludes the elder sergeant in a dour, matter-of-fact manner.

'OK,' I concede, my ammunition spent.

I left, head down and dejected. Did I honestly think they'd buy my argument? Who was I kidding? Lucy was waiting. We consoled each other.

---

* The National Service Law (1953) legislated national service for religious women only, but it has remained dormant since then.

Assuming my appeal was rejected, I would be left with one of three choices: conscript, face a jail sentence or go AWOL. Or, if I was really game, I could join God's Army, grow a beard (no trouble), brush up on my Torah studies (minor trouble, but possible) and then register in an ultra-Orthodox yeshivah on the grounds that I have just rediscovered myself (a long shot).

It sounded ridiculous, but then I had just tried to convince three sergeants, who had dedicated their lives to the military, of the merits of conscientious objection – which is tantamount to trying to persuade three ultra-Orthodox rabbis of the virtues of homosexuality.

CHAPTER FORTY-FIVE

MY FINAL DRAFT NOTICE arrived a week or so after my dismal appeal. It simply confirmed what I had already known when I walked out of that office: my last exit route had been closed. I'd blown my chances – if there had been any to begin with.

I had explored all avenues, considered every option in pursuit of an exemption. I had even entertained the notion of becoming ultra-Orthodox, and I was a heartbeat away from visiting a shrink and conceding that I was contemplating suicide.

They say that truth is the first casualty of war. I was prepared to sacrifice the truth to avoid going to war. In the end, the law is the law. And the law in Israel does not accommodate conscientious objectors. It felt strange to know that, finally, I had reached the end of the road. No matter how much I loved this country, I was unwilling to serve in the army. Or pay the price of jail. For me, but also for Lucy. We were fortunate enough to have another option.

I was still haunted by my conscience. What gave me the right to run? How could I sleep at night knowing that thousands of soldiers were out there preventing terrorist attacks? Young boys, barely pubescent, patrolling the borders, preventing enemy incursions, ensuring Israelis could sleep safely in their beds, not in bomb shelters.

Was I the only one scared of being ambushed by Hezbollah guerrillas? Or Hamas terrorists? Of leaving my beloved one morning and never returning?

In defence of the army, if I did serve I would be obligated by Israeli law to refuse an illegal command. This law dates back to 29 October 1956, when IDF troops opened fire on Israeli–Arab villagers from Kfar Kaseem, just near the then border with Jordan (now the Green Line), for breaking a curfew. Some forty-seven villagers were killed, most of them unaware of the imposed curfew because they had been out working the fields and were on their way home when they were shot. Eleven border policemen were court-martialled and charged; eight of them were convicted and sentenced to between eight and seventeen years in prison, although the sentences were appealed and no one served more that four years.

As a result, the military court ruled that soldiers were ordered to disobey illegal orders. Soldiers are only allowed to open fire in self-defence, if their life is in danger. It sounds clear in theory, but when faced with a horde of stone-throwing, Molotov-cocktail-wielding Palestinian youths, shades of grey may begin to blur that clarity.

But given that I would, by virtue of my age and health, be a B-grade soldier, the chances were slim that I'd ever have to contemplate pulling the trigger. Except in basic training. What was so morally troublesome about that? Nothing. And everything. I would gladly have served my country in another way. Just like in Germany, where conscientious objectors can perform national service as opposed to military service, I would have done so. Had I been eighteen, like most other Israeli conscripts, I have no doubt that I may have acted differently too. But I was twenty-eight and my value system was too deeply rooted.

How did the situation degenerate to such dismal depths? From (an albeit cold) peace with Egypt in 1979, a tentative agreement with the Palestinians to end the war in 1993 and peace with Jordan in 1994, the last few years had been stained with blood: Rabin's murder, suicide bombs, Lebanon . . .

I remembered my optimism on my arrival in 1994 and then again on the eve of the 1996 election. Now, here I was on the verge of packing up and heading into exile in 1998.

I was not being chased out. I was not leaving for fear of my life. I had decided, independently, to leave. To vote with my feet.

I did, however, discover that the government was waging a war on draft dodging at the time, after Defence Minister Yitzhak

Mordechai was stunned to learn of a 'crisis of motivation' when he heard soldiers at their induction tell him they wanted to serve close to home and return in one piece.

That's not the attitude with which soldiers are supposed to enter the army. Perhaps they were speaking up, for the first time, and expressing their concern that today's situation is different. The defence minister interpreted it as a sign of weakness, and ordered his staff to close the gates and block any draft dodging, which left me next to no chance of gaining 'Profile 21'. I never did find out what my profile was.

With the choice of army service or jail much like hell or purgatory, Lucy and I packed up our lives. The state did not exile me. If anything, I exiled myself.

CHAPTER FORTY-SIX

I BOOKED LUCY on a flight to London the day before mine. Just in case. If there were a chance of complications at the airport, the last thing I wanted was Lucy witnessing it. If I were caught by the military police going through passport control, I did not want her to watch me being escorted away.

I was on my own. Lucy was already in the air. I returned to Tel Hashomer to get an exit permit to leave the country. Once drafted, you can't go anywhere, not even to the Sinai, without getting an exit permit. It's understandable, I guess. The army needs to know your whereabouts in case they need you. Or in case you disappear.

It's usually a formality, and nine times out of ten, they issue a permit on the spot. I got mine without too much drama, lying that I would be back in three days after a brief business trip to London.

All the possible permutations percolated in my mind, some dripping through into my consciousness; most filtering straight into my subconscious. The army was still a rite of passage. It is the one thing in society that most Israelis do. Except Israeli Arabs and the ultra-Orthodox. Those who are physically or mentally sick. Waggers. And conscientious objectors like me.

I paid all our bills, but had to leave our bank account open so as not to arouse any suspicion. But I withdrew most of the little money we had in there and figured that we could wire the rest from exile.

On the morning of my flight I went to Jaffa to pay homage to my favourite local dish, hummous, at Abu Marouwan, one of my favourite parlours. Belly full, I rode home via the old part of Ajami, taking in some favourite backstreets where I could feast my eyes for the last time on the stunning architectural remnants and watch the waves crash onto Reef Beach.

I was going to leave my scooter for Ayal, my university friend, and had told him that I'd lock it up and hide the key in an envelope in my post box for him to collect. I would have given Sparky first choice on the bike, but he had gone travelling soon after he finished the army. Like most Israelis, his first mission upon leaving was to get out of the country and drown himself in every illicit substance possible to make up for three years of bad food and no sleep. In any case, he would have probably laughed at the suggestion that he ride a 49 cc scooter. Both Rose and Shira were too petite for it. They were coming over for a final farewell before I left.

I headed home through Neve Tzedek and the Yemenite Quarter for the last time.

Anat was one of those bubbly characters bursting with energy that made a habit of exploding with excitement whenever she met anyone close to her. She was moving into the flat, and we had arranged to meet, swap keys and organise the remaining paper-work. Her parents were Israeli but had moved to Australia years ago in search of the 'lucky' country. Lucy and Anat knew each other from when they were growing up in Australia.

She was sparkling, vivacious, energetic. True to form, she was over-excited; I was less than excited. In fact, I felt depressed and sorry for myself. She was thrilled to be moving into the roof flat. I was gutted to be leaving the country, my friends, my home.

'They'll probably come looking for me. If they do, tell them you've never heard of me.'

'No problem. I'll let you know if they do. I'll email you.'

Shira was there. So were Hannah and Rami. Rose arrived later. She didn't want to hang around in the gloom; she just wanted to say goodbye. We all knew we'd meet again, probably in Britain, and of course we'd remain in touch. Still, it was tough to part from close friends, people who had been part of my life for so long. Other friends arrived, but I just wanted to leave. I couldn't handle the morose atmosphere. I had my mind on one other thing: I still had to get beyond passport control.

I began feeling nervous as my taxi rolled past the army checkpoint on the road into the airport. Prior to that I was just emotional about leaving. I had built my life here. I had planted my hopes here. I had met Lucy here and fallen in love with her. This was where I belonged. This was where we belonged. This was where we had planned to have a family one day.

I declined the offer to engage in discussion with the taxi driver. I'd had my fair share of run-ins with them over the years. Lucy would have been proud of my silence. But I did wonder what he'd think of me if I told him I was about to go absent without leave. Once upon a time, I would have been considered a social pariah. Would he still excommunicate me?

As soon as I step across the threshold, I will be transformed from an Israeli citizen into an illegal draft dodger.

I check my bags in and head to passport control. Surprisingly, there's no queue. I hand over my British passport and my exit permit. The woman keys in my details and sits staring at her computer screen for what feels like several minutes. Normal procedure, I try to convince myself.

My palms are sweating. I pray that beads of sweat are not gathering on my forehead. Why didn't I shave? Jesus. How could I be so damned stupid? So I don't make a habit of shaving. But if there was ever a time to look smart, like I actually was going on a business trip, now was that time. I'd blown it.

'Where is your Israeli passport?'

'I don't have one.'

'But you are a citizen, no? You have an ID card, right?'

'Yes.'

'Can I see it please?'

'No problem. I just haven't had time to get to the Ministry of Interior to pick my passport up yet. I'll get it next week.'

I hand over my ID card.

'Where are you going?'

'London. Business trip.'

'Show me your ticket please.'

I oblige. I had to buy a return in order to get my exit permit, even though I knew I'd never be on that return flight.

'You have a three-day permit.'

'I know. I'm returning Thursday.'

She pauses, punches some keys and then stares at the screen for what seems like another excruciatingly long time. Then she stops.

I watch her closely as she lifts her hand, and then lowers it, stamp grasped firmly in her palm. She saturates the exit stamp in black ink and then bangs it firmly onto a page in my passport, permanently staining it. And with that she seals my destiny.

The round stamp simply states the date and the following: 'Ben-Gurion Border Patrol. Yetziah – exit.'

She was just a passport control officer, but as she handed me back my passport, I looked her in the eye as though she were the chief of staff of the IDF. I swallowed hard, bit my bottom lip, skipped a heartbeat and reached out to clutch my passport to freedom. I lowered my head before walking on.

In the departure lounge, my flight had already been called. I rushed to the gate and, as I boarded the plane, I took one last look behind me.

A security guard was mumbling something into a walkie-talkie.

I left home and entered exile.

EPILOGUE

OVER THREE YEARS have passed since May 1998 when I left Israel for the last time, and became a draft dodger living in exile for the first time. Since then, barely a day has passed when I have not, consciously or subconsciously, thought of home.

Looking back, I take no pride in being a draft dodger from the IDF. It may sound like a hip honour to hold, but under the surface it's a bitter reality. I did not depart Ben-Gurion international airport, just before my call-up, with a smile on my face. I left my soul behind.

But I have no shame either. I returned to Israel in 1994 to live in a country that had just embarked upon the road to peace, after Rabin and Arafat had signed the historic Oslo Accords and Israel and Jordan had just declared an end to war. I arrived home to become a living part of that peace crusade.

Some say I am a coward. Others say that I missed out on a great life experience. And there are those who admit that, while it wasn't great, it wasn't all that bad after all. Very few people think I made the right choice. So be it. I don't know. And I may never know.

What I do know is that I can sleep at night in the knowledge that I stood up for what I believe in and didn't conform just because the vast majority were, and still are, conscripting. I only wish that national service was an option. Then, my address would still be home, not exile.

Lucy and I spent a few weeks visiting my family in Britain and then headed across Asia to Australia. We landed in India, travelled overland up to Nepal and down to Thailand. Our last stop before Australia was Vietnam, where we backpacked from Saigon to Hanoi. It was good to be on the road again, travelling for the sake of travelling. But it was strange to know that we weren't returning to Israel, but were continuing south to Australia.

Shortly after, we landed in Sydney to begin our lives. Again.

There is a list. I guess it's a 'black' list. A list of people barred from entering Israel. Immigration officials at Ben-Gurion international airport have a copy of the list. Staff at the seaports and land crossings have one. So does every Israeli embassy the world over.

There are some obvious names on the list. They won't roll out the red carpet for Saddam Hussein. And there's no love lost for Libyan leader Muammar Gaddafi. But these guys are unlikely to make a personal appearance at Israeli immigration. They usually send someone – or something – in their stead. Like scud missiles or aeroplane hijackers.

The list isn't geared for the likes of Palestinian Authority Chairman Yasser Arafat. He has secretly sneaked into Israel several times to hold 'back-channel' meetings with prime ministers to try to complete the peace process.

No, this list is largely comprised of thousands of Islamic fundamentalists belonging to the military wings of Hamas, Islamic Jihad and Hezbollah, among other terrorist organisations. Like PFLP-GC leader Ahmad Jibril or his comrade in arms George Habash. Not to mention Fatah Revolutionary Council Leader Abu Nidal or Hezbollah militiamen like Sheikh Muhammas Hussein Fadlallah.

And me.

I'm up there alongside these thugs – and countless other draft dodgers who have fled the country, trading flak jackets for freedom.

I didn't know about the existence of the list, in its formal sense, until I decided to check with the Israeli Consul-General about the law regarding Israelis who had dodged the draft, who were AWOL or, as it is known in Hebrew, ARIK.

I had been led to believe that there was a general amnesty after seven years in exile. And, having endured three years, I wanted to be sure that if I sat tight and suffered another four years, I could return home. On a whim, I called one day to check on the score.

'Do you want me to see if you're on the list?' the woman on the end of the telephone asked in Hebrew.

'Y-y-y-yes,' I stuttered unconvincingly, trying to buy time.

What list? I knew I had broken the law, consigned myself to exile, would be imprisoned if I tried to re-enter the country, but I was amazed that there was someone around the corner who might know, by consulting a list, that I'd committed this crime.

'What's your name and date of birth?' she asked, matter-of-factly.

Midway through my vital statistics, a shiver ran down my spine and grabbed me by the genitals.

'Wait! Wait a minute,' I said in short, sharp Hebrew.

'If I give you my vitals, then, I guess, you guys could come and take away my . . . vitals. Right?' I suddenly began panicking that, by now, she knew my name and where I lived.

'No,' she replied, somewhat unconvincingly. 'We have no need.' At this point my left brain reminded my right brain that I had once suffered from a viral strain of pneumonia and a lung abscess, am chronically B-12 deficient, scream at the mere suggestion of an intravenous injection, faint at the sight of blood and that if the IDF wanted to flex its military muscle, I'd be at the very end of the queue. So why the hell would they trek all this way just to bring me home and then lock me up?

'OK,' I sighed, and parted way with my vitals. In an instant, I felt denuded.

There was silence. An eerie silence that seemed to last a lifetime. I could visualise the computer's database processing a check through the list, trying to find my name amid all these terrorists. The longer time went by, the safer I began to feel. My mind shifted effortlessly into overdrive. Maybe, after all, I had become one of the lost statistics, a mistake, a deletion, an accident. Human error. Any number of possibilities. All that worry, concern, fear, neurosis over nothing.

Ice-cold, with next to no hint of emotion that my future was in the balance, she finally cleared her throat.

'Ben – yes. You are on the list.'

It was official. Here, talking on the telephone to the Israeli embassy in Australia, having escaped military duty three years before, was the first official confirmation of my status.

I knew I was a draft dodger. I also knew that the military police had been looking for me after my conscription date. Anat had emailed me to say that days after I left, a draft order arrived in the mail and, later, a few messages were left on the answer phone and more orders arrived. Then an order was sent by registered post. The little old lady downstairs, who permanently smoked a plastic cigarette and limped around with a four-pronged walking stick, took the liberty of signing on my behalf. Anat got back from the beach to find her waiting, mail delivery in hand. Furious, Anat kindly asked her never to act on her behalf again (although it was very thoughtful, typically Israeli and came straight from the heart). The mail delivery lead to another barrage of phone calls and messages.

While I knew that they may have given up looking for me in Israel, I didn't realise I would be blacklisted on every single Israeli government computer terminal around the world. I didn't know whether to smile or sulk: on the one hand, it confirmed what I already knew deep inside. No big deal. No drama.

On the other hand, I felt a deep sense of despair. I was on a black list. And, to add insult to injury, my name was up there alongside some of the most notorious names on earth.

She asked me if that was all. 'Hell no!' I felt like yelling. Now that I knew I couldn't sneak into Israel with my British passport, I wanted to know how I could get back in without being banged up in a cell with a bunch of criminals who could smell the scent of fresh blood arriving.

Instead I tried to remain calm and said, 'Err . . . let's say, hypothetically of course, that I had to return urgently. What would I do?'

'You have to make a request in writing through the embassy. We send it on to the army and they will respond within two or three weeks. In all likelihood, they will let you enter.'

My eyebrows leaped toward my hairline, lines on my forehead immediately subsided, my ears pricked up.

'But,' she cautioned after a long pause, 'you will have to report to the army headquarters and resolve the issue with them when you are there.'

Having offered the prize, she immediately snatched it away again. My face sank.

'OK,' I said, pretending to be composed. 'So, let's say I did that. What would they do?'

'They may decide to close the case,' she said blankly, swinging the pendulum back in my favour again. 'Or they may take the matter to the military court.'

I suddenly felt like a kid who'd just been told that, in fact, after all these years of blind belief, Moses did not part the Red Sea. 'You m-m-m-ean,' I stuttered in Hebrew, 'that I could actually be let back into the country, but then wind up in prison?'

'Potentially,' she replied.

I required clarification. 'Let me understand. You're telling me that you can probably get me back into the country, but can't guarantee that I'll get out? Why on earth would I contemplate risking my free life for a life, or even a few months, no, one single day, behind bars?'

She responded on the defensive. 'Look, I'm just telling you the facts. If you want to apply to enter the country, write to us.'

'OK,' I said, trying to extract the heat out of the moment, but really wanting to re-confirm that I wouldn't get home to find a dodgy-looking car parked on the street outside my flat with two Mossad agents inside wearing sunglasses in mid-winter and pretending to read *Beano* magazine upside down.

'Is that all?' she queried, clearly fed up with my persistence.

'Yes. Well, actually, no. Would you happen to have my Israeli ID number on file?'

'2034 . . . ,' she began.

'23968,' I finished, my memory bank suddenly jolted into remembering my identification number which, for the duration of my time living in Israel, was my password – and passport – into civil life. Truth is, you can barely fart in the country without someone asking to see your ID card or, at least, what your number is. Without an ID card, the taps are turned off, all roads are closed, all avenues sealed. Life in Israel without an ID card is simply not worth the hassle.

'Thanks,' I said, trying to sound remotely thankful.

'Good luck,' she threw back at me, more as a convention than a courtesy.

I hung up, dazed by the sheer magnitude of the conversation. What was, supposedly, a mere phone call to confirm my seven-year exile, had evolved into a bureaucratic and legalistic nightmare.

While I already knew my status, there was still something disconcerting about having it confirmed, for the first time, by a state civil servant just around the corner.

And then the killer blow: they may let me in; but may not let me out again without serving time. Not only am I blacklisted, I have to return to the army to resolve the situation.

Maybe exile isn't so bad after all.

The first Palestinian I ever talked to for more than two minutes was a man by the name of Afif Safiyeh. He was the chief London representative of the PLO, and I was interviewing him for *Mancunion*, my university's student newspaper, while he was touring England in 1991.

We met in a small, dark room behind the stage of the main hall in the Student Union building. Two wooden chairs were all that furnished the room. Paint was peeling from the walls where a couple of anti-Thatcher posters, decrying the end of student loans peered down on us.

He was a smart-looking man in his late forties, perhaps early fifties. His black hair was neatly side-parted and he wore a jacket that failed to hide his potbelly. His English was impeccable, spoken in a deep guttural voice.

'Do you believe there will ever be peace in the Middle East?' I asked him.

He smiled, as though I had just asked the most predictable question possible. Then he responded with a joke: 'Presidents Bush and Gorbachev arrange a summit meeting with God in heaven. Bush and Gorbachev ask, "Will there ever be peace in the world?"

'God replies, "Yes, but not in your lifetimes".

'Yasser Arafat, upon hearing of this mission to heaven, arranges his own summit with God on the question of Palestine. Arafat asks, "Will there ever be peace in the Middle East?"

'God replies, "Yes, but not in *my* lifetime!"'

At the time of writing, while the negotiations continue, so too does the violence.

What has become known on the Palestinian streets as the Al-Aqsa Intifada, which began with riots on the Temple Mount at the end of September 2000, is not just another skirmish in this long, torrid affair.

At the Camp David summit in July 2000, Israeli Prime Minister Ehud Barak offered the Palestinians more than any other Israeli prime minister in history in his quest to leave 'no stone unturned' on the road to peace. He reportedly agreed to cede some 90 per cent of the West Bank to the Palestinians for a Palestinian state. In addition, he was willing to offer Palestinian sovereignty over Arab East Jerusalem and proffer a special status on the Old City of Jerusalem that would enable all religions free access to all holy sites, although Palestinians would be granted autonomous rule over the Al-Haram ash-Sharif (the Noble Sanctuary to the Arabs; Har HaBayit, the Temple Mount, to the Jews).

Arafat rejected the offer, lending yet more currency to former foreign minister Abba Eban's famous comment that the 'Palestinians never miss an opportunity to miss an opportunity'. So the Palestinians, provoked by a controversial visit by Likud leader Ariel Sharon to the Temple Mount on the eve of Rosh Hashanah (New Year), took to the streets for a second Intifada to demonstrate their determination that Al-Haram ash-Sharif in particular, and Jerusalem in general, belong to the Palestinians.

More than 350 lives, mostly Palestinian (including thirteen Israeli Arabs), have been lost in a battle that has been defined by two images: a 12-year-old Palestinian boy, cowering under his father's arm, before being shot dead in the Gaza Strip; and two Israeli reservists being lynched by a mob in Ramallah.

This may be the final battle for peace, the last stand over the most intractable final-status issue on the table: Jerusalem. But, when the forces of reason and rationalism finally manage to snuff the life from the flames of fury, Jerusalem will, one day, incorporate two capitals: Israeli and Palestinian, with a shared agreement over the holy sites of the Old City.

Already today, East and West Jerusalem are poles apart, reflecting the giant political, economic, cultural and social chasm that exists between the two peoples.

Inshallah – God willing, as they say in the Middle East, peace will one day prevail and this conflict will be read about in history books not newspaper headlines.

Then, perhaps, mandatory conscription will be cast into the dustbin.*

Then, perhaps, I will be able to return home.

Benjamin Black
Australia, January 2001

* In 1998, a group called 'Profile Hadash' (New Profile) was established with the aim of ending compulsory military service.

GLOSSARY

aliyah – literally 'ascent'; common usage for immigration to Israel

Ashkenazi – Jews of European descent (as opposed to Sephardi)

baklawah – a multi-layered, honey-soaked pastry filled with nuts

bar mitzvah – the rite of passage accorded to a 13-year-old Jewish boy who becomes a man in the community after he reads from the Torah in his bar mitzvah ceremony

Bedouin – nomadic Arabs who are desert dwellers

brit milah – circumcision of the male child after eight days

cohanim – descendants of the high priests and the highest 'rank' of Jew, followed by Levites

Druze – a member of an Arab splinter sect of Islam

felafel – a deep-fried chickpea ball mixed with parsley; classic street food wrapped in pita bread with tahina and salad

Green Line – so named because during an earlier round of troubles, a British officer drew a line in green ink to divide the Cypriot capital, Nicosia, into two sectors. After Israel occupied the West Bank in 1967, the term Green Line was used to refer to the 1949 cease-fire line in Palestine. Beirut acquired its own Green Line during the Lebanese civil war.

habibi – literally 'my love', but used more like *amigo*, my friend

haj – annual Muslim pilgrimage to Mecca

halachah – Jewish Law derived from oral tradition

halva – a sweet, chewy sesame seed block

Hamas – the Islamic Resistance Movement founded five days after the outbreak of the Intifada in December 1987 as an extremist opposition to Yasser Arafat's Al-Fatah organisation. Hamas promotes an Islamic State between the Mediterranean Sea and the Jordan River.

hamsa – a ceramic hand that is believed to ward off the evil eye; used largely by Sephardi Jews

hamseen – a heatwave that lasts for several days due to a hot wind blowing in from the desert

Hassidism – a Jewish ultra-Orthodox sect of Jews who followed the Ba'al Shem Tov, an eighteenth-century Polish Jew

haredi – literally God-fearing; refers to ultra-Orthodox Jews

Hezbollah – literally 'party of God', founded in Lebanon in 1982. The name is derived from a tortured Muslim scholar in Iran whose last words in 1973, allegedly, were: 'There is only one party, the party of God'.

hummous – a chickpea dip that is the staple diet in the Middle East

IDF – Israel Defence Forces

inshallah – Arabic for 'God willing'

Intifada – Arabic for 'shaking off', it refers to the 1987–93 Palestinian uprising in the West Bank and Gaza Strip; in September 2000 another uprising, dubbed the Al-Aqsa Intifada, began

jelabiyeh – an Arab ankle-length shirt-dress

jihad – Arabic for 'striving'; commonly associated with holy war against Israel

kaddish – memorial prayer for the dead, recited daily for eleven months and annually on the yahrzeit, the anniversary of the passing

katyusha – a rocket missile used in warfare

keffiyeh – an Arab headscarf

kibbutz – a cooperative-based settlement where all the members own all the property and share all the income

kibbutznik – a member of a kibbutz

Knesset – Israeli parliament

Koran – the Islamic holy text revealed to Mohammed by the archangel Gabriel

kosher – food prepared according to Jewish dietary laws

menorah – candelabra with seven branches; the emblem of Israel

mezuzah – a scroll of parchment in a case that is placed on the right-hand side of the doorpost to signal a Jewish home

mikveh – a ritual bath used for purification of women

mohel – an ordained rabbi who performs circumcision

moshav – a cooperative settlement similar to a kibbutz, except the profits of labour are not shared

Mossad – Israel's secret service agency which operates overseas; see also *Shabak*

nargilleh – a large Arab water pipe for smoking sweet tobacco; also known as hubbly-bubbly

peyot – side locks grown by ultra-Orthodox men

sabra – a native-born Israeli; pear-shaped prickly fruit grown on a cactus

Sephardi – Jews whose ancestors lived in Spain or Portugal before their expulsion in 1492 (as opposed to Ashkenazi). Thereafter many of these Jews fled to African or Arabian destinations, and nowadays Sephardi Jews also come from Oriental backgrounds

Shabak – a Hebrew acronym for *Sherut Bitachon Klali*, the internal security service. It is the sister agency of the Mossad, operating inside Israel.

Shabbat – the seventh day (when God rested), observed from sundown on Friday evening to one hour after sundown on Saturday evening

sharav – Hebrew for *hamseen*, a hot dry wind from the desert
sheitl – wigs worn by ultra-Orthodox women to cover their hair
sherut – a stretch taxi that carries seven passengers along main bus lines, but which waits to fill up prior to departing
Shin Bet – an abbreviated term for Shabak, the internal security service
shiva – the period of mourning after a death, lasting one week
shofar – a ram's horn blown every morning (Shabbat excepted) for the month prior to New Year, on New Year, and at the end of the fast of Yom Kippur, the Day of Atonement
shtetl – small Jewish towns or village in Eastern Europe
shtreimel – a fur-brimmed hat worn by *haredim* on Shabbat and festivals
shwarma – meat seasoned with herbs and spices and cooked on a spit
souk – an Arab market

tahina – a sesame seed dip; often served with falafel
Talmud – comprising the Mishnah and Gemara, it provides rabbinic commentaries and interpretations of the Torah
tefillin – phylacteries; two small boxes containing parchment from the Torah that are worn by men on the forearm and head during weekday morning prayers
Torah – the five books of Moses

wadi – a dry riverbed

yeshivah – an ultra-Orthodox Jewish seminary for the study of Torah

SOURCES & FURTHER READING

Aburish, Said. *Cry Palestine: Inside the West Bank.* London, Bloomsbury, 1991.

Bellow, Saul. *To Jerusalem and Back: A Personal Account.* London, Alison Press, 1976.

Binur, Yoram. *My Enemy, My Self.* New York, Doubleday, 1989.

Brook, Stephen. *Winner Takes All: A Season in Israel.* London, Penguin, 1990.

Buber, Martin. *The Tales of Rabbi Nachman.* Trans. Maurice Friedman. New York, Horizon, 1956.

Butt, Gerald. *Behind the Star: Inside Israel Today.* London, Constable, 1990.

Chapman, Colin. *Whose Promised Land?* Oxford, Lion, 1983.

Eisenberg, Robert. *Boychiks in the Hood: Travels in the Hassidic Underground.* San Francisco, HarperCollins, 1995.

Elon, Amos. *Jerusalem: City of Mirrors.* Boston, Little, Brown, 1989.

— *The Israelis: Founders and Sons.* New York, Penguin, 1971.

Friedman, Thomas. *From Beirut to Jerusalem.* New York, Farrar, Straus, Giroux, 1989.

Grossman, David. *The Yellow Wind.* Trans. Haim Watzmann. New York, Farrar, Straus, Giroux, 1988.

Hiro, Dilip. *Sharing The Promised Land: An Interwoven Tale of Israelis and Palestinians.* London, Hodder & Stoughton, 1996.

Hirst, David. *The Gun and the Olive Branch: The Roots of Violence in the Middle East.* London, Faber & Faber, 1977.

Horovitz, David. *A Little Too Close to God: The Thrills and Panic of a Life in Israel.* New York, Alfred A. Knopf, 2000.

Jacobson, Howard. *Roots Schmoots: Journey among Jews.* London, Viking, 1993.

Levi, Primo. *If This Is a Man.* Trans. Stuart Woolf. London, Abacus, 1987.

O'Brien, Conor Cruise. *The Siege: The Saga of Israel and Zionism.* London, Weidenfeld & Nicolson, 1986.

Oz, Amos. *In The Land Of Israel.* Trans. Maurice Goldberg-Bartura. London, Fontana, 1983.

— *The Slopes of Lebanon.* Trans. Maurie Goldberg-Bartura. London, Chatto & Windus, 1990.

Segev, Tom. *The Seventh Million: The Israelis and the Holocaust.* Trans. Haim Watzmann. New York, Hill and Wang, 1993.

Shapira, Avraham (ed.). *The Seventh Day: Soldiers' Talk about the Six-Day War.* Trans. Henry Near. London, Andre Deutsch, 1970.

Shipler, David. *Arab and Jew: Wounded Spirits in a Promised Land.* London, Bloomsbury, 1987.

Souss, Ibrahim. *Letter to a Jewish Friend.* Trans. John Howard Souss. London, Quartet, 1989.

Timerman, Jacobo. *The Longest War.* London, Chatto & Windus, 1982.

Twain, Mark. *The Innocents Abroad.* London, Century Hutchinson, 1988 (first published 1869).

Wiesel, Elie. *Night.* Trans. Stella Rodway. London, Penguin, 1981 (first published in English 1960).

Yehoshua, A.B. *The Continuing Silence of A Poet: The Collected Stories of A.B. Yehoshua.* London, Flamingo, 1990.